Rick Steves'

FRENCH

PHRASE BOOK
& DICTIONARY

D0972518

Avalon Travel
a member of the
Perseus Books Group
1700 Fourth Street
Berkeley, CA 94710, USA

Printed in Canada by Friesens.
Sixth edition. Ninth printing November 2012.

For the latest on Rick's lectures, guidebooks, tours, and public television
series, contact Europe Through the Back Door, P.O. Box 2009, Edmonds,
WA 98020, tel. 425/771-8303, fax 425/771-0833, www.ricksteves.com,
rick@ricksteves.com.

ISBN: 978-1-59880-186-6

Europe Through the Back Door Managing Editor: Risa Laib
Europe Through the Back Door Editors:
  Cameron Hewitt, Gretchen Strauch
Avalon Travel Editor: Jamie Andrade
Translation: Scott Bernhard, Paul Desloover,
  Sabine Leteinturier, Steve Smith
Phonetics: Risa Laib, Cameron Hewitt
Production: Darren Alessi
Cover Design: Kimberly Glyder Design
Maps & Graphics: David C. Hoerlein, Zoey Platt
Photography: Rick Steves
Cover Photo: © picturescolourlibrary.com

Distributed to the book trade by
Publishers Group West, Berkeley, California

Rick Steves' Guidebook Series

Country Guides

Rick Steves' Best of Europe
Rick Steves' Croatia & Slovenia
Rick Steves' Eastern Europe
Rick Steves' England
Rick Steves' France
Rick Steves' Germany
Rick Steves' Great Britain
Rick Steves' Ireland
Rick Steves' Italy
Rick Steves' Portugal
Rick Steves' Scandinavia
Rick Steves' Spain
Rick Steves' Switzerland

City and Regional Guides

Rick Steves' Amsterdam, Bruges & Brussels
Rick Steves' Athens & the Peloponnese (new in 2009)
Rick Steves' Budapest (new in 2009)
Rick Steves' Florence & Tuscany
Rick Steves' Istanbul
Rick Steves' London
Rick Steves' Paris
Rick Steves' Prague & the Czech Republic
Rick Steves' Provence & the French Riviera
Rick Steves' Rome
Rick Steves' Venice
Rick Steves' Vienna, Salzburg & Tirol (new in 2009)

Rick Steves' Phrase Books

French
French/Italian/German
German
Italian
Portuguese
Spanish

Other Books

Rick Steves' Europe Through the Back Door
Rick Steves' Europe 101: History and Art for the Traveler
Rick Steves' European Christmas
Rick Steves' Postcards from Europe

(Avalon Travel)

CONTENTS

vi

TABLE OF CONTENTS

Hi, I'm Rick Steves.

I'm the only monolingual speaker I know who's had the nerve to design a series of European phrase books. But that's one of the things that makes them better.

You see, after 30 summers of travel through Europe, I've learned first hand: (1) what's essential for communication in another country, and (2) what's not. I've assembled the most important words and phrases in a logical, no-frills format, and I've worked with native Europeans and seasoned travelers to give you the simplest, clearest translation possible.

But this book is more than just a pocket translator. The words and phrases have been carefully selected to help you have a smarter, smoother trip in France. The key to getting more out of every travel dollar is to get closer to the local people, and to rely less on entertainment, restaurants, and hotels that cater only to foreign tourists. This book will not only help you order a meal at a locals-only Parisian restaurant—but it will also help you talk with the family who runs the place . . . about their kids, travel dreams, politics, and favorite *fromage*. Long after your memories of châteaux have faded, you'll still treasure the personal encounters you had with your new French friends.

A good phrase book should help you enjoy your French experience—not just survive it—so I've added a healthy dose of humor. A few phrases are just for fun and aren't meant to be used at all. Most of the phrases are for real and should be used with "please." I know you can tell the difference.

To get the most out of this book, take the time to internalize and put into practice my French pronunciation tips. Don't worry too much about memorizing grammatical rules, like the gender of a noun—forget about sex, and communicate!

You'll notice this book has a handy dictionary and a nifty menu decoder. You'll also find tongue twisters, international words, telephone tips, and a tear-out "cheat sheet." Tear it out and tuck it in your beret, so you can easily memorize key phrases during otherwise idle moments. As you prepare for your trip, you may want to read this year's edition of my *Rick Steves' France*, *Rick Steves' Paris*, or *Rick Steves' Provence & the French Riviera* guidebooks.

Your French experience will be enriched by a basic understanding of French etiquette. This causes lots of needless frustration among Americans. Here's the situation in a nutshell. Americans feel that informality is friendly and formality is cold. The French feel that informality is rude and formality is polite. So, ironically, as the Americans and French are both doing their best to be nice, they accidentally offend one another. Remember you're the outsider, so watch the locals and try to incorporate some French-syle politeness into your routine. Walk into any shop in France and you will hear a cheery, *"Bonjour, Monsieur / Madame."* As you leave, you'll hear a lilting, *"Au revoir, Monsieur / Madame."* Always address a man as *Monsieur*, a woman as *Madame*, and an unmarried young woman or a girl as *Mademoiselle* (leaving this out is like addressing a French person as "Hey, you!"). For good measure, toss in *s'il vous plait* (please) whenever you can.

Adjust those cultural blinders. If you come to France expecting rudeness, you are sure to find it. If you respect the fine points of French culture and make an attempt to speak their language, you'll find the French as warm and friendly as anyone in Europe.

My goal is to help you become a more confident, extroverted traveler. If this phrase book helps make that happen, or if you have suggestions for making it better, I'd love to hear from you. I personally read and value all feedback.

You can reach me at Europe Through the Back Door, P.O. Box 2009, Edmonds, WA 98020, tel. 425/771-8303, fax 425/771-0833, rick@ricksteves.com.

Happy travels, and *bonne chance* (good luck) as you hurdle the language barrier!

GETTING STARTED

Challenging, Romantic French

...is spoken throughout Europe and thought to be one of the most beautiful languages in the world. Half of Belgium speaks French, and French rivals English as the handiest second language in Spain, Portugal, and Italy. Even your US passport is translated into French. You're probably already familiar with this poetic language. Consider: *bonjour, c'est la vie, bon appétit, merci, au revoir,* and *bon voyage!* The most important phrase is *s'il vous plaît* (please), pronounced see voo play. Use it liberally. The French will notice and love it.

As with any language, the key to communicating is to go for it with a mixture of bravado and humility. Try to sound like Maurice Chevalier or Inspector Clouseau.

French pronunciation differs from English in some key ways:

Ç sounds like S in sun.
CH sounds like SH in shine.
G usually sounds like G in get.
   But G followed by E or I sounds like S in treasure.
GN sounds like NI in onion.
H is always silent.
J sounds like S in treasure.
R sounds like an R being swallowed.

I sounds like EE in seed.

È and **Ê** sound like E in let.

É and **EZ** sound like AY in play.

ER, at the end of a word, sounds like AY in play.

Ô sounds like O in note.

In a Romance language, sex is unavoidable. A man is *content* (happy), a woman is *contente.* In this book, when you see a pair of words like "*content / contente,*" use the second word when talking about a woman.

French has four accents. The cedilla makes **Ç** sound like "s" (*façade*). The circumflex makes **Ê** sound like "eh" (*crêpe*), but has no effect on **Â, Î, Ô,** or **Û.** The grave accent stifles **È** into "eh" (*crème*), but doesn't change the stubborn **À** (*à la carte*). The acute accent opens **É** into "ay" (*café*).

French is tricky because the spelling and pronunciation seem to have little to do with each other. *Qu'est-ce que c'est?* (What is that?) is pronounced: kehs kuh say.

The final letters of many French words are silent, so *Paris* sounds like pah-ree. The French tend to stress every syllable evenly: pah-ree. In contrast, Americans say **Par**-is, emphasizing the first syllable.

In French, if a word that ends in a consonant is followed by a word that starts with a vowel, the consonant is frequently linked with the vowel. *Mes amis* (my friends) is pronounced: may-zah-mee. Some words are linked with an apostrophe. *Ce est* (It is) becomes *C'est,* as in *C'est la vie* (That's life). *Le* and *la* (the masculine and feminine "the") are intimately connected to words starting with a vowel. *La orange* becomes *l'orange.*

French has a few sounds that are unusual in English: the French *u* and the nasal vowels. To say the French *u,* round your lips to say "oh," but say "ee." Vowels combined with either *n* or *m* are often nasal vowels. As you nasalize a vowel, let the sound come through your nose as well as your mouth. The vowel is the important thing. The *n* or *m,* represented in this book by <u>n</u> for nasal, is not pronounced.

There are a total of four nasal sounds, all contained in the phrase *un bon vin blanc* (a good white wine).

Nasal vowels:	Phonetics:	To make the sound:
un	uh<u>n</u>	nasalize the U in lung.
bon	boh<u>n</u>	nasalize the O in bone.
vin	va<u>n</u>	nasalize the A in sack.
blanc	blah<u>n</u>	nasalize the A in want.

If you practice saying *un bon vin blanc,* you'll learn how to say the nasal vowels . . . and order a fine wine.

Here's a guide to the rest of the phonetics in this book:

ah	like A in father.
ay	like AY in play.
eh	like E in let.
ee	like EE in seed.
ehr, air	sounds like "air" (in *merci* and *extraordinaire*).
ew	pucker your lips and say "ee."
g	like G in go.
i	like I in light.
or	like OR in core.
oh	like O in note.
oo	like OO in too.
s	like S in sun.
uh	like U in but.
ur	like UR in purr.
zh	like S in treasure.

FRENCH BASICS

In 1945, American GIs helped liberate Paris using only these phrases.

Meeting and Greeting

Good day.	*Bonjour.*	bohn-zhoor
Good morning.	*Bonjour.*	bohn-zhoor
Good evening.	*Bonsoir.*	bohn-swar
Good night.	*Bonne nuit.*	buhn nwee
Hi / Bye. (informal)	*Salut.*	sah-lew
Welcome!	*Bienvenue!*	bee-an-vuh-new
Mr.	*Monsieur*	muhs-yur
Mrs.	*Madame*	mah-dahm
Miss	*Mademoiselle*	mahd-mwah-zehl
How are you?	*Comment allez-vous?*	koh-mahnt ah-lay-voo
Very well, thank you.	*Très bien, merci.*	treh bee-an mehr-see
And you?	*Et vous?*	ay voo
My name is___.	*Je m'appelle___.*	zhuh mah-pehl
What's your name?	*Quel est votre nom?*	kehl ay voh-truh nohn
Pleased to meet you.	*Enchanté.*	ahn-shahn-tay
Where are you from?	*D'où êtes-vous?*	doo eht voo
I am / We are...	*Je suis /*	zhuh swee /
	Nous sommes...	noo suhm
Are you...?	*Êtes-vous...?*	eht-vooz
...on vacation	*...en vacances*	ahn vah-kahns
...on business	*...en voyage*	ahn voy-yahzh
	d'affaires	dah-fair

4

See you later.	*À bientôt.*	ah bee-an-toh
So long! (informal)	*Salut!*	sah-lew
Goodbye.	*Au revoir.*	oh reh-vwar
Good luck!	*Bonne chance!*	buhn shahns
Have a good trip!	*Bon voyage!*	bohn voy-yahzh

The greeting "*Bonjour*" (Good day) turns to "*Bonsoir*" (Good evening) at sundown.

Essentials

Good day.	*Bonjour.*	bohn-zhoor
Do you speak English?	*Parlez-vous anglais?*	par-lay-voo ahn-glay
Yes. / No.	*Oui. / Non.*	wee / nohn
I don't speak French.	*Je ne parle pas français.*	zhuh nuh parl pah frahn-say
I'm sorry.	*Désolé.*	day-zoh-lay
Please.	*S'il vous plaît.*	see voo play
Thank you.	*Merci.*	mehr-see
Thank you very much.	*Merci beaucoup.*	mehr-see boh-koo
No problem.	*Pas de problème.*	pah duh proh-blehm
Good. / Very good. / Excellent.	*Bien. / Très bien. / Excellent.*	bee-an / treh bee-an / ehk-sehl-ahn
You are very kind.	*Vous êtes très gentil.*	vooz eht treh zhahn-tee
Excuse me. (to pass)	*Pardon.*	par-dohn
Excuse me. (to get attention)	*Excusez-moi.*	ehk-skew-zay-mwah
It doesn't matter.	*Ça m'est égal.*	sah meht ay-gal
You're welcome.	*Je vous en prie.*	zhuh vooz ahn pree
Sure.	*Bien sûr.*	bee-an suhr
O.K.	*D'accord.*	dah-kor
Let's go.	*Allons-y.*	ahl-lohn-zee
Goodbye.	*Au revoir.*	oh reh-vwar

FRENCH BASICS

Where?

Where is...?	*Où est...?*	oo ay
...the tourist information office	*...l'office du tourisme*	loh-fees dew too-reez-muh
...a cash machine	*...un distributeur automatique*	uhn dee-stree-bew-tur oh-toh-mah-teek
...the train station	*...la gare*	lah gar
...the bus station	*...la gare routière*	lah gar root-yehr
Where are the toilets?	*Où sont les toilettes?*	oo sohn lay twah-leht
men / women	*hommes / dames*	ohm / dahm

You'll find some French words are similar to English if you're looking for a *banque*, *pharmacie*, *hôtel*, or *restaurant*.

How Much?

How much is it, please?	*Combien, s'il vous plaît?*	kohn-bee-an see voo play
Write it?	*Ecrivez?*	ay-kree-vay
Is it free?	*C'est gratuit?*	say grah-twee
Included?	*Inclus?*	an-klew
Do you have...?	*Avez-vous...?*	ah-vay-voo
Where can I buy...?	*Où puis-je acheter...?*	oo pwee-zhuh ah-shuh-tay
I would like...	*Je voudrais...*	zhuh voo-dray
We would like...	*Nous voudrions...*	noo voo-dree-ohn
...this.	*...ceci.*	suh-see
...just a little.	*...un petit peu.*	uhn puh-tee puh
...more.	*...plus.*	plew
...a ticket.	*...un billet.*	uhn bee-yay
...a room.	*...une chambre.*	ewn shahn-bruh
...the bill.	*...l'addition.*	lah-dee-see-ohn

How Many?

one	*un*	uhn
two	*deux*	duh

three	*trois*	twah
four	*quatre*	kah-truh
five	*cinq*	sa<u>n</u>k
six	*six*	sees
seven	*sept*	seht
eight	*huit*	weet
nine	*neuf*	nuhf
ten	*dix*	dees

FRENCH BASICS

You'll find more to count on in the "Numbers" section (page 14).

When?

At what time?	*À quelle heure?*	ah kehl ur
open / closed	*ouvert / fermé*	oo-vehr / fehr-may
Just a moment.	*Un moment.*	uh<u>n</u> moh-mah<u>n</u>
Now.	*Maintenant.*	ma<u>n</u>-tuh-nah<u>n</u>
Soon.	*Bientôt.*	bee-an-toh
Later.	*Plus tard.*	plew tar
Today.	*Aujourd'hui.*	oh-zhoor-dwee
Tomorrow.	*Demain.*	duh-ma<u>n</u>

Be creative! You can combine these phrases to say: "Two, please," or "No, thank you," or "Open tomorrow?" or "Please, where can I buy a ticket?" Please is a magic word in any language, but especially in French. The French love to hear it. If you want to buy something and you don't know the word for it, just point and say, "*S'il vous plaît*" (Please). If you know the word for what you want, such as the bill, simply say, "*L'addition, s'il vous plaît*" (The bill, please).

Struggling with French

Do you speak English?	*Parlez-vous anglais?*	par-lay-voo ah<u>n</u>-glay
A teeny weeny bit?	*Un tout petit peu?*	uh<u>n</u> too puh-tee puh
Please speak English.	*Parlez anglais, s'il vous plaît.*	par-lay ah<u>n</u>-glay see voo play

FRENCH BASICS

You speak English well.	*Vous parlez bien anglais.*	voo par-lay bee-an ahn-glay
I don't speak French.	*Je ne parle pas français.*	zhuh nuh parl pah frahn-say
We don't speak French.	*Nous ne parlons pas français.*	noo nuh par-lon pah frahn-say
I speak a little French.	*Je parle un petit peu français.*	zhuh parl uhn puh-tee puh frahn-say
Sorry, I speak only English.	*Désolé, je ne parle qu'anglais.*	day-zoh-lay zhuh nuh parl kahn-glay
Sorry, we speak only English.	*Désolé, nous ne parlons qu'anglais.*	day-zoh-lay noo nuh par-lon kahn-glay
Does somebody nearby speak English?	*Quelqu'un près d'ici parle anglais?*	kehl-kuhn preh dee-see parl ahn-glay
Who speaks English?	*Qui parle anglais?*	kee parl ahn-glay
What does this mean?	*Qu'est-ce-que ça veut dire?*	kehs-kuh sah vuh deer
How do you say this in French / English?	*Comment dit-on en français / anglais?*	koh-mahn dee-tohn ahn frahn-say / ahn-glay
Repeat?	*Répétez?*	ray-pay-tay
Speak slowly, please.	*Parlez lentement, s'il vous plaît.*	par-lay lahn-tuh-mahn see voo play
Slower.	*Plus lentement.*	plew lahn-tuh-mahn
I understand.	*Je comprends.*	zhuh kohn-prahn
I don't understand.	*Je ne comprends pas.*	zhuh nuh kohn-prahn pah
Do you understand?	*Vous comprenez?*	voo kohn-preh-nay
Write it?	*Ecrivez?*	ay-kree-vay

A French person who is asked, "Do you speak English?" assumes you mean, "Do you speak English fluently?" and will likely answer no. But if you just keep on struggling in French, you'll bring out the English in most any French person.

Handy Questions

How much?	*Combien?*	kohn-bee-an
How many?	*Combien?*	kohn-bee-an

How long is the trip?	*Combien de temps dure le voyage?*	kohn-bee-an duh tahn dewr luh voy-yahzh
How many minutes?	*Combien de minutes?*	kohn-bee-an duh mee-newt
How many hours?	*Combien d'heures?*	kohn-bee-an dur
How far?	*C'est loin?*	say lwan
How?	*Comment?*	koh-mahn
Can you help me?	*Vous pouvez m'aider?*	voo poo-vay may-day
Can you help us?	*Vous pouvez nous aider?*	voo poo-vay nooz ay-day
Can I...?	*Puis-je...?*	pwee-zhuh
Can we...?	*Pouvons-nous...?*	poo-vohn-noo
...have one	*...avoir un*	ah-vwar uhn
...go in for free	*...aller gratuitement*	ah-lay grah-tweet-mahn
...borrow that for a moment / an hour	*...emprunter ça pour un moment / une heure*	ahn-pruhn-tay sah poor uhn moh-mahn / ewn ur
...use the toilet	*...utiliser les toilettes*	oo-tee-lee-zay lay twah-leht
What? (didn't hear)	*Comment?*	koh-mahn
What is this?	*Qu'est-ce que c'est?*	kehs kuh say
What is better?	*Qu'est-ce qui vaut mieux?*	kehs kee voh mee-uh
What's going on?	*Qu'est-ce qui se passe?*	kehs kee suh pahs
When?	*Quand?*	kahn
What time is it?	*Quelle heure est-il?*	kehl ur ay-teel
At what time?	*À quelle heure?*	ah kehl ur
On time? / Late?	*A l'heure? /En retard?*	ah lur / ahn ruh-tar
How long will it take?	*Ça prend combien de temps?*	sah prahn kohn-bee-an duh tahn
At what time does this open / close?	*À quelle heuere c'est ouvert / fermé?*	ah kehl ur say oo-vehr / fehr-may
Is this open daily?	*C'est ouvert tous les jours?*	say oo-vehr too lay zhoor
What day is this closed?	*C'est fermé quel jour?*	say fehr-may kehl zhoor

FRENCH BASICS

Do you have...?	*Avez-vous...?*	ah-vay-voo
Where is...?	*Où est...?*	oo ay
Where are...?	*Où sont...?*	oo soh<u>n</u>
Where can I find / buy...?	*Où puis-je trouver / acheter...?*	oo pwee-zhuh troo-vay / ah-shuh-tay
Where can we find / buy...?	*Où pouvons-nous trouver / acheter...?*	oo poo-vah<u>n</u>-noo troo-vay / ah-shuh-tay
Is it necessary?	*C'est nécessaire?*	say nay-suh-sair
Is it possible...?	*C'est possible...?*	say poh-see-bluh
...to enter	*...d'entrer*	dah<u>n</u>-tray
...to picnic here	*...de pique-niquer ici*	duh peek-neek-ay ee-see
...to sit here	*...de s'assoir ici*	duh sah-swar ee-see
...to look	*...de regarder*	duh ray-gar-day
...to take a photo	*...de prendre une photo*	duh prah<u>n</u>-druh ewn foh-toh
...to see a room	*...de voir une chambre*	duh vwar ewn shah<u>n</u>-bruh
Who?	*Qui?*	kee
Why?	*Pourquoi?*	poor-kwah
Why not?	*Pourquoi pas?*	poor-kwah pah
Yes or no?	*Oui ou non?*	wee oo noh<u>n</u>

To prompt a simple answer, ask, "*Oui ou non?*" (Yes or no?). To turn a word or sentence into a question, ask it in a questioning tone. "*C'est bon*" (It's good) becomes "*C'est bon?*" (Is it good?). An easy way to say, "Where is the toilet?" is to ask, "*Toilette?*"

Le Yin et le Yang

good / bad	*bon / mauvais*	boh<u>n</u> / moh-vay
best / worst	*le meilleur / le pire*	luh meh-yur / luh peer
a little / lots	*un peu / beaucoup*	uh<u>n</u> puh / boh-koo
more / less	*plus / moins*	plew / mwa<u>n</u>
cheap / expensive	*bon marché / cher*	boh<u>n</u> mar-shay / shehr
big / small	*grand / petit*	grah<u>n</u> / puh-tee
hot / cold	*chaud / froid*	shoh / frwah
warm / cool	*tiede / frais*	tee-ehd / fray

cool (nice) / not cool	sympa / pas sympa	sahn-pah / pah sahn-pah
open / closed	ouvert / fermé	oo-vehr / fehr-may
entrance / exit	entrée / sortie	ahn-tray / sor-tee
push / pull	pousser / tirer	poo-say / tee-ray
arrive / depart	arriver / partir	ah-ree-vay / par-teer
early / late	tôt / tard	toh / tar
soon / later	bientôt / plus tard	bee-an-toh / plew tar
fast / slow	vite / lent	veet / lahn
here / there	ici / là-bas	ee-see / lah-bah
near / far	près / loin	preh / lwan
indoors / outdoors	l'intérieur / dehors	lan-tay-ree-yoor / duh-or
mine / yours	le mien / le vôtre	luh mee-an / luh voh-truh
this / that	ce / cette	suh / seht
everybody / nobody	tout le monde / personne	too luh mohnd / pehr-suhn
easy / difficult	facile / difficile	fah-seel / dee-fee-seel
left / right	à gauche / à droite	ah gohsh / ah dwaht
up / down	en haut / en bas	ahn oh / ahn bah
above / below	au-dessus / en-dessous	oh-duh-sew / ahn-duh-soo
young / old	jeune / vieux	zhuhn / vee-uh
new / old	neuf / vieux	nuhf / vee-uh
heavy / light	lourd / léger	loor / lay-zhay
dark / light	sombre / clair	sohn-bruh / klair
happy (m, f) / sad	content, contente / triste	kohn-tahn, kohn-tahnt / treest
beautiful / ugly	beau / laid	boh / leh
nice / mean	gentil / méchant	zhahn-tee / may-shahn
intelligent / stupid	intelligent / stupide	an-teh-lee-zhahn / stew-peed
vacant / occupied	libre / occupé	lee-bruh / oh-kew-pay
with / without	avec / sans	ah-vehk / sahn

Big Little Words

I	*je*	zhuh
you (formal)	*vous*	voo
you (informal)	*tu*	tew
we	*nous*	noo
he	*il*	eel
she	*elle*	ehl
they	*ils*	eel
and	*et*	ay
at	*à*	ah
because	*parce que*	pars kuh
but	*mais*	may
by (train, car, etc.)	*par*	par
for	*pour*	poor
from	*de*	duh
here	*ici*	ee-see
if	*si*	see
in	*en*	ahn
it (m / f)	*le / la*	luh / lah
not	*pas*	pah
now	*maintenant*	man-tuh-nahn
only	*seulement*	suhl-mahn
or	*ou*	oo
this / that	*ce / cette*	suh / seht
to	*à*	ah
very	*très*	treh

Quintessentially French Expressions

Bon appétit!	*bohn ah-pay-tee*	Enjoy your meal!
Ça va?	*sah vah*	How are you? (informal)
Ça va. (response to Ça va?)	*sah vah*	I'm fine.
Sympa. / Pas sympa.	*sahn-pah / pah sahn-pah*	Nice. / Not nice.
C'est chouette. ("That's a female owl.")	*say shweht*	That's cool.

Ce n'est pas vrai!	*suh nay pah vray*	It's not true!
C'est comme ça.	*say kohm sah*	That's the way it is.
Comme ci,	*kohm see*	So so.
comme ça.	*kohm sah*	
D'accord.	*dah-kor*	O.K.
Formidable!	*for-mee-dah-bluh*	Great!
Mon Dieu!	*mohn dee-uh*	My God!
Tout de suite.	*toot sweet*	Right away.
Voilà.	*vwah-lah*	Here it is.

COUNTING

NUMBERS

0	*zéro*	zay-roh
1	*un*	uh<u>n</u>
2	*deux*	duh
3	*trois*	twah
4	*quatre*	kah-truh
5	*cinq*	sa<u>n</u>k
6	*six*	sees
7	*sept*	seht
8	*huit*	weet
9	*neuf*	nuhf
10	*dix*	dees
11	*onze*	oh<u>n</u>z
12	*douze*	dooz
13	*treize*	trehz
14	*quatorze*	kah-torz
15	*quinze*	ka<u>n</u>z
16	*seize*	sehz
17	*dix-sept*	dee-seht
18	*dix-huit*	deez-weet
19	*dix-neuf*	deez-nuhf
20	*vingt*	va<u>n</u>
21	*vingt et un*	va<u>n</u>t ay uh<u>n</u>
22	*vingt-deux*	va<u>n</u>t-duh

23	*vingt-trois*	vant-twah
30	*trente*	trahnt
31	*trente et un*	trahnt ay uhn
40	*quarante*	kah-rahnt
41	*quarante et un*	kah-rahnt ay uhn
50	*cinquante*	san-kahnt
51	*cinquante et un*	san-kahnt ay uhn
60	*soixante*	swah-sahnt
61	*soixante et un*	swah-sahnt ay uhn
70	*soixante-dix*	swah-sahnt-dees
71	*soixante et onze*	swah-sahnt ay ohnz
72	*soixante-douze*	swah-sahnt-dooz
73	*soixante-treize*	swah-sahnt-trehz
74	*soixante-quatorze*	swah-sahnt-kah-torz
75	*soixante-quinze*	swah-sahnt-kanz
76	*soixante-seize*	swah-sahnt-sehz
77	*soixante-dix-sept*	swah-sahnt-dee-seht
78	*soixante-dix-huit*	swah-sahnt-deez-weet
79	*soixante-dix-neuf*	swah-sahnt-deez-nuhf
80	*quatre-vingts*	kah-truh-van
81	*quatre-vingt-un*	kah-truh-van-uhn
82	*quatre-vingt-deux*	kah-truh-van-duh
83	*quatre-vingt-trois*	kah-truh-van-twah
84	*quatre-vingt-quatre*	kah-truh-van-kah-truh
85	*quatre-vingt-cinq*	kah-truh-van-sank
86	*quatre-vingt-six*	kah-truh-van-sees
87	*quatre-vingt-sept*	kah-truh-van-seht
88	*quatre-vingt-huit*	kah-truh-van-weet
89	*quatre-vingt-neuf*	kah-truh-van-nuhf
90	*quatre-vingt-dix*	kah-truh-van-dees
91	*quatre-vingt-onze*	kah-truh-van-ohnz
92	*quatre-vingt-douze*	kah-truh-van-dooz
93	*quatre-vingt-treize*	kah-truh-van-trehz
94	*quatre-vingt-quatorze*	kah-truh-van-kah-torz
95	*quatre-vingt-quinze*	kah-truh-van-kanz
96	*quatre-vingt-seize*	kah-truh-van-sehz
97	*quatre-vingt-dix-sept*	kah-truh-van-dee-seht

COUNTING

98	*quatre-vingt-dix-huit*	kah-truh-van-deez-weet
99	*quatre-vingt-dix-neuf*	kah-truh-van-deez-nuhf
100	*cent*	sahn
101	*cent un*	sahn uhn
102	*cent deux*	sahn duh
200	*deux cents*	duh sahn
1000	*mille*	meel
2000	*deux mille*	duh meel
2001	*deux mille un*	duh meel uhn
2002	*deux mille deux*	duh meel duh
2003	*deux mille trois*	duh meel twah
2004	*deux mille quatre*	duh meel kah-truh
2005	*deux mille cinq*	duh meel sank
2006	*deux mille six*	duh meel sees
2007	*deux mille sept*	duh meel seht
2008	*deux mille huit*	duh meel weet
2009	*deux mille neuf*	duh meel nuhf
2010	*deux mille dix*	duh meel dees
million	*million*	meel-yohn
billion	*milliard*	meel-yar
number one	*numéro un*	new-may-roh uhn
first	*premier*	pruhm-yay
second	*deuxième*	duhz-yehm
third	*troisième*	twahz-yehm
once / twice	*une fois / deux fois*	ewn fwah / duh fwah
a quarter	*un quart*	uhn kar
a third	*un tiers*	uhn tee-ehr
half	*demi*	duh-mee
this much	*comme ça*	kohm sah
a dozen	*une douzaine*	ewn doo-zayn
some	*quelques*	kehl-keh
enough	*suffisament*	soo-fee-zah-mahn
a handful	*une poignée*	ewn pwahn-yay
50%	*cinquante pour cent*	san-kahnt poor sahn
100%	*cent pour cent*	sahn poor sahn

French numbering is a little quirky from the seventies through the nineties. Let's pretend momentarily that the French speak English. Instead of saying 70, 71, 72, up to 79, the French say, "sixty ten," "sixty eleven," "sixty twelve" up to "sixty nineteen." Instead of saying 80, the French say, "four twenties." The numbers 81 and 82 are literally "four twenty one" and "four twenty two." It gets stranger. The number 90 is "four twenty ten." To say 91, 92, up to 99, the French say, "four twenty eleven," "four twenty twelve" on up to "four twenty nineteen." But take heart. If little French children can learn these numbers, so can you. Besides, didn't Abe Lincoln say, "Four score and seven..."?

MONEY

Where is a cash machine?	*Oú est un distributeur automatique?*	oo ay uhn dee-stree-bew-tur oh-toh-mah-teek
My ATM card has been...	*Ma carte a été...*	mah kart ah ay-tay
...demagnetized.	*...démagnétisée.*	day-mag-neht-ee-zay
...stolen.	*...volée.*	voh-lay
...eaten by the machine.	*...avalée par la machine.*	ah-vah-lee par lah mah-sheen
My card doesn't work.	*Ma carte ne marche pas.*	mah kart neh marsh pah
Do you accept credit cards?	*Vous prenez les cartes de crédit?*	voo preh-nay lay kart duh kray-dee
Can you change dollars?	*Pouvez-vous changer les dollars?*	poo-vay-voo shahn-zhay lay doh-lar
What is your exchange rate for dollars...?	*Quel est le cours du dollar...?*	kehl ay luh koor dew doh-lar
...in traveler's checks	*...en cheques de voyage*	ahn shehk duh voy-yahzh
What is the commission?	*Quel est la commission?*	kehl ay lah koh-mee-see-ohn

Key Phrases: Money

euro (€)	euro	eh-oo-roo
money	argent	ar-zhah<u>n</u>
cash	liquide	lee-keed
credit card	carte de crédit	kart duh kray-dee
bank	banque	bah<u>n</u>k
cash machine	distributeur automatique	dee-stree-bew-tur oh-toh-mah-teek
Where is a cash machine?	Oú est un distributeur automatique?	oo ay uh<u>n</u> dee-stree-bew-tur oh-toh-mah-teek
Do you accept credit cards?	Vous prenez les cartes de crédit?	voo preh-nay lay kart duh kray-dee

Any extra fee?	Il y a d'autre frais?	eel yah doh-truh fray
Can you break this? (large into small bills)	Vous pouvez casser ça?	voo poo-vay kas-ay sah
I would like...	Je voudrais...	zhuh voo-dray
...small bills.	...des petits billets.	day puh-tee bee-yay
...large bills.	...des gros billets.	day groh bee-yay
...coins.	...des pièces.	day pee-ehs
€ 50	cinquante euros	seeng-kwayn-tah eh-oo-roo
Is this a mistake?	C'est une erreur?	sayt ewn er-ror
This is incorrect.	C'est incorrect.	say in-koh-rehkt
Did you print these today?	Vous les avez imprimés aujourd'hui?	voo layz ah-vay an-pree-may oh-zhoor-dwee
I'm broke / poor / rich.	Je suis fauché / pauvre / riche.	zhuh swee foh-shay / poh-vruh / reesh
I'm Bill Gates.	Je suis Bill Gates.	zhuh swee "Bill Gates"
Where is the nearest casino?	Oú se trouve le casino le plus proche?	oo suh troov luh kah-see-noh luh plew prohsh

France uses the euro currency. Euros (€) are divided into 100 cents.
Use your common cents—cents are like pennies, and the currency
has coins like nickels, dimes, and half-dollars.

Money Words

euro (€)	*euro*	eh-oo-roo
cents	*centimes*	sah<u>n</u>-teem
money	*argent*	ar-zhah<u>n</u>
cash	*liquide*	lee-keed
cash machine	*distributeur automatique*	dee-stree-bew-tur oh-toh-mah-teek
bank	*banque*	bah<u>n</u>k
credit card	*carte de crédit*	kart duh kray-dee
change money	*changer de l'argent*	shah<u>n</u>-zhay duh lar-zhah<u>n</u>
exchange	*bureau de change*	bew-roh duh shah<u>n</u>zh
buy / sell	*acheter / vendre*	ah-shuh-tay / vah<u>n</u>-druh
commission	*commission*	koh-mee-see-oh<u>n</u>
traveler's check	*cheque de voyage*	shehk duh voy-yahzh
cash advance	*crédit de caisse*	kray-dee duh kehs
cashier	*caisse*	kehs
bills	*billets*	bee-yay
coins	*pièces*	pee-ehs
receipt	*reçu*	ruh-sew

COUNTING

At French banks, you may encounter a security door that allows one
person to enter at a time. Push the *entrez* (enter) button, then
attendez (wait), and *voilà!*, the door opens. Every *distributeur
automatique* (cash machine) is multilingual, but if you'd like to learn
French under pressure, look for these three buttons: *annuler* (cancel),
modifier (change), *valider* (affirm). Your PIN code is a *code.*

TIME

What time is it?	*Quelle heure est-il?*	kehl ur ay-teel
It's...	*Il est...*	eel ay

...8:00 in the morning.	...huit heures du matin.	weet ur doo mah-tahn
...16:00.	...seize heures.	sehz ur
...4:00 in the afternoon.	...quatre heures de l'après-midi.	kah-truh ur duh lah-preh-mee-dee
...10:30 in the evening.	...dix heures et demie du soir.	deez ur ayd-mee dew swar
...a quarter past nine.	...neuf heures et quart.	nuhv ur ay kar
...a quarter to eleven.	...onze heures moins le quart.	ohnz ur mwan luh kar
...noon.	...midi.	mee-dee
...midnight.	...minuit.	meen-wee
...early / late.	...tôt / tard.	toh / tar
...on time.	...à l'heure.	ah lur
...sunrise.	...l'aube.	lohb
...sunset.	...le coucher de soleil.	luh koo-shay duh soh-lay
It's my bedtime.	C'est l'heure où je me couche.	say lur oo zhuh muh koosh

COUNTING

Timely Expressions

I'll return / We'll return...	Je reviens / Nous revenons...	zhuh reh-vee-an / noo ruh-vuh-nohn
...at 11:20.	...à onze heures vingt.	ah ohnz ur van
I'll be / We'll be...	Je serai / Nous serons...	zhuh suh-ray / noo suh-rohn
...there by 18:00.	...là avant dix huit heures.	lah ah-vahn deez-weet ur
When is checkout time?	À quelle heure on doit libérer la chambre?	ah kehl ur ohn dwah lee-bay-ray lah shahn-bruh
At what time does...?	À quelle heure...?	ah kehl ur
...this open / close	...c'est ouvre / ferme	say oov-reh / fehrm
...this train / bus leave for ___	...ce train / bus part pour ___	seh tran / bews par poor

Key Phrases: Time

minute	*minute*	mee-newt
hour	*heure*	ur
day	*jour*	zhoor
week	*semaine*	suh-mehn
What time is it?	*Quelle heure est-il?*	kehl ur ay-teel
It's...	*Il est...*	eel ay
...8:00.	*...huit heures.*	weet ur
...16:00.	*...seize heures.*	sehz ur
At what time does this open / close?	*À quelle heuere c'est ouvert / fermé?*	ah kehl ur say oo-vehr / fehr-may

...the next train / bus leave for ___	*...le prochain train / bus part pour ___*	luh proh-shan tran / bews par poor
...the train / bus arrive in ___	*...le train / bus arrive à ___*	luh tran / bews ah-reev ah
I want / We want...	*Je veux / Nous voulons...*	zhuh vuh / noo voo-lohn
...to take the 16:30 train.	*...prendre le train de seize heures trente.*	prahn-druh luh tran duh sehz ur trahnt
Is the train...?	*Le train est...?*	luh tran ay
Is the bus...?	*Le bus est...?*	luh bews ay
...early / late	*...en avance / en retard*	ahn ah-vahns / ahn ruh-tar
...on time	*...à l'heure*	ah lur

In France, the 24-hour clock (military time) is used by hotels and stores, and for train, bus, and ferry schedules. Informally, the French use the 24-hour clock and "our clock" interchangeably— 17:00 is also 5:00 *de l'après-midi* (in the afternoon).

About Time

minute	*minute*	mee-newt
hour	*heure*	ur

COUNTING

in the morning	*dans le matin*	dahn luh mah-tan
in the afternoon	*dans l'après-midi*	dahn lah-preh-mee-dee
in the evening	*dans le soir*	dahn luh swar
at night	*la nuit*	lah nwee
at 6:00 sharp	*à six heures précises*	ah sees ur preh-see
from 8:00 to 10:00	*de huit heures à dix heures*	duh weet ur ah dees ur
in half an hour	*dans une demie heure*	dahnz ewn duh-mee ur
in one hour	*dans une heure*	dahnz ewn ur
in three hours	*dans trois heures*	dahn twahz ur
anytime	*n'importe quand*	nan-port kahn
immediately	*immédiatement*	ee-may-dee-aht-mahn
every hour	*toutes les heures*	toot layz ur
every day	*tous les jours*	too lay zhoor
last	*dernier*	dehrn-yay
this (m / f)	*ce / cette*	suh / seht
next	*prochain*	proh-shan
May 15	*le quinze mai*	luh kanz may
high season	*haute saison*	oht say-zohn
low season	*basse saison*	bahs say-zohn
in the future	*dans l'avenir*	dahn lah-vahn-eer
in the past	*dans le passé*	dahn luh pah-say

The Day

day	*jour*	zhoor
today	*aujourd'hui*	oh-zhoor-dwee
yesterday	*hier*	yehr
tomorrow	*demain*	duh-man
tomorrow morning	*demain matin*	duh-man mah-tan
day after tomorrow	*après demain*	ah-preh duh-man

The Week

week	*semaine*	suh-mehn
last week	*la semaine dernière*	lah suh-mehn dehrn-yehr
this week	*cette semaine*	seht suh-mehn

next week	*la semaine d'avance*	lah suh-mehn dah-vah<u>n</u>s
Monday	*lundi*	luh<u>n</u>-dee
Tuesday	*mardi*	mar-dee
Wednesday	*mercredi*	mehr-kruh-dee
Thursday	*jeudi*	zhuh-dee
Friday	*vendredi*	vah<u>n</u>-druh-dee
Saturday	*samedi*	sahm-dee
Sunday	*dimanche*	dee-mah<u>n</u>sh

The Month

month	*mois*	mwah
January	*janvier*	zhah<u>n</u>-vee-yay
February	*février*	fay-vree-yay
March	*mars*	mars
April	*avril*	ahv-reel
May	*mai*	may
June	*juin*	zhwa<u>n</u>
July	*juillet*	zhwee-yay
August	*août*	oot
September	*septembre*	sehp-tah<u>n</u>-bruh
October	*octobre*	ohk-toh-bruh
November	*novembre*	noh-vah<u>n</u>-bruh
December	*décembre*	day-sah<u>n</u>-bruh

The Year

year	*année*	ah-nay
spring	*printemps*	pra<u>n</u>-tah<u>n</u>
summer	*été*	ay-tay
fall	*automne*	oh-tuh<u>n</u>
winter	*hiver*	ee-vehr

Holidays and Happy Days

holiday	*jour férié*	zhoor fay-ree-ay
national holiday	*fête nationale*	feht nah-see-oh-nahl
school holiday	*vacance scolaire*	vah-kah<u>n</u>s skoh-lair
religious holiday	*fête religieuse*	feht ruh-lee-zhuhz

Bastille Day (July 14)	*le quatorze juillet*	luh kah-torz zhwee-yay
Is it a holiday today / tomorrow?	*C'est un jour férié aujourd'hui / demain?*	say tuhn zhoor fay-ree-ay oh-zhoor-dwee / duh-man
What is the holiday?	*C'est quel jour férié?*	say kehl zhoor fay-ree-ay
Is a holiday coming up soon?	*C'est bientôt un jour férié?*	say bee-an-toh uhn zhoor fay-ree-ay
When?	*Quand?*	kahn
Merry Christmas!	*Joyeux Noël!*	zhwah-yuh noh-ehl
Happy New Year!	*Bonne année!*	buhn ah-nay
Easter	*Pâques*	pahk
Happy anniversary!	*Bon anniversaire de mariage!*	bohn ah-nee-vehr-sair duh mah-ree-yahzh
Happy birthday!	*Bon anniversaire!*	bohn ah-nee-vehr-sair

The French sing "Happy Birthday" to the same tune we do. Here are the words: *Joyeux anniversaire, joyeux anniversaire, joyeux anniversaire* (fill in name), *nos voeux les plus sincères.*

Other celebrations include May 1 (Labor Day), May 8 (Liberation Day), and August 15 (Assumption of Mary). France's biggest holiday is on July 14, Bastille Day. Festivities begin on the evening of the 13th and rage throughout the country.

If a holiday falls on a Thursday, many get Friday off as well: The Friday is called *le pont,* or the bridge, between the holiday and the weekend. On school holidays (*vacances scolaires*), families head for the beach, jamming resorts.

TRAVELING

FLIGHTS

All of France's airports have bilingual signage with French and English. Also, nearly all airport service personnel and travel agents speak English these days. Still, these words and phrases could conceivably come in handy.

Making a Reservation

I'd like to...	*Je voudrais...*	zhuh voo-dray
my reservation /	*ma réservation /*	mah ray-zehr-vah-see-ohn /
my ticket.	*mon billet.*	mohn bee-yay
We'd like to...	*Nous voudrions...*	noo voo-dree-ohn
our reservation /	*notre réservation /*	noh-truh ray-zehr-vah-see-
our tickets.	*nos billet.*	ohn / noh bee-yay
...confirm	*...confirmer*	kohn-feer-may
...reconfirm	*...reconfirmer*	ray-kohn-feer-may
...change	*...modifier*	moh-dee-fee-ay
...cancel	*...annuler*	ah-noo-lay
a seat near the	*un siège côté*	uhn see-ehzh koh-tay
aisle / window	*couloir / fenêtre*	kool-wahr / fuh-neh-truh

At the Airport

Which terminal?	*Quel terminal?*	kehl tehr-mee-nahl
international flights	*vols*	vohl
	internationaux	een-tehr-nah-see-ohn-oh

25

domestic flights	vols domestiques	vohl doh-mehs-teek
arrival	arrivée	ah-ree-vay
departure	départ	day-par
baggage check	inspection des bagages	een-spehk-see-ohn day bah-gahzh
baggage claim	caroussel des bagages	kah-roo-sehl day bah-gahzh
Nothing to declare.	Rien à déclarer.	ree-an ah day-klah-ray
I have only carry-on luggage.	J'ai juste un bagage en cabine.	zhay zhoost uhn bah-gahzh ahn kah-been
flight number	numéro de vol	noo-mehr-oh duh vohl
departure gate	la porte de départ	lah port duh day-par
duty free	hors taxe	or tahks
luggage cart	chariot à bagages	shah-ree-oh ah bah-gahzh
jet lag	décalage horaire	day-kah-lahzh oh-rair

Getting to/from the Airport

Approximately how much is a taxi ride to...?	C'est combien environ un taxi pour...?	say kohn-bee-an ahn-vee-rohn uhn tahk-see poor
...downtown	...le centre-ville	luh sahn-truh-veel
...the train station	...la gare	lah gar
...the airport	...l'aéroport	lah-ay-roh-por
Is there a bus (or train)...?	Il y a un bus (ou un train)...?	eel yah uhn bews (oo uhn tran)
...from the airport to downtown	...de l'aéroport au centre-ville	duh lah-ay-roh-por oh sahn-truh-veel
...from downtown to the airport	...du centre-ville à l'aéroport	dew sahn-truh-veel ah lah-ay-roh-por
How much is it?	C'est combien?	say kohn-bee-an
Where does it leave from...?	Il part d'où...?	eel par doo
Where does it arrive...?	Il arrive où...?	eel ah-ree-vay oo
...at the airport	...à l'aéroport	ah lah-ay-roh-por

| ...downtown | *...au centre-ville* | oh sahn-truh-veel |
| How often does it run? | *Quand est-ce qu'il circule?* | kahn ehs keel seer-kewl |

TRAINS

The Train Station

Where is...?	*Où est... ?*	oo ay
...the train station	*...la gare*	lah gar
French State Railways	*SNCF*	S N say F
train information	*renseignements SNCF*	rahn-sehn-yuh-mahn S N say F
train	*train*	tran
high-speed train	*TGV*	tay zhay vay
fast / faster	*rapide / plus rapide*	rah-peed / plew rah-peed
arrival	*arrivée*	ah-ree-vay
departure	*départ*	day-par
delay	*retard*	ruh-tar
toilet	*toilette*	twah-leht
waiting room	*salle d'attente*	sahl dah-tahnt
lockers	*consigne automatique*	kohn-seen-yuh oh-toh-mah-teek
baggage check room	*consigne de bagages*	kohn-seen-yuh duh bah-gahzh
lost and found office	*bureau des objets trouvés*	bew-roh dayz ohb-zhay troo-vay
tourist information	*office du tourisme*	oh-fees dew too-reez-muh
platform	*quai*	kay
to the platforms	*accès aux quais*	ahk-seh oh kay
track	*voie*	vwah
train car	*voiture*	vwah-tewr
dining car	*voiture restaurant*	vwah-tewr rehs-toh-rahn
sleeper car	*voiture-lit*	vwah-tewr-lee
conductor	*conducteur*	kohn-dewk-tur

Key Phrases: Trains

train station	*gare*	gar
train	*train*	tran
ticket	*billet*	bee-yay
transfer (n)	*correspondance*	kor-rehs-pohn-dahns
supplement	*supplément*	sew-play-mahn
arrival	*arrivée*	ah-ree-vay
departure	*départ*	day-par
platform	*quai*	kay
track	*voie*	vwah
train car	*voiture*	vwah-tewr
A ticket to ___.	*Un billet pour ___.*	uhn bee-yay poor
Two tickets to ___.	*Deux billets pour ___.*	duh bee-yay poor
When is the next train?	*Le prochain train part á quelle heure?*	luh proh-shan tran par ah kehl ur
Where does the train leave from?	*Il le train part d'où?*	eel luh tran par doo
Which train to ___?	*Quel train pour ___?*	kehl tran poor

You'll encounter several types of trains in France. Along with the various local and milk-run trains, there are:

- the slow *Regionale* trains
- the medium-speed *Trains Express Regionaux*
- the fast *EuroCity* international trains
- the super-fast trains: *TGV* (within France and to Switzerland), *Thalys* (to Belgium), and *Artesia* (to Italy)

Railpasses cover travel on all of these trains, but you'll be required to pay for a reservation (€3 per trip) on *TGV* and *Artesia* trains. On *Thalys* trains, you'll pay a Passholder Fare (about €15 second class or €30 first class) if your railpass covers all of the countries on the route you'll be taking. The French railway system

limits the number of TGV and international train reservations sold
to railpass holders, so plan ahead or be flexible. See www.ricksteves
.com/rail for more advice and information about the Eurostar train
that connects Paris to London.

Getting a Ticket

Where can I buy a ticket?	*Où puis-j'acheter un billet?*	oo pweezh ah-shuh-tay uhn bee-yay
A ticket to ___.	*Un billet pour ___.*	uhn bee-yay poor
Where can we buy tickets?	*Où pouvons-nous acheter les billets?*	oo poo-vohn-nooz ah-shuh-tay lay bee-yay
Two tickets to ___.	*Deux billets pour ___.*	duh bee-yay poor
Is this the line for...?	*C'est la file pour...?*	say lah feel poor
...tickets	*...les billets*	lay bee-yay
...reservations	*...les réservations*	lay ray-zehr-vah-see-ohn
How much is the fare to ___?	*C'est combien pour aller à ___?*	say kohn-bee-an poor ah-lay ah
Is this ticket valid for ___?	*Ce billet est bon pour ___?*	suh bee-yay ay bohn poor
How long is this ticket valid?	*Ce billet est bon pour combien de temps?*	suh bee-yay ay bohn poor kohn-bee-an duh tahn
When is the next train?	*Le prochain train part á quelle heure?*	luh proh-shan tran par ah kehl ur
Do you have a schedule for all trains departing for ___ today / tomorrow?	*Avez-vous un horaire pour tous les trains qui partent pour ___ aujourd'hui / demain?*	ah-vay-vooz uhn oh-rair poor too lay tran kee par-tahn poor ___ oh-zhoor-dwee / duh-man
I'd like to leave...	*Je voudrais partir...*	zhuh voo-dray par-teer
We'd like to leave...	*Nous voudrions partir...*	noo voo-dree-ohn par-teer
I'd like to arrive...	*Je voudrais arriver...*	zhuh voo-dray ah-ree-vay
We'd like to arrive...	*Nous voudrions arriver...*	noo voo-dree-ohn ah-ree-vay
...by ___.	*...avant ___.*	ah-vahn
...in the morning.	*...le matin.*	luh mah-tan
...in the afternoon.	*...l'après-midi.*	lah-preh-mee-dee

TRAVELING

...in the evening.	...le soir.	luh swahr
Is there a...?	Il y a un...?	eel yah uhn
...earlier train	...train plus tôt	tran plew toh
...later train	...train plus tard	tran plew tar
...overnight train	...train de nuit	tran duh nwee
...cheaper train	...train moins cher	tran mwahn shehr
...cheaper option	...solution meilleure marché	soh-lew-see-ohn may-ur mar-shay
...local train	...TER (train express régional)	tay ay ehr (tran ehk-sprehs ray-zhee-oh-nahl)
...express train	...train direct	tran dee-rehkt
What track does the train leave from?	Le train part de quel voie?	luh tran par duh kel vwah
On time?	À l'heure?	ah lur
Late?	En retard?	ahn ruh-tar

TRAVELING

Reservations, Supplements, and Discounts

Is a reservation required?	Une réservation est obligatoire?	ewn ray-zehr-vah-see-ohn ay oh-blee-gah-twahr
I'd like to reserve...	Je voudrais réserver...	zhuh voo-dray ray-zehr-vay
...a seat.	...une place.	ewn plahs
...a berth.	...une couchette.	ewn koo-sheht
...a sleeper.	...un compartiment privé.	uhn kohn-par-tuh-mahn pree-vay
...the entire train.	...le train entier.	luh tran ahn-tee-ay
We'd like to reserve...	Nous voudrions réserver...	noo voo-dree-ohn ray-zehr-vay
...two seats.	...deux places.	duh plahs
...two couchettes.	...deux couchettes.	duh koo-sheht
...two sleepers.	...un compartiment privé pour deux personnes.	uhn kohn-par-tuh-mahn pree-vay poor duh pehr-suhn
Is there a supplement?	Il y a un supplément?	eel yah uhn sew-play-mahn

Does my railpass cover the supplement?	*Le supplément est inclus dans mon pass?*	luh sew-play-mahn ay an-klew dahn mohn pahs
Is there a discount for...?	*Il y a une réduction pour les...?*	eel yah ewn ray-dewk-see-ohn poor lay
...youth	*...jeunes*	zhuhn
...seniors	*...gens âgés*	zhahn ah-zhay
...families	*...familles*	fah-mee

Ticket Talk

ticket window	*guichet*	gee-shay
reservations window	*comptoir des réservations*	kohn-twahr day ray-zehr-vah-see-ohn
national	*en France*	ahn frahns
international	*internationaux*	een-tehr-nah-see-ohn-oh
ticket	*billet*	bee-yay
one way	*aller simple*	ah-lay san-pluh
round trip	*aller retour*	ah-lay-ruh-toor
first class	*première classe*	pruhm-yehr klahs
second class	*deuxième classe*	duhz-yehm klahs
non-smoking	*non fumeur*	nohn few-mur
validate	*composter*	kohn-poh-stay
schedule	*horaire*	oh-rair
departure	*départ*	day-par
direct	*direct*	dee-rehkt
transfer (n)	*correspondance*	kor-rehs-pohn-dahns
with supplement	*avec supplément*	ah-vehk sew-play-mahn
reservation	*réservation*	ray-zehr-vah-see-ohn
seat...	*place...*	plahs
...by the window	*...côté fenêtre*	koh-tay fuh-neh-truh
...on the aisle	*...côté couloir*	koh-tay kool-wahr
berth...	*couchette...*	koo-sheht
...upper	*...en haut*	ahn oh
...middle	*...milieu*	meel-yuh
...lower	*...en bas*	ahn bah
refund	*remboursement*	rahn-boor-suh-mahn
reduced fare	*tarif réduit*	tah-reef ray-dwee

TRAVELING

Changing Trains

Is it direct?	C'est direct?	say dee-rehkt
Must I /	Je dois /	zhuh dwah /
Must we...?	Nous devons...?	noo duh-voh<u>n</u>
...make a transfer	...prendre une	prah<u>n</u>-druh ewn
	correspondance	kor-rehs-poh<u>n</u>-dah<u>n</u>s
When? / Where?	À quelle heure? / Où?	ah kehl ur / oo
Do I change	Je transfère	zhuh trah<u>n</u>s-fehr
here for ___?	ici pour ___?	ee-see poor
Do we change	Nous transférons	noo trah<u>n</u>s-fehr-oh<u>n</u>
here for ___?	ici pour ___?	ee-see poor
Where do I	Où je transfère	oo zhuh trah<u>n</u>s-fehr
change for ___?	pour ___?	poor
Where do we	Où nous transférons	oo noo trah<u>n</u>s-fehr-oh<u>n</u>
change for ___?	pour ___?	poor
At what time?	À quelle heure?	ah kehl ur
From what track	Le train part de	luh tra<u>n</u> par duh
does the train	quelle voie?	kehl vwah
leave?		
How many	Combien de	koh<u>n</u>-bee-a<u>n</u> duh
minutes in ___ to	minutes à ___ pour	mee-newt ah ___ poor
change trains?	changer de train?	shah<u>n</u>-zhay duh tra<u>n</u>

On the Platform

Where is...?	Où est...?	oo ay
Is this...?	C'est...?	say
...the train to ___	...le train pour ___	luh tra<u>n</u> poor
Which train to ___?	Quel train pour ___?	kehl tra<u>n</u> poor
Which train	Quelle voiture	kehl vwah-tewr
car to ___?	pour ___?	poor
Where is first	Où est la première	oo ay lah pruhm-yehr
class?	classe?	klahs
front	à l'avant	ah lah-vah<u>n</u>
middle	au milieu	oh meel-yuh
back	au fond	oh foh<u>n</u>

Arrive at the station well before your departure to find the right platform. In small towns, your train may depart before the station opens; go directly to the tracks and find the overhead sign that confirms your train stops at that track.

For security reasons, all luggage (including day packs) must carry a tag with the traveler's first and last name and current address. Free tags are available at all train stations in France.

On the Train

Is this seat free?	C'est libre?	say lee-bruh
May I...?	Je peux...?	zhuh puh
May we...?	Nous pouvons...?	noo poo-vohn
...sit here	...s'asseoir ici	sah-swar ee-see
...open the window	...ouvrir la fenêtre	oo-vreer lah fuh-neh-truh
...eat your meal	...manger votre repas	mahn-zhay voh-truh ruh-pah
Save my place?	Garder ma place?	gar-day mah plahs
Save our places?	Garder nos places?	gar-day noh plahs
That's my seat.	C'est ma place.	say mah plahs
These are our seats.	Ce sont nos places.	suh sohn noh plahs
Where are you going?	Où allez-vous?	oo ah-lay-voo
I'm going to ___.	Je vais à ___.	zhuh vay ah
We're going to ___.	Nous allons à ___.	nooz ah-lohn ah
Tell me when to get off?	Dîtes-moi quand je descends?	deet-mwah kahn zhuh day-sahn
Tell us when to get off?	Dîtes-nous quand on descend?	deet-noo kahn ohn day-sahn
Where is a (good-looking) conductor?	Où est un (beau) conducteur?	oo ay uhn (boh) kohn-dewk-tur
Does this train stop in ___?	Ce train s'arrête à ___?	suh tran sah-reht ah
When will it arrive in ___?	Il va arriver à ___ à quelle heure?	eel vah ah-ree-vay ah ___ ah kehl ur
When will it arrive?	Il va arriver à quelle heure?	eel vah ah-ree-vay ah kehl ur

Reading Train and Bus Schedules

European schedules use the 24-hour clock. It's like American time until noon. After that, subtract twelve and add P.M. So 13:00 is 1 P.M., 20:00 is 8 P.M., and 24:00 is midnight. One minute after midnight is 00:01.

French train schedules show blue (quiet), white (normal), and red (peak and holiday) times. You can save money if you get the blues (travel during off-peak hours).

à, pour	to
arrivée	arrival
de	from
départ	departure
dimanche	Sunday
en retard	late
en semaine	workdays (Monday-Saturday)
et	and
heure	hour
horaire	timetable
jour férié	holiday
jours	days
jusqu'à	until
la semaine	weekdays
par	via
pas	not
samedi	Saturday
sauf	except
seulement	only
tous	every
tous les jours	daily
vacances	holidays
voie	track
1-5	Monday-Friday
6, 7	Saturday, Sunday

Major Transportation Lines in France

Going Places

France	*la France*	lah frahns
Belgium	*la Belgique*	lah behl-zheek
English Channel	*la Manche*	lah mahnsh
Austria	*l'Autriche*	loh-treesh
Czech Republic	*la République Tcheque*	lah reh-poob-leek chehk

TRAVELING

Great Britain	*la Grande-Bretagne*	lah grah<u>n</u> breh-tah<u>n</u>-yuh
Germany	*l'Allemagne*	lahl-mah<u>n</u>-yuh
Greece	*la Grèce*	lah grehs
Ireland	*l'Irlande*	leer-lah<u>n</u>d
Italy	*l'Italie*	lee-tah-lee
Netherlands	*les Pays-Bas*	lay peh-ee-bah
Portugal	*le Portugal*	luh por-tew-gal
Scandinavia	*la Scandinavie*	lah skah<u>n</u>-dee-nah-vee
Spain	*l'Espagne*	luh-spah<u>n</u>-yuh
Switzerland	*la Suisse*	lah swees
Turkey	*la Turquie*	lah tehr-kee
Europe	*l'Europe*	lur-rohp
EU	*UE*	ew uh
(European	(*l'Union*	(lewn-yoh<u>n</u>
Union)	*Européenne*)	ur-oh-pay-ehn)
Russia	*la Russie*	lah roo-see
Africa	*l'Afrique*	laf-reek
United States	*les États-Unis*	layz ay-tah-zew-nee
Canada	*le Canada*	luh kah-nah-dah
world	*le monde*	luh moh<u>n</u>d

Places Within France

If you're using the *Rick Steves' France* guidebook, you're also likely to see these place names. When French clerks at train stations and train conductors don't understand your pronunciation, write the town name on a piece of paper.

Alsace	ahl-sahs
Amboise	ahm-bwahz
Annecy	ahn-see
Antibes	ahn-teeb
Arles	arl
Arromanches	ah-roh-mahnsh
Avignon	ah-veen-yohn
Bayeux	bah-yuh
Beaune	bohn
Beynac	bay-nak

Bordeaux	bor-doh
Calais	kah-lay
Carcassonne	kar-kah-suhn
Chambord	shahn-bor
Chamonix	shah-moh-nee
Chartres	shart
Chenonceau	shuh-nohn-soh
Cherbourg	shehr-boor
Chinon	shee-nohn
Collioure	kohl-yoor
Colmar	kohl-mar
Côte d'Azur	koht dah-zewr
Dijon	dee-zhohn
Dordogne	dor-dohn-yuh
Giverny	zhee-vehr-nee
Grenoble	gruh-noh-bluh
Honfleur	ohn-floor
Le Havre	luh hah-vruh
Loire	lwar
Lyon	lee-ohn
Marseille	mar-say
Mont Blanc	mohn blahn
Mont St. Michel	mohn san mee-shehl
Nantes	nahnt
Nice	nees
Normandy	nor-mahn-dee
Paris	pah-ree
Provence	proh-vahns
Reims	rans (rhymes with France)
Rouen	roo-ahn
Roussillon	roo-see-yohn
Sarlat	sar-lah
Strasbourg	strahs-boorg
Verdun	vehr-duhn
Versailles	vehr-sī
Villefranche	veel-frahnsh

BUSES AND SUBWAYS

At the Bus Station or Métro Stop

ticket	*ticket*	tee-kay
city bus	*bus*	bews
long-distance bus	*car*	kar
bus stop	*arrêt de bus*	ah-reh duh bews
bus station	*gare routière*	gar root-yehr
subway	*Métro*	may-troh
subway station	*station de Métro*	stah-see-ohn duh may-troh
subway map	*plan du Métro*	plahn dew may-troh
subway entrance	*l'entrée du Métro*	lahn-tray dew may-troh
subway stop	*arrêt de Métro*	ah-reh duh may-troh
subway exit	*sortie*	sor-tee
direct	*direct*	dee-rehkt
connection	*correspondance*	kor-rehs-pohn-dahns
pickpocket	*voleur*	voh-loor
batch of 10 tickets	*carnet*	kar-nay

In Paris, you'll save money by buying a *carnet* (batch of 10 tickets) at virtually any Métro station. The tickets, which are sharable, are valid on the buses, Métro, and RER (underground rail lines) within the city limits.

Taking Buses and Subways

How do I get to ___?	*Comment je vais à ___?*	koh-mahn zhuh vay ah
How do we get to ___?	*Comment nous allons à ___?*	koh-mahn nooz ah-lohn ah
How much is a ticket?	*C'est combien le ticket?*	say kohn-bee-an luh tee-kay
Where can I buy a ticket?	*Où puis-je acheter un ticket?*	oo pwee-zhuh ah-shuh-tay uhn tee-kay
Where can we buy tickets?	*Où pouvons-nous acheter les tickets?*	oo poo-vohn-noo ah-shuh-tay lay tee-kay

TRAVELING

Key Phrases: Buses and Subways

bus	*bus*	bews
subway	*Métro*	may-troh
ticket	*ticket*	tee-kay
How do I get to ___?	*Comment je vais à ___?*	koh-mahn zhuh vay ah
Which stop for ___?	*Quel arrêt pour ___?*	kehl ah-reh poor
Tell me when to get off?	*Dîtes-moi quand je descends?*	deet-mwah kahn zhuh day-sahn

One ticket, please.	*Un billet, s'il vous plaît.*	uhn bee-yay see voo play
Two tickets.	*Deux billets.*	duh bee-yay
Is this ticket valid (for ___)?	*Ce ticket est bon (pour ___)?*	suh tee-kay ay bohn (poor)
Is there...?	*Il y a...?*	eel yah
...a one-day pass	*...un pass à la journée*	uhn pahs ah lah zhoor-nay
...a discount if I buy more tickets	*...une réduction si j'achet plusieurs tickets*	ewn ray-dewk-see-ohn see zhah-shay plewz-yur tee-kay
Which bus to ___?	*Quel bus pour ___?*	kehl bews poor
Does it stop at ___?	*Il s'arrête à ___?*	eel sah-reht ah
Which bus stop for ___?	*Quel arrêt pour ___?*	kehl ah-reh poor
Which subway stop for ___?	*Quel arrêt de Métro pour ___?*	kehl ah-reh duh may-troh poor
Which direction for ___?	*Quelle direction pour ___?*	kehl dee-rehk-see-ohn poor
Must I / Must we...?	*Je dois / Nous devons...?*	zhuh dwah / noo duh-vohn
...transfer	*...prendre une correspondance*	prahn-druh ewn kor-rehs-pohn-dahns

TRAVELING

When does the... leave?	Le... part quand?	luh... par kahn
...first / next / last	...premier / prochain / dernier	pruhm-yay / proh-shan / dehrn-yay
...bus / subway	...bus / Métro	bews / may-troh
What's the frequency per hour / day?	Combien de fois par heure / jour?	kohn-bee-an duh fwah par ur / zhoor
Where does it leave from?	D'où il part?	doo eel par
What time does it leave?	Il part à quelle heure?	eel par ah kehl ur
I'm going to ___.	Je vais à ___.	zhuh vay ah
We're going to ___.	Nous allons à ___.	nooz ah-lohn ah
Tell me when to get off?	Dîtes-moi quand je descends?	deet-mwah kahn zhuh day-sahn
Tell us when to get off?	Dîtes-nous quand on descend?	deet-noo kahn ohn day-sahn

TAXIS

Getting a Taxi

Taxi!	Taxi!	tahk-see
Can you call a taxi?	Pouvez-vous appeler un taxi?	poo-vay-voo ah-puh-lay uhn tahk-see
Where is a taxi stand?	Où est une station de taxi?	oo ay ewn stah-see-ohn duh tahk-see
Where can I get a taxi?	Où puis-je trouver un taxi?	oo pwee-zhuh troo-vay uhn tahk-see
Where can we get a taxi?	Où pouvons-nous trouver un taxi?	oo poo-vohn-noo troo-vay uhn tahk-see
Are you free?	Vous êtes libre?	vooz eht lee-bruh
Occupied.	Occupé.	oh-kew-pay
To ___, please.	À ___, s'il vous plaît.	ah ___ see voo play
To this address.	À cette adresse.	ah seht ah-drehs
Take me to ___.	Amenez-moi à ___.	ah-muh-nay-mwah ah
Take us to ___.	Amenez-nous à ___.	ah-muh-nay-nooz ah

Key Phrases: Taxis

Taxi!	*Taxi!*	tahk-see
Are you free?	*Vous êtes libre?*	vooz eht lee-bruh
To ___ , please.	*À ___ , s'il vous plaît.*	ah ___ see voo play
meter	*compteur*	kohn-tur
Stop here.	*Arrêtez-vous ici.*	ah-reh-tay-voo ee-see
Keep the change.	*Gardez la monnaie.*	gar-day lah moh-nay

Approximately how much will it cost to go...?	*C'est environ combien d'aller...?*	say ahn-vee-rohn kohn-bee-an dah-lay
...to ___	*...à ___*	ah
...to the airport	*...à l'aéroport*	ah lah-ay-roh-por
...to the train station	*...à la gare*	ah lah gar
...to this address	*...à cette adresse*	ah seht ah-drehs
Any extra supplement?	*Il y a un supplément?*	eel yah uhn sew-play-mahn
It's too much.	*C'est trop.*	say troh
Can you take ___ people?	*Pouvez-vous prendre ___ passagers?*	poo-vay-voo prahn-druh ___ pah-sah-zhay
Any extra fee?	*Il y a d'autres frais?*	eel yah doh-truh fray
Do you have an hourly rate?	*Avez-vous un taux par heure?*	ah-vay-vooz uhn toh par ur
How much for a one-hour city tour?	*Combien pour une visite d'une heure en ville?*	kohn-bee-an poor ewn vee-zeet dewn ur ahn veel

TRAVELING

So you'll know what to expect, ask your hotelier about typical taxi fares. Fares go up at night (7:00 P.M. to 7:00 A.M.) and on Sundays, and drivers always charge for loading baggage in the trunk. Your fare can nearly double if you're taking a short trip with lots of bags. In smaller towns, cabbies are few and customer satisfaction is important. Strike up a conversation and make a new friend.

If you're having a tough time hailing a taxi, ask for the nearest taxi stand (*station de taxi*). The simplest way to tell a cabbie where you want to go is by stating your destination followed by "please" ("*Louvre, s'il vous plaît*"). Tipping isn't expected, but it's polite to round up. So if the fare is €19, round up to €20.

In the Taxi

The meter, please.	Le compteur, s'il vous plaît.	luh kohn-tur see voo play
Where is the meter?	Où est le compteur?	oo ay luh kohn-tur
I'm in a hurry.	Je suis pressé.	zhuh swee preh-say
We're in a hurry.	Nous sommes pressés.	noo suhm preh-say
Slow down.	Ralentissez.	rah-lahn-tee-say
If you don't slow down, I'll throw up.	Si vous ne ralentissez pas, je vais vomir.	see voo nuh rah-lahn-tee-say pah, zhuh vay voh-meer
Left / Right / Straight.	À gauche / À droite / Tout droit.	ah gohsh / ah dwaht / too dwah
I'd like to stop here for a moment.	J'aimerais m'arrêter ici un moment.	zhehm-uh-ray mah-reh-tay ee-see uhn moh-mahn
We'd like to stop here for a moment.	Nous aimerions nous arrêter ici un moment.	nooz ehm-uh-rohn nooz ah-reh-tay ee-see uhn moh-mahn
Please stop here for ___ minutes.	S'il vous plaît arrêtez-vous ici pour ___ minutes.	see voo play ah-reh-tay-voo ee-see poor ___ mee-newt
Can you wait?	Pouvez-vous attendre?	poo-vay vooz ah-tahn-druh
Crazy traffic, isn't it?	C'est fou, cette circulation, non?	say foo seht seer-kewl-ah-see-ohn nohn
You drive like ...	Vous conduisez comme...	voo kohn-dwee-zay kohm
...a madman!	...un fou!	uhn foo
...Michael Schumacher.	...Michel Schumacher.	mee-shehl "Schumacher"

You drive very well.	*Vous conduisez très bien.*	voo kohn-dwee-zay treh bee-an
Where did you learn to drive?	*Où avez-vous appris à conduire?*	oo ah-vay-vooz ah-preez ah kohn-dweer
Stop here.	*Arrêtez-vous ici.*	ah-reh-tay-voo ee-see
Here is fine.	*Ici c'est bien.*	ee-see say bee-an
At this corner.	*À ce coin.*	ah say kwan
The next corner.	*Au coin prochain.*	oh kwan proh-shan
My change, please.	*La monnaie, s'il vous plaît.*	lah moh-nay see voo play
Keep the change.	*Gardez la monnaie.*	gar-day lah moh-nay
This ride is / was more fun than Disneyland.	*Ce trajet est / était plus drôle que Disneyland.*	suh trah-zhay ay / ay-tay plew drohl kuh "Disneyland"

DRIVING

Rental Wheels

car rental agency	*agence de location de voiture*	ah-zhahns duh loh-kah-see-ohn duh vwah-tewr
I'd like to rent...	*Je voudrais louer...*	zhuh voo-dray loo-ay
We'd like to rent...	*Nous voudrions louer...*	noo voo-dree-ohn loo-ay
...a car.	*...une voiture.*	ewn vwah-tewr
...a station wagon.	*...un break.*	uhn brayk
...a van.	*...un van.*	uhn vahn
...a motorcycle.	*...une motocyclette.*	ewn moh-toh-see-kleht
...a motor scooter.	*...un vélomoteur.*	uhn vay-loh-moh-tur
...the Concorde.	*...le Concorde.*	luh kohn-kord
How much per...?	*Combien par...?*	kohn-bee-an par
...hour	*...heure*	ur
...half day	*...demie-journée*	duh-mee zhoor-nay
...day	*...jour*	zhoor
...week	*...semaine*	suh-mehn
Unlimited mileage?	*Kilométrage illimité?*	kee-loh-may-trahzh eel-lee-mee-tay

TRAVELING

Key Phrases: Driving

car	*voiture*	vwah-tewr
gas station	*station service*	stah-see-oh<u>n</u> sehr-vees
parking lot	*parking*	par-keeng
accident	*accident*	ahk-see-dah<u>n</u>
left / right	*à gauche / à droite*	ah gohsh / ah dwaht
straight ahead	*tout droit*	too dwah
downtown	*centre-ville*	sah<u>n</u>-truh-veel
How do I get	*Comment je*	koh-mah<u>n</u> zhuh
to ___?	*vais à ___?*	vay ah
Where can I park?	*Où puis-je me*	oo pwee-zhuh muh
	garer?	gah-ray

When must I bring	*Je dois le ramener*	zhuh dwah luh rah-muh-nay
it back?	*à quelle heure?*	ah kehl ur
Is there...?	*Est-ce qu'il y a...?*	ehs keel yah
...a helmet	*...un casque*	uh<u>n</u> kahsk
...a discount	*...une réduction*	ewn ray-dewk-see-oh<u>n</u>
...a deposit	*...une caution*	ewn koh-see-oh<u>n</u>
...insurance	*...une assurance*	ewn ah-sewr-rah<u>n</u>s

At the Gas Station

gas station	*station service*	stah-see-oh<u>n</u> sehr-vees
The nearest	*La plus proche*	lah plew prohsh
gas station?	*station service?*	stah-see-oh<u>n</u> sehr-vees
Self-service?	*Libre service?*	lee-bruh sehr-vees
Fill the tank.	*Faites le plein.*	feht luh pla<u>n</u>
Wash the windows.	*Lavez le pare-brise.*	lah-vay luh pah-ruh-breez
I need...	*Il me faut...*	eel muh foh
We need...	*Il nous faut...*	eel noo foh
...gas.	*...de l'essence.*	duh leh-sah<u>n</u>s
...unleaded.	*...sans plomb.*	sah<u>n</u> ploh<u>n</u>
...regular.	*...normale.*	nor-mahl
...super.	*...du super.*	dew sew-pehr

...diesel.	...gazoil.	gah-zoyl
Check...	Vérifiez...	vay-ree-fee-ay
...the oil.	...l'huile.	lweel
...the air in the tires.	...la pression dans les pneus.	lah pruh-see-ohn dahn lay puh-nuh
...the radiator.	...le radiateur.	luh rahd-yah-tur
...the battery.	...la batterie.	lah bah-tuh-ree
...the sparkplugs.	...les bougies.	lay boo-zhee
...the headlights.	...les phares.	lay fahr
...the tail lights.	...les feux arrières.	lay fuh ah-ree-ehr
...the directional signal.	...le clignotant.	luh klee-noh-tahn
...the brakes.	...les freins.	lay fran
...the transmission fluid.	...la liquide de transmission.	lah lee-keed duh trahnz-mee-see-ohn
...the windshield wipers.	...les essuie-glaces.	layz ehs-wee-glahs
...the fuses.	...les fusibles.	lay few-zee-bluh
...the fanbelt.	...la courroie du ventilateur.	lah koor-wah dew vahn-tee-lah-tur
...my pulse.	...mon poul.	mohn pool
...my husband / my wife.	...mon mari / ma femme.	mohn mah-ree / mah fahm

(side tab: **TRAVELING**)*

The cheapest gas in France is sold in *hypermarché* (supermarket) parking lots. Prices are listed per liter; there are about four liters in a gallon.

Car Trouble

accident	accident	ahk-see-dahn
breakdown	en panne	ahn pahn
dead battery	batterie morte	bah-tuh-ree mort
funny noise	bruit curieux	brwee kew-ree-uh
electrical problem	problème d'électricité	proh-blehm day-lehk-tree-see-tay
flat tire	pneu crevé	puh-nuh kruh-vay

shop with auto parts	*magasin de pièces detachées auto*	mah-gah-za<u>n</u> duh pee-ehs duh-tah-shay oh-toh
dealership	*concessionaire*	koh<u>n</u>-seh-see-oh-nair
My car won't start.	*Ma voiture ne démarre pas.*	mah vwah-tewr nuh day-mar pah
My car is broken.	*Ma voiture est cassée.*	mah vwah-tewr ay cah-say
This doesn't work.	*Ça ne marche pas.*	sah nuh marsh pah
It's overheating.	*Le moteur surchauffe.*	luh moh-tur sewr-shohf
It's a lemon (rattletrap).	*C'est un tas de féraille.*	say uh<u>n</u> tah duh fay-ray-y<u>ī</u>
I need...	*J'ai besoin...*	zhay buh-swa<u>n</u>
We need...	*Nous avons besoin...*	nooz ah-voh<u>n</u> buh-swa<u>n</u>
...a tow truck.	*...d'un dépanneur.*	duh<u>n</u> day-pah-nur
...a mechanic.	*...d'un mécanicien.*	duh<u>n</u> may-kah-nee-see-a<u>n</u>
...a stiff drink.	*...d'un bon coup à boire.*	duh<u>n</u> boh<u>n</u> koo ah bwahr

In France, people with car problems go to the dealership. If you're renting a troubled Renault, your rental agency may direct you to the nearest *concessionaire Renault*. For help with repair, see "Repair" in the Services chapter on page 160.

Parking

parking lot	*parking*	par-keeng
parking garage	*garage de stationement*	gah-rahzh duh stah-see-ohn-mah<u>n</u>
parking meter	*horodateur*	oh-roh-dah-tur
Where can I park?	*Où puis-je me garer?*	oo pwee-zhuh muh gah-ray
Is parking nearby?	*Il y a un parking près d'ici?*	eel yah uh<u>n</u> par-keeng preh dee-see
Can I park here?	*Je peux me garer ici?*	zhuh puh muh gah-ray ee-see
Is this a safe place to park?	*C'est prudent de se garer ici?*	say prew-dah<u>n</u> duh suh gah-ray ee-see

How long can I park here?	*Je peux me garer ici pour combien de temps?*	zhuh puh muh gah-ray ee-see poor kohn-bee-an duh tahn
Must I pay to park here?	*Je dois payer pour me garer ici?*	zhuh dwah pay-yay poor muh gah-ray ee-see
How much per hour / day?	*Combien heure / jour?*	kohn-bee-an par ur / zhoor

Many French cities use remote meters for curbside parking. After you park, look for a meter at the street corner and buy a ticket to place on the dash. If you're not certain you need a ticket, look at the dashboards of cars parked nearby. If they have tickets, you'll need one, too. Ask a local for help finding the *horodateur* (parking meter).

FINDING YOUR WAY

I am going to ___.	*Je vais à ___.*	zhuh vay ah
We are going to ___.	*Nous allons à ___.*	nooz ah-lohn ah
How do I get to ___?	*Comment je vais à ___?*	koh-mahn zhuh vay ah
How do we get to ___?	*Comment nous allons à ___?*	koh-mahn nooz ah-lohn ah
Do you have...?	*Avez-vous...?*	ah-vay-vooz
...a city map	*...un plan de la ville*	uhn plahn duh lah veel
...a road map	*...une carte routière*	ewn kart root-yehr
How many minutes...?	*Combien de minutes...?*	kohn-bee-an duh mee-newt
How many hours...?	*Combien d'heures...?*	kohn-bee-an dur
...on foot	*...à pied*	ah pee-yay
...by bicycle	*...à bicyclette*	ah bee-see-kleht
...by car	*...en voiture*	ahn vwah-tewr
How many kilometers to ___?	*Combien de kilomètres à ___?*	kohn-bee-an duh kee-loh-meh-truh ah
What's the...	*Quelle est la...*	kehl eh lah...
route to Paris?	*route pour Paris?*	root poor pah-ree
...most scenic	*...plus belle*	plew behl

...fastest	*...plus directe*	plew dee-rehkt
...most interesting	*...plus intéressante*	plewz a<u>n</u>-tay-reh-sah<u>n</u>t
Point it out?	*Montrez-moi?*	moh<u>n</u>-tray mwah
I'm lost.	*Je suis perdu.*	zhuh swee pehr-dew
We're lost.	*Nous sommes perdu.*	noo suhm pehr-dew
Where am I?	*Où suis-je?*	oo swee-zhuh
Where is...?	*Où est...?*	oo ay
The nearest...?	*Le plus proche...?*	luh plew prohsh
Where is this address?	*Où se trouve cette adresse?*	oo suh troov seht ah-drehs

Route-Finding Words

city map	*plan de la ville*	plah<u>n</u> duh lah veel
road map	*carte routière*	kart root-yehr
downtown	*centre-ville*	sah<u>n</u>-truh-veel
left	*à gauche*	ah gohsh
right	*à droite*	ah dwaht
straight ahead	*tout droit*	too dwah
first	*premier*	pruhm-yay
next	*prochain*	proh-sha<u>n</u>
intersection	*carrefour*	kar-foor
corner	*au coin*	oh kwa<u>n</u>
block	*paté de maisons*	pah-tay duh may-zoh<u>n</u>
roundabout	*rondpoint*	roh<u>n</u>-pwa<u>n</u>
ring road	*rocade*	roh-kahd
stoplight	*feu*	fuh
square	*place*	plahs
street	*rue*	rew
bridge	*pont*	poh<u>n</u>
tunnel	*tunnel*	tew-nehl
highway	*grande route*	grah<u>n</u>d root
national highway	*route nationale*	root nah-see-oh-nahl
freeway	*autoroute*	oh-toh-root
north	*nord*	nor
south	*sud*	sewd
east	*est*	ehs
west	*ouest*	wehs

The shortest distance between any two points in France is the *autoroute*, but the tolls add up. You'll travel cheaper, but slower, on a *route nationale*. Along the *autoroute*, electronic signs flash messages to let you know what's ahead: *bouchon* (traffic jam), *circulation* (traffic), and *fluide* (no traffic).

The Police

As in any country, the flashing lights of a patrol car are a sure sign that someone's in trouble. If it's you, try this handy phrase: "*Pardon, je suis touriste*" (Sorry, I'm a tourist). Or, for the adventurous: "*Si vous n'aimez pas ma conduite, vous n'avez que descendre du trottoir.*" (If you don't like how I drive, get off the sidewalk.)

I'm late for my tour.	*Je suis en retard pour mon tour.*	zhuh swee ah<u>n</u> ruh-tar poor moh<u>n</u> toor
Can I buy your hat?	*Je peux acheter votre chapeau?*	zhuh puh ah-shuh-tay voh-truh shah-poh
What seems to be the problem?	*Quel est le problème?*	kehl ay luh proh-blehm
Sorry, I'm a tourist.	*Pardon, je suis touriste.*	par-doh<u>n</u> zhuh swee too-reest

Reading Road Signs

attention travaux	workers ahead
autres directions (follow when leaving a town)	other directions
céder le passage	yield
centre-ville	to the center of town
déviation	detour
entrée	entrance
péage	toll
prochaine sortie	next exit
ralentir	slow down
réservé aux piétons	pedestrians only
sans issue	dead end
sauf riverains	local access only

Standard Road Signs

 AND LEARN THESE ROAD SIGNS

Speed Limit (km/hr)

Yield

No Passing

End of No Passing Zone

One Way

Intersection

Main Road

Freeway

Danger

No Entry

No Entry for Cars

All Vehicles Prohibited

Parking

No Parking

Customs

Peace

sens unique	one-way street
sortie	exit
stationnement interdit	no parking
stop	stop
toutes directions	all directions
(follow when leaving a town)	
travaux	construction
virages	curves

Other Signs You May See

à louer	for rent or for hire
à vendre	for sale
chambre libre	vacancy
chien méchant	mean dog
complet	no vacancy
dames	women
danger	danger
défense de fumer	no smoking
défense de toucher	do not touch
défense d'entrer	keep out
eau non potable	undrinkable water
entrée libre	free admission
entrée interdite	no entry
en panne	out of service
fermé	closed
fermé pour restauration	closed for restoration
fermeture annuelle	closed for vacation
guichet	ticket window
hommes	men
hors service	out of service
interdit	forbidden
occupé	occupied
ouvert	open
ouvert de___ à___	open from___ to___
poussez / tirez	push / pull
prudence	caution

solde	sale
sortie de secours	emergency exit
tirez / poussez	pull / push
toilettes	toilets
WC	toilet

SLEEPING

Places to Stay

hotel	hôtel	oh-tehl
small hotel	pension	pah**n**-see-oh**n**
small hotel with restaurant	auberge	ow-behrzh
castle hotel	hôtel-château	oh-tehl-shah-toh
room in a private home	chambre d'hôte	shah**n**-bruh doht
youth hostel	auberge de jeunesse	oh-behrzh duh zhuh-nehs
country home rental	gîte	zheet
vacancy	chambre libre	shah**n**-bruh lee-bruh
no vacancy	complet	koh**n**-play

Reserving a Room

I like to reserve rooms a few days in advance as I travel. But if my itinerary is set, I reserve before I leave home. To reserve from home by fax or email, use the handy form in the appendix (online at www.ricksteves.com/reservation).

Hello.	Bonjour.	boh**n**-zhoor
Do you speak English?	Parlez-vous anglais?	par-lay-voo ah**n**-glay

Key Phrases: Sleeping

I want to make / confirm a reservation.	Je veux faire / confirmer une réservation.	zhuh vuh fair / kohn-feer-may ewn ray-zehr-vah-see-ohn
I'd like a room (for two people), please.	Je voudrais une chambre (pour deux personnes) s'il vous plaît.	zhuh voo-dray ewn shahn-bruh (poor duh pehr-suhn) see voo play
...with / without / and	...avec / sans / et	ah-vehk / sahn / ay
...toilet	...WC	vay say
...shower	...douche	doosh
Can I see the room?	Je peux voir la chambre?	zhuh puh vwar lah shahn-bruh
How much is it?	Combien?	kohn-bee-an
Credit card O.K.?	Carte de crédit O.K.?	kart duh kray-dee "O.K."

SLEEPING

Do you have a room...?	Avez-vous une chambre...?	ah-vay-vooz ewn shahn-bruh
...for one person	...pour une personne	poor ewn pehr-suhn
...for two people	...pour deux personnes	poor duh pehr-suhn
...for tonight	...pour ce soir	poor suh swar
...for two nights	...pour deux nuits	poor duh nwee
...for this Friday	...pour ce vendredi	poor suh vahn-druh-dee
...for June 21	...pour le vingt et un juin	poor luh vant ay uhn zhwan
Yes or no?	Oui ou non?	wee oo nohn
I'd like...	Je voudrais...	zhuh voo-dray
We'd like...	Nous voudrions...	noo voo-dree-ohn
...a private bathroom.	...une salle de bains.	ewn sahl duh ban
...your cheapest room.	...la chambre la moins chère.	lah shahn-bruh lah mwan shehr
...___ beds for ___ people in ___ rooms.	...___ lits par ___ personnes dans ___ chambres.	___ lee par ___ pehr-suhn dahn ___ shahn-bruh

How much is it?	*Combien?*	kohn-bee-an
Anything cheaper?	*Rien de moins cher?*	ree-an duh mwan shehr
I'll take it.	*Je la prends.*	zhuh lah prahn
My name is ___.	*Je m'appelle ___.*	zhuh mah-pehl
I'll stay...	*Je reste...*	zhuh rehst
We'll stay...	*Nous restons...*	noo rehs-tohn
...one night.	*...une nuit.*	ewn nwee
...___ nights.	*...___ nuits.*	___ nwee
I'll come...	*J'arrive...*	zhah-reev
We'll come...	*Nous arrivons...*	nooz ah-ree-vohn
...in the morning.	*...dans la matinée.*	dahn lah mah-tee-nay
...in the afternoon.	*...dans l'après-midi.*	dahn lah-preh-mee-dee
...in the evening.	*...dans la soirée.*	dahn lah swah-ray
...in one hour.	*...dans une heure.*	dahnz ewn ur
...before 4:00 in the afternoon.	*...avant quatre heures dans l'après-midi.*	ah-vahn kah-truh ur dahn lah-preh-mee-dee
...Friday before 6 P.M.	*...vendredi avant six heures du soir.*	vahn-druh-dee ah-vahn seez ur dew swar
Thank you.	*Merci.*	mehr-see

L'Alphabet

If phoning, you can use the code alphabet below to spell out your name if necessary. Unless you're giving the hotelier your name as it appears on your credit card, consider using a shorter version of your name to make things easier.

a	*ah*	Anatole	ahn-ah-tohl
b	*bay*	Berthe	behrt
c	*say*	Célestin	say-luh-steen
d	*day*	Désiré	day-zee-ray
e	*uh*	Emile	eh-meel
f	*"f"*	François	frahn-swah
g	*zhay*	Gaston	gah-stohn
h	*ahsh*	Henri	ahn-ree
i	*ee*	Irma	eer-mah
j	*zhee*	Joseph	zhoh-zuhf

k	*kah*	Kléber	klay-behr
l	*"l"*	Louis	loo-ee
m	*"m"*	Marcel	mar-sehl
n	*"n"*	Nicolas	nee-koh-lahs
o	*"o"*	Oscar	ohs-kar
p	*pay*	Pierre	pee-yehr
q	*kew*	Quintal	kween-tahl
r	*ehr*	Raoul	rah-ool
s	*"s"*	Suzanne	soo-zah<u>n</u>
t	*tay*	Thérèse	tay-rehs
u	*ew*	Ursule	oor-sool
v	*vay*	Victor	veek-tor
w	*doo-bluh vay*	William	weel-yahm
x	*"x"*	Xavier	zhahv-yehr
y	*ee grehk*	Yvonne	ee-vuh<u>n</u>
z	*zehd*	Zoé	zoh-ay

Using a Credit Card

If you need to secure your reservation with a credit card, here's the lingo.

Is a deposit required?	*Je dois verser un accompte?*	zhuh dwah vehr-say uh<u>n</u> ah-kohnt
Credit card O.K.?	*Carte de crédit O.K.?*	kart duh kray-dee "O.K."
credit card	*carte de crédit*	kart duh kray-dee
debit card	*carte bancaire*	kart bah<u>n</u>-kair
The name on the card is ___.	*Le nom sur la carte est ___.*	luh noh<u>n</u> sewr lah kart ay
The credit card number is...	*Le numéro de carte de crédit est...*	luh noo-mehr-oh duh kart duh kray-dee ay
0	*zéro*	zay-roh
1	*un*	uh<u>n</u>
2	*deux*	duh
3	*trois*	twah
4	*quatre*	kah-truh
5	*cinq*	sa<u>n</u>k

SLEEPING

6	*six*	sees
7	*sept*	seht
8	*huit*	weet
9	*neuf*	nuhf
The expiration date is...	*La date d'expiration est...*	lah daht dehks-pee-rah-see-oh<u>n</u> ay
January	*janvier*	zhah<u>n</u>-vee-yay
February	*février*	fay-vree-yay
March	*mars*	mars
April	*avril*	ahv-reel
May	*mai*	may
June	*juin*	zhwa<u>n</u>
July	*juillet*	zhwee-yay
August	*août*	oot
September	*septembre*	sehp-tah<u>n</u>-bruh
October	*octobre*	ohk-toh-bruh
November	*novembre*	noh-vah<u>n</u>-bruh
December	*décembre*	day-sah<u>n</u>-bruh
2009	*deux mille neuf*	duh meel nuhf
2010	*deux mille dix*	duh meel dees
2011	*deux mille onze*	duh meel ohnz
2012	*deux mille douze*	duh meel dooz
2013	*deux mille treize*	duh meel trehz
2014	*deux mille quatorze*	duh meel kah-torz
2015	*deux mille quinze*	duh meel kanz
2016	*deux mille seize*	duh meel sehz
2017	*deux mille dix-sept*	duh meel dee-seht
Can I reserve with a credit card and pay in cash?	*Je peux réserver avec une carte de crédit et payer en liquide?*	zhuh puh ray-zehr-vay ah-vehk ewn kart duh kray-dee ay pay-yay ah<u>n</u> lee-keed
I have another card.	*J'ai une autre carte.*	zhay ewn oh-truh kart

SLEEPING

If your *carte de crédit* is not approved, say, "*J'ai une autre carte*" (I have another card)—if you do.

Just the Fax, Ma'am

If you're booking a room by fax...

I want to send a fax.	*J'aimerais vous envoyer un fax.*	zhehm-uh-ray vooz ahn-voy-ay uhn fahks
What is your fax number?	*Quel est votre numéro de fax?*	kehl ay voh-truh noo-mehr-oh duh fahks
Your fax number is not working.	*Votre numéro de fax ne marche pas.*	voh-truh noo-mehr-oh duh fahks nuh marsh pah
Please turn on your fax machine.	*Vous pourriez brancher votre fax, s'il vous plaît.*	voo poor-yay brahn-shay voh-truh fahks see voo play

Getting Specific

I'd like a room...	*Je voudrais une chambre...*	zhuh voo-dray ewn shahn-bruh
We'd like a room...	*Nous voudrions une chambre...*	noo voo-dree-ohn ewn shahn-bruh
...with / without / and	*...avec / sans / et*	ah-vehk / sahn / ay
...toilet	*...WC*	vay say
...shower	*...douche*	doosh
...sink and toilet	*...cabinet de toilette*	kah-bee-nay duh twah-leht
...shower and toilet	*...salle d'eau*	sahl doh
...shower down the hall	*...douche sur le palier*	doosh sewr luh pahl-yay
...bathtub and toilet	*...salle de bains*	sahl duh ban
...double bed	*...grand lit*	grahn lee
...twin beds	*...deux petits lits, lits jumeaux*	duh puh-tee lee, lee zhew-moh
...balcony	*...balcon*	bahl-kohn
...view	*...vue*	vew
...only a sink	*...lavabo seulement*	lah-vah-boh suhl-mahn
...on the ground floor	*...au rez-de-chaussée*	oh ray-duh-shoh-say
...television	*...télévision*	tay-lay-vee-zee-ohn
...telephone	*...téléphone*	tay-lay-fohn

SLEEPING

...air conditioning	...climatisation	klee-mah-tee-zah-see-ohn
...kitchenette	...kitchenette	keet-chehn-eht
Is there an elevator?	Il y a un ascenseur?	eel-yah uhn ah-sahn-sur
Do you have a swimming pool?	Vous avez une piscine?	vooz ah-vay ewn pee-seen
I arrive Monday, depart Wednesday.	J'arrive lundi, et pars mercredi.	zhah-reev luhn-dee ay par mehr-kruh-dee
We arrive Monday, depart Wednesday.	Nous arrivons lundi, et partons mercredi.	nooz ah-ree-vohn luhn-dee ay par-tohn mehr-kruh-dee
I'm desperate.	Je suis désespéré.	zhuh swee day-zuh-spay-ray
We're desperate.	Nous sommes désespérés.	noo suhm day-zuh-spay-ray
I'll sleep anywhere.	Je peux dormir n'importe où.	zhuh puh dor-meer nan-port oo
We'll sleep anywhere.	Nous pouvons dormir n'importe où.	noo poo-vohn dor-meer nan-port oo
I have a sleeping bag.	J'ai un sac de couchage.	zhay uhn sahk duh koo-shahzh
We have sleeping bags.	Nous avons les sacs de couchage.	nooz ah-vohn lay sahk duh koo-shahzh
Will you call another hotel for me?	Vous pourriez contacter un autre hôtel pour moi?	voo poor-yay kohn-tahk-tay uhn oh-truh oh-tehl poor mwah

Offering some of the best budget beds in Europe, French hotels are rated from one to four stars (check the blue-and-white plaque by the front door). For budget travelers, one or two stars is the best value. Prices vary widely under one roof. A room with a double bed (**grand lit**) is cheaper than a room with twin beds (**deux petits lits**), and a bathroom with a shower (**salle d'eau**) is cheaper than a bathroom with a bathtub (**salle de bains**). Rooms with just a toilet and sink (**cabinet de toilette,** abbreviated **C. de T.**) are even cheaper, and a room with only a sink (**lavabo seulement**) is the cheapest.

Families

Do you have...?	*Vous avez...?*	vooz ah-vay
...a family room	*...une grande chambre, une suite*	ewn grahn shahn-bruh, ewn sweet
...a family rate	*...un tarif famille*	uhn tah-reef fah-mee-yee
...a discount for children	*...un tarif réduit pour enfants*	uhn tah-reef ray-dwee poor ahn-fahn
I have...	*J'ai...*	zhay
We have...	*Nous avons...*	nooz ah-vohn
...one child, ___ months / years old.	*...un enfant, de ___ mois / ans.*	uhn ahn-fahn duh ___ mwah / ahn
...two children, ___ and ___ years old.	*...deux enfants, de ___ et ___ ans.*	duhz ahn-fahn duh ___ ay ___ ahn
I'd like...	*Je voudrais...*	zhuh voo-dray
We'd like...	*Nous voudrions...*	noo voo-dree-ohn
...a crib.	*...un berceau.*	uhn behr-soh
...a cot.	*...un lit de camp.*	uhn lee duh kahn
...bunk beds.	*...lits superposés.*	lee sew-pehr-poh-zay
babysitting service	*service de babysitting*	sehr-vees duh "babysitting"
Is... nearby?	*Il y a... près d'ici?*	eel-yah... preh dee-see
...a park	*...un parc*	uhn park
...a playground	*...un parc avec des jeux*	uhn park ah-vehk day zhuh
...a swimming pool	*...une piscine*	ewn pee-seen

Equivalent to our word "kids," the French say *les gamins* or *les gosses*. Snot-nosed kids are *les morveux* and brats are called *les momes*.

Mobility Issues

Stairs are... for me / us / my husband / my wife.	*Les escaliers sont... pour moi / nous / mon mari / ma femme.*	layz ehs-kahl-yay sohn... poor mwah / noo / mohn mah-ree / mah fahm
...impossible	*...impossible*	an-poh-see-bluh
...difficult	*...difficile*	dee-fee-seel

Do you have...?	*Vous avez...?*	vooz ah-vay
...an elevator	*...un ascenseur*	uhn ah-sahn-sur
...a ground floor room	*...une chambre au rez-de-chaussée*	ewn shahn-bruh oh ray-duh-shoh-say
...a wheelchair-accessible room	*...une chambre accessible à un fauteuil roulant*	ewn shahn-bruh ahk-seh-see-bluh ah uhn foh-toy roo-lahn

Confirming, Changing, and Canceling Reservations

You can use this template for your telephone call.

I have a reservation.	*J'ai une réservation.*	zhay ewn ray-zehr-vah-see-ohn
We have a reservation.	*Nous avons une réservation.*	nooz ah-vohn ewn ray-zehr-vah-see-ohn
My name is ___.	*Je m'appelle ___.*	zhuh mah-pehl
I'd like to... my reservation.	*Je voudrais... ma réservation.*	zhuh voo-dray... mah ray-zehr-vah-see-ohn
...confirm	*...confirmer*	kohn-feer-may
...reconfirm	*...reconfirmer*	ray-kohn-feer-may
...cancel	*...annuler*	ah-noo-lay
...change	*...modifier*	moh-dee-fee-ay
The reservation is / was for...	*La réservation est / était pour...*	lah ray-zehr-vah-see-ohn ay / ay-tay poor
...one person	*...une personne*	ewn pehr-suhn
...two people	*...deux personnes*	duh pehr-suhn
...today / tomorrow	*...aujourd'hui / demain*	oh-zhoor-dwee / duh-man
...the day after tomorrow	*...après demain*	ah-preh duh-man
...August 13	*...le treize août*	luh trehz oot
...one night / two nights	*...une nuit / deux nuits*	ewn nwee / duh nwee
Did you find my / our reservation?	*Avez-vous trouvé ma / notre réservation?*	ah-vay-voo troo-vay mah / noh-truh ray-zehr-vah-see-ohn

What is your cancellation policy?	*Quel est le règlement pour annuler?*	kehl ay luh reh-gluh-mahn poor ah-noo-lay
Will I be billed for the first night if I can't make it?	*Je dois payer la première nuit si je ne peux pas venir?*	zhuh dwah pay-yay lah pruhm-yehr nwee see zhuh nuh puh pah vuh-neer
I'd like to arrive instead on ___.	*Je préfère arriver le ___.*	zhuh pray-fehr ah-ree-vay luh
We'd like to arrive instead on ___.	*Nous préférerions arriver le ___.*	noo pray-fay-ree-ohn ah-ree-vay luh
Is everything O.K.?	*Ça va marcher?*	sah vah mar-shay
Thank you. See you then.	*Merci. À bientôt.*	mehr-see ah bee-an-toh
I'm sorry, I need to cancel.	*Je suis désolé, car je dois annuler.*	zhuh swee day-zoh-lay kar zhuh dwah ah-noo-lay

Nailing Down the Price

How much is...?	*Combien...?*	kohn-bee-an
...a room for ___ people	*...une chambre pour ___ personnes*	ewn shahn-bruh poor ___ pehr-suhn
...your cheapest room	*...la chambre la moins chère*	lah shahn-bruh lah mwan shehr
Is breakfast included?	*Le petit déjeuner est compris?*	luh puh-tee day-zhuh-nay ay kohn-pree
Is breakfast required?	*Le petit déjeuner est obligatoire?*	luh puh-tee day-zhuh-nay ay oh-blee-gah-twar
How much without breakfast?	*Combien sans le petit déjeuner?*	kohn-bee-an sahn luh puh-tee day-zhuh-nay
Is half-pension required?	*La demi-pension est obligatoire?*	lah duh-mee-pahn-see-ohn ay oh-blee-gah-twar
Complete price?	*Tout compris?*	too kohn-pree
Is it cheaper if I stay three nights?	*C'est moins cher si je reste trois nuits?*	say mwan shehr see zhuh rehst twah nwee
I will stay three nights.	*Je vais rester trois nuits.*	zhuh vay rehs-tay twah nwee
We will stay three nights.	*Nous allons rester trois nuits.*	nooz ah-lohn rehs-tay twah nwee

SLEEPING

| Is it cheaper if I pay in cash? | C'est moins cher si je paie en liquide? | say mwan shehr see zhuh pay ahn lee-keed |
| What is the cost per week? | Quel est le prix à la semaine? | kehl ay luh pree ah lah suh-mehn |

In resort towns, some hotels offer *demi-pension* (half-pension), of two meals per day served at the hotel: breakfast and your choice of lunch or dinner. The price for half-pension is often listed per person rather than per room. Hotels that offer half-pension often require it in summer. The meals are usually good, but if you want more freedom, look for hotels that don't push half-pension.

Choosing a Room

Can I see the room?	Je peux voir la chambre?	zhuh puh vwar lah shahn-bruh
Can we see the room?	Nous pouvons voir la chambre?	noo poo-vohn vwar lah shahn-bruh
Show me another room?	Montrez-moi une autre chambre?	mohn-tray-mwah ewn oh-truh shahn-bruh
Show us another room?	Montrez-nous une autre chambre?	mohn-tray-nooz ewn oh-truh shahn-bruh
Do you have something...?	Avez-vous quelque chose de...?	ah-vay-voo kehl-kuh shohz duh
...larger / smaller	...plus grand / moins grand	plew grahn / mwan grahn
...better / cheaper	...meilleur / moins cher	meh-yur / mwan shehr
...brighter	...plus clair	plew klair
...in the back	...derrière	dehr-yehr
...quieter	...plus tranquille	plew trahn-keel
Sorry, it's not right for me.	Désolé, ça ne me convient pas.	day-zoh-lay sah nuh muh kohn-vee-ahn pah
Sorry, it's not right for us.	Désolé, ça ne nous convient pas.	day-zoh-lay sah nuh noo kohn-vee-ahn pah
I'll take it.	Je la prends.	zhuh lah prahn
We'll take it.	Nous la prenons.	noo lah prahn-nohn
The key, please.	La clef, s'il vous plaît.	lah klay see voo play

Breakfast

Breakfast is rarely included, but at least coffee refills are free.

How much is breakfast?	*Combien coûte petit déjeuner?*	kohn-bee-an koot puh-tee day-zhuh-nay
Is breakfast included?	*Petit déjeuner compris?*	puh-tee day-zhuh-nay kohn-pree
When does breakfast start?	*Le petit déjeuner commence à quelle heure?*	luh puh-tee day-zhuh-nay koh-mahns ah kehl ur
When does breakfast end?	*Le petit déjeuner termine à quelle heure?*	luh puh-tee day-zhuh-nay tehr-meen ah kehl ur
Where is breakfast served?	*Le petit déjeuner est servi où?*	luh puh-tee day-zhuh-nay ay sehr-vee oo

Hotel Help

I'd like...	*Je voudrais...*	zhuh voo-dray
We'd like...	*Nous voudrions...*	noo voo-dree-ohn
...a / another...	*...un / un autre...*	uhn / uhn oh-truh
...towel.	*...serviette de bain.*	sehrv-yeht duh ban
...clean towel.	*...serviette propre.*	sehrv-yeht proh-puh
...pillow.	*...oreiller.*	oh-reh-yay
...fluffy pillow.	*...coussin.*	koo-san
...clean sheets.	*...draps propres.*	drah proh-pruh
...blanket.	*...couverture.*	koo-vehr-tewr
...glass.	*...verre.*	vehr
...sink stopper.	*...bouchon pour le lavabo.*	boo-shohn poor luh lah-vah-boh
...soap.	*...savon.*	sah-vohn
...toilet paper.	*...papier hygiénique.*	pahp-yay ee-zhay-neek
...electrical adapter.	*...adaptateur électrique.*	ah-dahp-tah-tewr ay-lehk-treek
...brighter light bulb.	*...ampoule plus forte.*	ahn-pool plew fort
...lamp.	*...lampe.*	lahmp
...chair.	*...chaise.*	shehz

SLEEPING

...roll-away bed.	...lit pliant.	lee plee-ah<u>n</u>
...table.	...table.	tah-bluh
...Internet access.	...accès internet.	ahk-sehs a<u>n</u>-tehr-neht
...different room.	...autre chambre.	oh-truh shah<u>n</u>-bruh
...silence.	...le calme.	luh kahlm
...to speak to the manager.	...parler à la direction.	par-lay ah lah dee-rehk-see-oh<u>n</u>
I've fallen and I can't get up.	Je suis tombé et je ne peux pas me lever.	zhuh swee toh<u>n</u>-bay ay zhuh nuh puh pah muh lay-vay
How can I make the room warmer / cooler?	Comment rendre la chambre plus chaude / plus fraiche?	koh-mah<u>n</u> rah<u>n</u>-druh lah shah<u>n</u>-bruh plew shohd / plew frehsh
Where can I wash / hang my laundry?	Où puis-je faire / étendre ma lessive?	oo pwee-zhuh fair / ay-tah<u>n</u>-druh mah luh-seev
Is a... nearby?	Il y a une... près d'ici?	eel-yah ewn... preh dee-see
...self-service laundry	...laverie automatique	lah-vah-ree oh-toh-mah-teek
...full service laundry	...blanchisserie	blah<u>n</u>-shee-suh-ree
I'd like / We'd like...	Je voudrais / Nous voudrions...	zhuh voo-dray / noo voo-dree-oh<u>n</u>
...to stay another night.	...rester encore une nuit.	rehs-tay ah<u>n</u>-kor ewn nwee
Where can I park?	Je peux me garer où?	zhuh puh muh gah-ray oo
What time do you lock up?	Vous fermez à quelle heure?	voo fehr-may ah kehl ur
Please wake me at 7:00.	Réveillez-moi à sept heures, s'il vous plaît.	ray-veh-yay-mwah ah seht ur see voo play
Where do you go for lunch / dinner / coffee?	Vous allez où pour déjeuner / dîner / un café?	vooz ah-lay oo poor day-zhuh-nay / dee-nay / uh<u>n</u> kah-fay

If you'd rather not struggle all night with a log-style French pillow, check in the closet to see if there's a fluffier American-style pillow, or ask for a "*coussin.*"

Chill Out

Many hotel rooms in the Mediterranean part of Europe come with air-conditioning that you control—often with a stick (like a TV remote). Various sticks have basically the same features:

- fan icon (click to toggle through the wind power from light to gale)
- louver icon (click to choose: steady air flow or waves)
- snowflakes and sunshine icons (heat or cold, generally just one or the other is possible: cool air in summer, heat in winter)
- two clock settings (to determine how many hours the air-conditioning will stay on before turning off, or stay off before turning on)
- temperature control (20° or 21° is a comfortable temperature in Celsius—see the thermometer on page 187)

Hotel Hassles

Come with me.	Venez avec moi.	vuh-nayz ah-vehk mwah
I have a problem	J'ai un problème	zhay uhn proh-blehm
in the room.	dans la chambre.	dahn lah shahn-bruh
It smells bad.	Elle sent mauvaise.	ehl sahn moh-vehz
bugs	insectes	an-sehkt
mice	souris	soo-ree
cockroaches	cafards	kah-far
prostitutes	prostituées	proh-stee-tew-ay
I'm covered with	Je suis couvert de	zhuh swee koo-vehr duh
bug bites.	piqures d'insectes.	pee-kewr dan-sehkt
The bed is too	Le lit est trop	luh lee eh troh
soft / hard.	mou / dur.	moo / dewr
I can't sleep.	Je ne peux pas	zhuh nuh puh pah
	dormir.	dor-meer
The room is too...	La chambre est trop...	lah shahn-bruh ay troh
...hot / cold.	...chaude / froide.	shohd / frwahd
...noisy / dirty.	...bruyante / sale.	brew-yahnt / sahl
I can't	Je ne peux pas	zhuh nuh puh pah
open / shut...	ouvrir / fermer...	oov-reer / fehr-may
...the door /	...la porte /	lah port /
the window.	la fenêtre.	lah fuh-neh-truh

SLEEPING

Air conditioner...	*Climatisation...*	klee-mah-tee-zah-see-oh<u>n</u>
Lamp...	*Lampe...*	lahmp
Lightbulb...	*Ampoule...*	ah<u>n</u>-pool
Electrical outlet...	*Prise...*	preez
Key...	*Clef...*	klay
Lock...	*Serrure...*	suh-roor
Window...	*Fenêtre...*	fuh-neh-truh
Faucet...	*Robinet...*	roh-bee-nay
Sink...	*Lavabo...*	lah-vah-boh
Toilet...	*Toilette...*	twah-leht
Shower...	*Douche...*	doosh
...doesn't work.	*...ne marche pas.*	nuh marsh pah
There is no	*Il n'y a pas*	eel nee yah pah
hot water.	*d'eau chaude.*	doh shohd
When is the	*L'eau sera chaude*	loh suh-rah shohd
water hot?	*à quelle heure?*	ah kehl ur

Checking Out

When is check-out	*A quelle heure on*	ah kehl ur oh<u>n</u>
time?	*doit libérer*	dwah lee-bay-ray
	la chambre?	lah shah<u>n</u>-bruh
I'll leave...	*Je pars...*	zhuh par
We'll leave...	*Nous partons...*	noo par-toh<u>n</u>
...today /	*...aujourd'hui /*	oh-zhoor-dwee /
tomorrow.	*demain.*	duh-ma<u>n</u>
...very early.	*...très tôt.*	treh toh
Can I / Can we...?	*Je peux /*	zhuh puh /
	Nous pouvons...?	noo poo-voh<u>n</u>
...pay now	*...régler la note*	ray-glay lah noht
	maintenant	ma<u>n</u>-tuh-nah<u>n</u>
The bill, please.	*La note, s'il vous plaît.*	lah noht see voo play
Credit card O.K.?	*Carte de crédit O.K.?*	kart duh kray-dee "O.K."
Everything was great.	*C'était super.*	say-tay sew-pehr
I slept like a baby.	*J'ai dormi comme*	zhay dor-mee kohm
	un enfant.	uh<u>n</u> ah<u>n</u>-fah<u>n</u>

SLEEPING

Will you call my next hotel...?	Pourriez-vous appeler mon prochain hotel...?	poor-yay-vooz ah-puh-lay mohn proh-shahn oh-tehl
...for tonight	...pour ce soir	poor suh swar
...to make a reservation	...pour faire une réservation	poor fair ewn ray-zehr-vah-see-ohn
...to confirm a reservation	...pour confirmer une réservation	poor kohn-feer-may ewn ray-zehr-vah-see-ohn
I will pay for the call	Je paierai l'appel.	zhuh pay-uh-ray lah-pehl
Can I / Can we...?	Je peux / Nous pouvons...?	zhuh puh / noo poo-vohn
...leave baggage here until ___	...laisser les baggages ici jusqu'à ___	lay-say lay bah-gahzh ee-see zhews-kah

I never tip beyond the included service charges in hotels or for hotel services.

Camping

camping	camping	kahn-peeng
campsite	emplacement	ahn-plahs-mahn
tent	tente	tahnt
The nearest campground?	Le camping le plus proche?	luh kahn-peeng luh plew prohsh
Can I / Can we...?	Je peux / Nous pouvons...?	zhuh puh / noo poo-vohn
...camp here for one night	...camper ici pour une nuit	kahn-pay ee-see poor ewn nwee
Are showers included?	Les douches sont comprises?	lay doosh sohn kohn-preez
shower token	jeton	zhuh-tohn

In some French campgrounds and hostels, you need to buy a *jeton* (token) to activate a hot shower. To avoid a sudden cold rinse, buy two *jetons* before getting undressed.

EATING

RESTAURANTS

Types of Restaurants and Cuisine

Diners around the world recognize French food as a work of art. French cuisine is sightseeing for your tastebuds.

Styles of cooking include *haute cuisine* (classic, elaborately prepared, multi-course meals); *cuisine bourgeoise* (the finest-quality home cooking); *cuisine des provinces* (traditional dishes of specific regions, using the best ingredients); and *nouvelle cuisine* (the "new style" from the 1970s, which breaks from tradition with a focus on small portions and close attention to the texture and color of the ingredients).

Here are the types of restaurants you're likely to encounter:

Restaurant—Generally elegant, expensive eatery serving *haute cuisine*

Brasserie—Large café with quick, simple food and drink

Bistro—Small, usually informal neighborhood restaurant offering mainly *cuisine bourgeoise*

Auberge, Hostellerie, or *Relais*—Country inn serving high-quality traditional food

Routier—Truck stop dishing up basic, decent food

Crêperie—Street stand or café specializing in crêpes (thin pancakes, usually served with sweet fillings such as chocolate, Nutella, jam, or butter and sugar)

Salon de thé—Tea and coffee house offering pastries, desserts, and sometimes light meals

Buffet-express or *snack bar*—Cafeteria, usually near a train or bus station

Cabaret—Supper club featuring entertainment

Finding a Restaurant

Where's a good...	*Où se trouve un*	oo suh troov uhn
restaurant nearby?	*bon restaurant...*	bohn rehs-toh-rahn
	près d'ici?	preh dee-see
...cheap	*...bon marché*	bohn mar-shay
...local-style	*...cuisine*	kwee-zeen
	régionale	ray-zhee-oh-nahl
...untouristy	*...pas touristique*	pah too-ree-steek
...vegetarian	*...végétarien*	vay-zhay-tah-ree-an
...fast food	*...service rapide*	sehr-vees rah-peed
...self-service buffet	*...buffet de libre*	boo-fay duh lee-bruh
	service	sehr-vees
...Chinese	*...chinois*	sheen-wah
with terrace	*avec terrace*	ah-vehk tehr-rahs
with a salad bar	*avec un buffet*	ah-vehk uhn boo-fay
	salade	sah-lahd
with candles	*avec bougies*	ah-vehk boo-zhee
romantic	*romantique*	roh-mahn-teek
moderate price	*prix modéré*	pree moh-day-ray
splurge	*faire une folie*	fair ewn foh-lee
Is it better than	*C'est mieux que*	say mee-uh kuh
McDonald's?	*Mac Do?*	mahk doh

Restaurants normally serve from 12:00 P.M. to 2:00 P.M., and from 7:00 P.M. until about 10:00 P.M. Cafés are generally open throughout the day. The menu is posted right on the front door or window, and "window shopping" for your meal is a fun, important part of the experience. While the slick self-service restaurants are easy to use, you'll often eat better for the same money in a good little family bistro. The inside seating in all French restaurants is now non-smoking.

Key Phrases: Restaurants

Where's a good restaurant nearby?	Où se trouve un bon restaurant près d'ici?	oo suh troov uhn bohn rehs-toh-rahn preh dee-see
I'd like...	Je voudrais...	zhuh voo-dray
We'd like...	Nous voudrions...	noo voo-dree-ohn
...a table for one / two.	...une table pour un / deux.	ewn tah-bluh poor uhn / duh
inside / outside	à l'intérieur / dehors.	ah lan-tay-ree-yoor / duh-or
Is this seat free?	C'est libre?	say lee-bruh
The menu (in English), please.	La carte (en anglais), s'il vous plaît.	lah kart (ahn ahn-glay) see voo play
The bill, please.	L'addition, s'il vous plaît.	lah-dee-see-ohn see voo play
Credit card O.K.?	Carte de crédit O.K.?	kart duh kray-dee "O.K."

Getting a Table

At what time does this open / close?	À quelle heure c'est ouvert / fermé?	ah kehl ur say oo-vehr / fehr-may
Are you open...?	Vous êtes ouvert...?	vooz eht oo-vehr...
...today / tomorrow	...aujourd'hui / demain	oh-zhoor-dwee / duh-man
...for lunch / dinner	...pour déjeuner / dîner	poor day-zhuh-nay / dee-nay
Are reservations recommended?	Les réservations sont conseillé?	lay ray-zehr-vah-see-ohn sohn kohn-seh-yay
I'd like...	Je voudrais...	zhuh voo-dray
We'd like...	Nous voudrions...	noo voo-dree-ohn
...a table for one / two.	...une table pour un / deux.	ewn tah-bluh poor uhn / duh
...to reserve a table for two people...	...réserver une table pour deux personnes...	ray-zehr-vay ewn tah-bluh poor duh pehr-suhn

EATING

...for today / tomorrow	...pour aujourd'hui / demain	poor oh-zhoor-dwee / duh-man
...at 8 P.M.	...à huit heures du soir	ah weet ur duh swar
My name is ___.	Je m'appelle ___.	zhuh mah-pehl
I have a reservation for ___ people.	J'ai une réservation pour ___ personnes.	zhay ewn ray-zehr-vah-see-ohn poor ___ pehr-suhn
I'd like to sit...	J'aimerais s'asseoir...	zhehm-uh-ray sah-swar
We'd like to sit...	Nous aimerions nous asseoir...	nooz ehm-uh-rohn nooz ah-swar
...inside / outside.	...à l'intérieur / dehors.	ah lan-tay-ree-yoor / duh-or
...by the window.	...à côté de la fenêtre.	ah koh-tay duh lah fuh-neh-truh
...with a view.	...avec une vue.	ah-vehk ewn vew
...where it's quiet.	...dans un coin tranquille.	dahnz uhn kwan trahn-keel
Is this table free?	Cette table est libre?	seht tah-bluh ay lee-bruh
Can I sit here?	Je peux s'asseoir ici?	zhuh puh sah-swar ee-see
Can we sit here?	Nous pouvons nous asseoir ici?	noo poo-vohn nooz ah-swar ee-see

Better restaurants routinely take telephone reservations. Guidebooks include phone numbers and the process is simple. If you want to eat at a normal French dinnertime (later than 7:30 P.M.), it's smart to call and reserve a table. Many of my favorite restaurants are filled with Americans at 7:30 P.M. and can feel like tourist traps. But if you drop in at (or reserve ahead for) 8:30 or 9:00 P.M., when the French are eating, the restaurants feel completely local.

The Menu

menu	carte	kart
special of the day	plat du jour	plah dew zhoor
specialty of the house	spécialité de la maison	spay-see-ah-lee-tay duh lah may-zohn

fast service special	*formule rapide*	for-mewl rah-peed
fixed-price meal	*menu, prix fixe*	muh-new, pree feeks
breakfast	*petit déjeuner*	puh-tee day-zhuh-nay
lunch	*déjeuner*	day-zhuh-nay
dinner	*dîner*	dee-nay
appetizers	*hors-d'oeuvre*	or-duh-vruh
sandwiches	*sandwichs*	sahnd-weech
bread	*pain*	pan
salad	*salade*	sah-lahd
soup	*soupe*	soop
first course	*entrée*	ahn-tray
main course	*plat principal*	plah pran-see-pahl
meat	*viande*	vee-ahnd
poultry	*volaille*	voh-lī
fish	*poisson*	pwah-sohn
seafood	*fruits de mer*	frwee duh mehr
children's plate	*assiette d'enfant*	ahs-yeht dahn-fahn
vegetables	*légumes*	lay-gewm
cheese	*fromage*	froh-mahzh
dessert	*dessert*	duh-sehr
munchies	*amuse bouche*	ah-mewz boosh
	("mouth amusements")	
drink menu	*carte des*	kart day
	consommation	kohn-soh-mah-see-ohn
beverages	*boissons*	bwah-sohn
beer	*bière*	bee-ehr
wine	*vin*	van
service included	*service compris*	sehr-vees kohn-pree
service not included	*service non compris*	sehr-vees nohn kohn-pree
hot / cold	*chaud / froid*	shoh / frwah
with / and /	*avec / et /*	ah-vehk / ay /
or / without	*ou / sans*	oo / sahn

EATING

In France, a menu is a ***carte***, and a fixed-price meal is a ***menu*** (also called ***menu touristique***). So, if you ask for a ***menu*** (instead of the ***carte***), you'll get this fixed-price meal, which includes your choice of an appetizer, entrée, and dessert for one set price. The *menu* is usually a good value, though most locals prefer to order à la carte (from the *carte*, what we would call the menu). *Service compris (s.c.)* means the tip is included. For a complete culinary language guide, travel with the excellent *Marling Menu-Master* for France.

Ordering

waiter	*Monsieur*	muhs-yur
waitress	*Mademoiselle, Madame*	mahd-mwah-zehl, mah-dahm
I'm / We're ready to order.	*Je suis /Nous sommes prêt à commander.*	zhuh swee / noo suhm preh ah koh-mah<u>n</u>-day
I'd like / We'd like...	*Je voudrais / Nous voudrions...*	zhuh voo-dray / noo voo-dree-oh<u>n</u>
...just a drink.	*...une consommation seulement.*	ewn koh<u>n</u>-soh-mah-see-oh<u>n</u> suhl-mah<u>n</u>
...a snack.	*...un snack.*	uh<u>n</u> snahk
...just a salad.	*...qu'une salade.*	kewn sah-lahd
...a half portion.	*...une demi-portion.*	ewn duh-mee-por-see-oh<u>n</u>
...the tourist *menu.* (fixed-price meal)	*...le menu touristique.*	luh muh-new too-ree-steek
...to see the menu.	*...voir la carte.*	vwar lah kart
...to order.	*...commander.*	koh-mah<u>n</u>-day
...to pay.	*...payer.*	pay-yay
...to throw up.	*...vomir.*	voh-meer
Do you have...?	*Avez-vous...?*	ah-vay-voo
...an English menu	*...une carte en anglais*	ewn kart ah<u>n</u> ah<u>n</u>-glay
...a lunch special	*...un plat du jour*	uh<u>n</u> plah dew zhoor
What do you recommend?	*Qu'est-ce que vous recommandez?*	kehs kuh voo ruh-koh-mah<u>n</u>-day
What's your favorite dish?	*Quel est votre plat favori?*	kehl eh voh-truh plah fah-voh-ree
Is it...?	*C'est...?*	say
...good	*...bon*	boh<u>n</u>
...expensive	*...cher*	shehr
...light	*...léger*	lay-zhay

EATING

...filling	...copieux	kohp-yuh
What is...?	Qu'est-ce...?	kehs
...that	...que c'est	kuh say
...local	...que vous avez de la région	kuh vooz ah-vay duh lah ray-zhee-ohn
...fresh	...qu'il y a de frais	keel yah duh fray
...cheap and filling	...qu'il y a de bon marché et de copieux	keel yah duh bohn mar-shay ay duh kohp-yuh
...fast (already prepared)	...qui est déjà préparé	kee ay day-zhah pray-pah-ray
Can we split this and have an extra plate?	Nous pouvons partager et avoir une assiette de plus?	noo poo-vohn par-tah-zhay ay ah-vwar ewn ahs-yeht duh plew
I've changed my mind.	J'ai changé d'avis.	zhay shahn-zhay dah-vee
Nothing with eyeballs.	Rien avec des yeux.	ree-an ah-vehk dayz yuh
Can I substitute (something) for __?	Je peux substituer (quelque chose) pour __?	zhuh puh soob-stee-too-ay (kehl-kuh shohz) poor
Can I / Can we get it "to go"?	Je peux / Nous pouvons prendre ça "à emporter"?	zhuh puh / noo poo-vohn prahn-druh sah ah ahn-por-tay
"To go"?	"À emporter"?	ah ahn-por-tay

Once you're seated, the table is yours for the entire lunch or dinner period. The waiter or waitress is there to serve you, but only when you're ready. To get his or her attention, simply ask, "*S'il vous plaît?*" ("Please?").

This is the sequence of a typical restaurant experience: The waiter will give you a menu (*carte*) and then ask what you'd like to drink (*Vous voulez quelque choses à boire?*), if you're ready to order (*Vous êtes prets à commander?*) or what you'd like to eat (*Qu'est ce que je vous sers?*), if everything is okay (*Tout va bien?*), if you'd like dessert (*Vous voulez un dessert?*), and if you're finished (*Vous avez terminer?*). You ask for the bill (*L'addition, s'il vous plaît*).

Tableware and Condiments

plate	assiette	ahs-yeht
extra plate	une assiette de plus	ewn ahs-yeht duh plew
napkin	serviette	sehrv-yeht
silverware	couverts	koo-vehr
knife	couteau	koo-toh
fork	fourchette	foor-sheht
spoon	cuillère	kwee-yehr
cup	tasse	tahs
glass	verre	vehr
carafe	carafe	kah-rahf
water	l'eau	loh
bread	pain	pan
butter	beurre	bur
margarine	margarine	mar-gah-reen
salt / pepper	sel / poivre	sehl / pwah-vruh
sugar	sucre	sew-kruh
artificial sweetener	édulcorant	ay-dewl-koh-rahn
honey	miel	mee-ehl
mustard	moutarde	moo-tard
ketchup	ketchup	"ketchup"
mayonnaise	mayonnaise	mah-yuh-nehz
toothpick	cure-dent	kewr-dahn

The Food Arrives

Is it included with the meal?	C'est inclus avec le repas?	say an-klew ah-vehk luh ruh-pah
I did not order this.	Je n'ai pas commandé ça.	zhuh nay pah koh-mahn-day sah
We did not order this.	Nous n'avons pas commandé ça.	noo nah-vohn pah koh-mahn-day sah
Heat this up?	Vous pouvez réchauffer ça?	voo poo-vay ray-shoh-fay sah
A little.	Un peu.	uhn puh

More. / Another.	*Plus. / Un autre.*	plew / uhn oh-truh
One more please.	*Encore un*	ahn-kor uhn
	s'il vous plaît.	see voo play
The same.	*La même chose.*	lah mehm shohz
Enough.	*Assez.*	ah-say
Finished.	*Terminé.*	tehr-mee-nay

After bringing your meal, your server might wish you a cheery
"*Bon appétit!*" (pronounced bohn ah-pay-tee).

Complaints

This is...	*C'est...*	say
...dirty.	*...sale.*	sahl
...greasy.	*...graisseux.*	gray-suh
...salty.	*...salé.*	sah-lay
...undercooked.	*...pas assez cuit.*	pah ah-say kwee
...overcooked.	*...trop cuit.*	troh kwee
...inedible.	*...immangeable.*	an-mahn-zhah-bluh
...cold.	*...froid.*	frwah
Do any of your	*Avez-vous des*	ah-vay-voo day
customers return?	*clients qui*	klee-ahn kee
	reviennent?	ruh-vee-an
Yuck!	*Pouah!*	pwah

Compliments to the Chef

Yummy!	*Miam-miam!*	myahm-myahm
Delicious!	*Délicieux!*	day-lee-see-uh
Magnificent!	*Magnifique!*	mahn-yee-feek
Very tasty!	*Très bon!*	treh bohn
I love French food /	*J'aime la cuisine*	zhehm lah kwee-zeen
this food.	*française /*	frahn-sehz /
	cette cuisine.	seht kwee-zeen
Better than my	*Meilleur que la*	meh-yur kuh lah
mom's cooking.	*cuisine de ma mère.*	kwee-zeen duh mah mehr
My compliments	*Mes compliments*	may kohn-plee-mahn
to the chef!	*au chef!*	oh shehf

Paying for Your Meal

The bill, please.	L'addition, s'il vous plaît.	lah-dee-see-ohn see voo play
Together.	Ensemble.	ahn-sahn-bluh
Separate checks.	Notes séparées.	noht say-pah-ray
Credit card O.K.?	Carte de crédit O.K.?	kart duh kray-dee "O.K."
This is not correct.	Ce n'est pas exact.	suh nay pah ehg-zahkt
Explain this?	Expliquez ça?	ehk-splee-kay sah
Can you explain / itemize the bill?	Vous pouvez expliquer / détailler cette note?	voo poo-vay ehk-splee-kay / day-tay-yay seht noht
What if I wash the dishes?	Et si je lave la vaisselle?	ay see zhuh lahv lah veh-sehl
Is tipping expected?	Je dois laisser un pourboire?	zhuh dwah lay-say uhn poor-bwar
What percent?	Quel pourcentage?	kehl poor-sahn-tahzh
tip	pourboire	poor-bwar
Keep the change.	Gardez la monnaie.	gar-day lah moh-nay
This is for you.	C'est pour vous.	say poor voo
May I have a receipt, please?	Je peux avoir une fiche, s'il vous plaît?	zhuh puh ah-vwar ewn feesh see voo play

In France, slow service is good service (fast service would rush the diners). Out of courtesy, your waiter will not bring your bill until you ask for it. While a service charge is included in the bill, it's polite to round up for a drink or meal well-served. This bonus tip is usually about 5 percent of the bill (e.g., if your bill is €19, leave €20). When you hand your payment plus a tip to your waiter, you can say, "*C'est bon*" (say bohn), meaning, "It's good." If you order your food at a counter, don't tip.

SPECIAL CONCERNS

In a Hurry

I'm / We're in a hurry.	Je suis / Nous sommes pressé.	zhuh swee / noo suhm preh-say

I need / We need...	J'ai besoin / Nous avons besoin...	zhay buh-swan / nooz ah-vohn buh-swan
...to be served quickly.	...d'être servi vite.	deh-truh sehr-vee veet
Is that possible?	C'est possible?	say poh-see-bluh
I must / We must...	Je dois / Nous devons...	zhuh dwah / noo duh-vohn
...leave in 30 minutes / one hour.	...partir dans trente minutes / une heure.	par-teer dahn trahnt mee-newt / ewn ur
Will the food be ready soon?	Ce sera prêt bientôt?	suh suh-rah preh bee-an-toh

If you are in a rush, seek out a brasserie or restaurant that offers *service rapide* (fast food).

Dietary Restrictions

I'm allergic to...	Je suis allergique à...	zhuh sweez ah-lehr-zheek ah
I cannot eat...	Je ne peux pas manger de...	zhuh nuh puh pah mahn-zhay duh
He / She cannot eat...	Il / Elle ne peut pas manger de...	eel / ehl nuh puh pah mahn-zhay duh
...dairy products.	...produits laitiers.	proh-dwee lay-tee-yay
...wheat.	...blé.	blay
...meat / pork.	...viande / porc.	vee-ahnd / por
...salt / sugar.	...sel / sucre.	sehl / sew-kruh
...shellfish.	...crustacés.	krew-stah-say
...spicy foods.	...nourriture épicée.	noo-ree-tewr ay-pee-say
...nuts.	...noix.	nwah
I'm a diabetic.	Je suis diabétique.	zhuh swee dee-ah-bay-teek
I'd like / We'd like...	Je voudrais / Nous voudrions...	zhuh voo-dray / noo voo-dree-ohn
...a kosher meal.	...repas kasher.	ruh-pah kah-shay
...a low-fat meal.	...repas allege en matières grasses.	ruh-pah ah-lehzh ahn mah-tee-yehr grahs

I eat only insects.	Je ne mange que les insectes.	zhuh nuh mahnzh kuh layz an-sehkt
No salt.	Sans sel.	sahn sehl
No sugar.	Sans sucre.	sahn sew-kruh
No fat.	Sans matière grasse.	sahn mah-tee-yehr grahs
Minimal fat.	Léger en matière grasse.	lay-zhay ahn mah-tee-yehr grahs
Low cholesterol.	Allégé.	ah-lay-zhay
No caffeine.	Décaféiné.	day-kah-fay-nay
No alcohol.	Sans alcool.	sahnz ahl-kohl
Organic.	Biologique.	bee-oh-loh-zheek
I'm a...	Je suis...	zhuh swee
...vegetarian. (male)	...végétarien.	vay-zhay-tah-ree-an
...vegetarian. (female)	...végétarienne.	vay-zhay-tah-ree-ehn
...strict vegetarian.	...strict végétarien.	streekt vay-zhay-tah-ree-an
...carnivore.	...carnivore.	kar-nee-vor
...big eater.	...gourmand.	goor-mahn
Is any meat or animal fat used in this?	Il y a des produits ou dérivés animaux dans ça?	eel yah dayz proh-dwee oo day-ree-vay ah-nee-moh dahn sah

Children

Do you have...?	Vous avez...?	vooz ah-vay
...a children's portion	...une assiette enfant	ewn ahs-yeht ahn-fahn
...a half portion	...une demi-portion	ewn duh-mee-por-see-ohn
a high chair / a booster seat	une chaise enfant / un réhausseur	oon shehz ahn-fahn / uhn ray-oh-sur
plain noodles / plain rice	pâtes natures / riz nature	paht nah-toor / ree nah-toor
with butter	avec beurre	ah-vehk bur
no sauce	pas de sauce	pah duh sohs

sauce or dressing on the side	*sauce à part*	sohs ah par
pizza	*pizza*	"pizza"
...cheese only	*...juste fromage*	zhoost froh-mahzh
...pepperoni and cheese	*...chorizo et fromage*	shoh-ree-zoh ay froh-mahzh
toasted cheese sandwich	*croque monsieur*	krohk muhs-yur
hot dog and fries	*saucisse-frites*	soh-sees-freet
hamburger	*hamburger*	ahm-boor-gehr
cheeseburger	*cheeseburger*	sheez-boor-gehr
French fries	*frites*	freet
ketchup	*ketchup*	"ketchup"
crackers	*crackers*	krah-kehr
Nothing spicy.	*Rien d'épicé.*	ree-a<u>n</u> day-pee-say
Not too hot.	*Pas trop chaud.*	pah troh shoh
Don't let the food mix together on the plate.	*Merci d'eviter que la nourriture se mêle sur l'assiette.*	mehr-see duh-vee-tay kuh lah noo-ree-tewr suh mehl sewr lahs-yeht
He will / She will / They will...	*Il va / Elle va / Ils vont...*	eel vah / ehl vah / eel voh<u>n</u>
...share our meal.	*...partager notre repas.*	par-tah-zhay noh-truh ruh-pah
We need our food quickly, please.	*Nous avons besoin de notre repas très vite, s'il vous plaît.*	nooz ah-voh<u>n</u> buh-swa<u>n</u> duh noh-truh ruh-pah tray veet see voo play
Can I / Can we have an extra...?	*Je peux / Nous pouvons avoir une... de plus?*	zhuh puh / noo poo-voh<u>n</u> ah-vwar ewn... duh plew
...plate	*...assiette*	ahs-yeht
...cup	*...tasse*	tahs
...spoon / fork	*...cuillère / fourchette*	kwee-yehr / foor-sheht
Can I / Can we have two extra...?	*Je peux / Nous pouvons deux... de plus?*	zhuh puh / noo poo-voh<u>n</u> duh... duh plew
...plates	*...assiettes*	ahs-yeht

...cups	...tasses	tahs
...spoons / forks	...cuillères / fourchettes	kwee-yehr / foor-sheht
Milk (in a plastic cup).	Du lait (dans une verre plastique).	doo lay (dah<u>n</u>z oon vehr plah-steek)
Straw(s).	Paille(s)	pī-yee
More napkins, please.	Des serviettes, s'il vous plaît.	day sehrv-yeht see voo play
Sorry for the mess.	Désolé pour le désordre.	day-zoh-lay poor luh day-zor-druh

WHAT'S COOKING?

Breakfast

breakfast	petit déjeuner	puh-tee day-zhuh-nay
bread	pain	pa<u>n</u>
roll	petit pain	puh-tee pa<u>n</u>
little loaf of bread	baguette	bah-geht
toast	toast	"toast"
butter	beurre	bur
jelly	confiture	koh<u>n</u>-fee-tewr
pastry	pâtisserie	pah-tee-suh-ree
croissant	croissant	kwah-sah<u>n</u>
cheese	fromage	froh-mahzh
yogurt	yaourt	yah-oort
cereal	céréale	say-ray-ahl
milk	lait	lay
hot chocolate	chocolat chaud	shoh-koh-lah shoh
fruit juice	jus de fruit	zhew duh frwee
orange juice (fresh)	jus d'orange (pressé)	zhew doh-rah<u>n</u>zh (preh-say)
coffee / tea	café / thé	kah-fay / tay
Is breakfast included?	Le petit déjeuner est compris?	luh puh-tee day-zhuh-nay ay koh<u>n</u>-pree

EATING

Key Phrases: What's Cooking?

food	*nourriture*	noo-ree-tewr
breakfast	*petit déjeuner*	puh-tee day-zhuh-nay
lunch	*déjeuner*	day-zhuh-nay
dinner	*dîner*	dee-nay
bread	*pain*	pan
cheese	*fromage*	froh-mahzh
soup	*soupe*	soop
salad	*salade*	sah-lahd
meat	*viande*	vee-ahnd
fish	*poisson*	pwah-sohn
fruit	*fruit*	frwee
vegetables	*légumes*	lay-gewm
dessert	*dessert*	duh-sehr
Delicious!	*Délicieux!*	day-lee-see-uh

What's Probably Not for Breakfast

omelet	*omelette*	oh-muh-leht
eggs	*des oeufs*	dayz uh
fried eggs	*oeufs au plat*	uh oh plah
scrambled eggs	*oeufs brouillés*	uh broo-yay
boiled egg...	*oeuf à la coque...*	uhf ah lah kohk
...soft / hard	*...mollet / dur*	moh-lay / dewr
ham	*jambon*	zhahn-bohn

EATING

French hotel breakfasts are small, expensive, and often optional. They normally include coffee and a fresh *croissant* or a chunk of *baguette* with butter and jelly. Being a juice and cheese man, I keep a liter box of O.J. in my rooms for a morning eye-opener and a wedge of "Laughing Cow" cheese in my bag for a moo-vable feast. You can also save money by breakfasting at a *bar* or *café*, where it's acceptable to bring in a *croissant* from the neighboring *boulangerie* (bakery). You can get an *omelette* almost any time of day at a café.

Snacks and Quick Lunches

crêpe	crêpe	krehp
buckwheat crêpe	galette	gah-leht
omelet	omelette	oh-muh-leht
quiche...	quiche...	keesh
...with cheese	...au fromage	oh froh-mahzh
...with ham	...au jambon	oh zhahn-bohn
...with mushrooms	...aux champignons	oh shahn-peen-yohn
...with bacon, cheese, and onions	...lorraine	lor-rehn
paté	pâté	pah-tay
onion tart	tarte à l'oignon	tart ah loh-yohn
cheese tart	tarte au fromage	tart oh froh-mahzh

Light meals are quick and easy at *cafés* and *bars* throughout France. A *salade*, *crêpe*, *quiche*, or *omelette* is a fairly cheap way to fill up, even in Paris. Each can be made with various extras like ham, cheese, mushrooms, and so on. *Crêpes* come in dinner or dessert varieties.

Hors d'Oeuvres

hors-d'oeuvres	or-duh-vruh	appetizers
escargots	ehs-kar-goh	snails baked in the shell w/ garlic butter
pâté de foie gras	pah-tay duh fwah grah	goose- or duck-liver spread
huîtres	wee-truh	oysters (usually served on the half shell)
terrine	tehr-reen	type of pâté served in a deep pot—made w/ fish, poultry, game, or pork
crudités	krew-dee-tay	raw vegetables served w/ vinaigrette
artichauts à la vinaigrette	ar-tee-shoh ah lah vee-nay-greht	artichokes in a vinaigrette dressing
quenelles	kehn-ehl	dumplings w/meat or fish in white sauce

EATING

bouchée à la reine	*boo-shay ah lah rehn*	pastry shell filled with creamed veal brains and mushrooms
soufflé	*soo-flay*	fluffy eggs baked w/ savory fillings (cheese, meat, and vegetables)
tapenade	*tah-puh-nahd*	paste made from olives, anchovies, lemon, and olive oil

Sandwiches

I'd like a sandwich.	*Je voudrais un sandwich.*	zhuh voo-dray uhn sahnd-weech
We'd like two sandwiches.	*Nous voudrions deux sandwichs.*	noo voo-dree-ohn duh sahnd-weech
toasted	*grillé*	gree-yay
toasted ham and cheese sandwich	*croque monsieur*	krohk muhs-yur
toasted ham, cheese, and fried egg sandwich	*croque madame*	krohk mah-dahm
cheese	*fromage*	froh-mahzh
tuna	*thon*	tohn
fish	*poisson*	pwah-sohn
chicken	*poulet*	poo-lay
turkey	*dinde, dindon*	dand, dan-dohn
ham	*jambon*	zhahn-bohn
salami	*salami*	sah-lah-mee
boiled egg	*oeuf à la coque*	uhf ah lah kohk
garnished with veggies	*crudités*	krew-dee-tay
lettuce	*laitue*	lay-too
tomato	*tomate*	toh-maht
onions	*oignons*	oh-yohn
mustard	*moutarde*	moo-tard
mayonnaise	*mayonnaise*	mah-yuh-nehz

peanut butter	*beurre de cacahuètes*	bur duh kah-kah-weet
jelly	*confiture*	koh<u>n</u>-fee-tewr
pork sandwich	*sandwich au porc*	sah<u>nd</u>-weech oh por
Does this come cold or warm?	*C'est servi froid ou chaud?*	say sehr-vee frwah oo shoh
Heated, please.	*Réchauffé, s'il vous plaît.*	ray-shoh-fay see voo play

Sandwiches, as well as small quiches, often come ready-made at *boulangeries* (bakeries).

If You Knead Bread

bread	*pain*	pa<u>n</u>
thin, long loaf	*baguette*	bah-geht
sweet, soft bun	*brioche*	bree-osh
crescent roll	*croissant*	kwah-sah<u>n</u>
lace-like bread (Riviera)	*fougasse*	foo-gahs
dark-grain bread	*pain bisse, pain de seigle*	pa<u>n</u> bees, pa<u>n</u> duh seh-gluh
onion and anchovy pizza	*pissaladière*	pees-ah-lah-dee-yehr
cheese pastry	*croûte au fromage*	kroot oh froh-mahzh

Say Cheese

cheese...	*fromage...*	froh-mahzh
...mild	*...doux*	doo
...sharp	*...fort*	for
...goat	*...chèvre*	sheh-vruh
...bleu	*...bleu*	bluh
...with herbs	*...aux herbes*	ohz ehrb
...cream	*...à la crème*	ah lah krehm
...of the region	*...de la région*	duh lah ray-zhee-oh<u>n</u>
Swiss cheese	*gruyère, emmenthal*	grew-yehr, eh-mehn-tahl
Laughing Cow	*La vache qui rit*	lah vahsh kee ree
cheese platter	*le plâteau de fromages*	luh plah-toh duh froh-mahzh

| **May I taste a little?** | *Je peux goûter* | zhuh puh goo-tay |
| | *un peu?* | uhn puh |

In France, the cheese course is served just before (or instead of) dessert. It not only helps with digestion, it gives you a great opportunity to sample the tasty regional cheeses. There are over 500 different French cheeses to try. You've heard of *Camembert* and *Brie. Port Salut* comes in a sweet, soft wedge, and *Roquefort* is strong and blue-veined. *Boursin* is a soft cheese with herbs. Some cheeses are named after the city they come from (*pont l'éveque*—flavorful and smooth; *liverot*—strong fragrance and a rich, creamy taste). *Fromage aux cindres* (cheese with cinders) is ash-ually better than it sounds. Visit a *fromagerie* (cheese shop) and experiment. Ask for a *fromage de la région* (of the region), and specify mild, sharp, goat, or bleu (see list above).

Soups and Salads

soup (of the day)	*soupe (du jour)*	soop (dew zhoor)
broth	*bouillon*	boo-yohn
...chicken	*...de poulet*	duh poo-lay
...beef	*...de boeuf*	duh buhf
...with noodles	*...aux nouilles*	oh noo-ee
...with rice	*...au riz*	oh ree
thick vegetable soup	*potage de légumes*	poh-tahzh duh lay-gewm
Provençal vegetable soup	*soupe au pistou*	soop oh pees-too
onion soup	*soupe à l'oignon*	soop ah lohn-yohn
cream of asparagus soup	*crème d'asperges*	krehm dah-spehrzh
potato and leek soup	*vichyssoise*	vee-shee-swah
shellfish chowder	*bisque*	beesk
seafood stew	*bouillabaisse*	boo-yah-behs
meat and vegetable stew	*pot au feu*	poht oh fuh

EATING

salad...	salade...	sah-lahd
...green / mixed	...verte / mixte	vehrt / meekst
...with goat cheese	...au chèvre chaud	oh sheh-vruh shoh
...chef's	...composée	koh<u>n</u>-poh-zay
...seafood	...océane	oh-shay-ah<u>n</u>
...tuna	...de thon	duh toh<u>n</u>
...veggie	...crudités	krew-dee-tay
...with ham / cheese / egg	...avec jambon / fromage / oeuf	ah-vehk zhah<u>n</u>-boh<u>n</u> / froh-mahzh / uh
lettuce	laitue	lay-too
tomatoes	tomates	toh-maht
onions	oignons	oh<u>n</u>-yoh<u>n</u>
cucumber	concombre	koh<u>n</u>-koh<u>n</u>-bruh
oil / vinegar	huile / vinaigre	weel / vee-nay-gruh
dressing on the side	sauce à part	sohs ah par
What is in this salad?	Qu'est-ce qu'il ya dans cette salade?	kehs keel yah dah<u>n</u> seht sah-lahd

Salads are usually served with a vinaigrette dressing and often eaten after the main course.

Seafood

seafood	fruits de mer	frwee duh mehr
assorted seafood	assiette de fruits de mer	ahs-yeht duh frwee duh mehr
fish	poisson	pwah-soh<u>n</u>
anchovies	anchois	ah<u>n</u>-shwah
clams	palourdes	pah-loord
cod	cabillaud	kah-bee-yoh
crab	crabe	krahb
herring	hareng	ah-rah<u>n</u>
lobster	homard	oh-mar
mussels	moules	mool
oysters	huîtres	wee-truh
prawns	scampi	skah<u>n</u>-pee
salmon	saumon	soh-moh<u>n</u>

salty cod	morue	moh-rew
sardines	sardines	sar-deen
scallops	coquilles	koh-keel
shrimp	crevettes	kruh-veht
squid	calamar	kahl-mar
trout	truite	trweet
tuna	thon	toh<u>n</u>
What's fresh today?	Qu'est-ce frais aujourd'hui?	kehs kay fray oh-joord-wee
Do you eat this part?	Ça se mange?	sah suh mah<u>n</u>zh
Just the head, please.	Seulement la tête, s'il vous plaît.	suhl-mah<u>n</u> lah teht see voo play

Poultry

poultry	volaille	voh-lī
chicken	poulet	poo-lay
duck	canard	kah-nar
turkey	dinde, dindon	da<u>n</u>d, da<u>n</u>-doh<u>n</u>
How long has this been dead?	Il est mort depuis longtemps?	eel ay mor duh-pwee loh<u>n</u>-tah<u>n</u>

Meat

meat	viande	vee-ah<u>n</u>d
beef	boeuf	buhf
flank steak	faux-filet	foh-fee-lay
ribsteak	entrecôte	ah<u>n</u>-truh-koht
bunny	lapin	lah-pa<u>n</u>
cutlet	côtelette	koh-tuh-leht
frog's legs	cuisses de grenouilles	kwees duh greh-noo-ee
ham	jambon	zhah<u>n</u>-boh<u>n</u>
lamb	agneau	ah<u>n</u>-yoh
meat stew	ragoût	rah-goo
mixed grill	grillades	gree-yahd
pork	porc	por
roast beef	rosbif	rohs-beef

EATING

Avoiding Mis-Steaks

By American standards, the French undercook meats. In France, rare (*saignant*) is nearly raw, medium (*à point*) is rare, and well-done (*bien cuit*) is medium.

tenderloin	*médaillon*	may-dÉyohn
T-bone	*côte de boeuf*	koht duh buhf
tenderloin of T-bone	*tournedos*	toor-nah-doh
alive	*vivant*	vee-vahn
raw	*cru*	krew
very rare	*bleu*	bluh
rare	*saignant*	sayn-yahn
medium	*à point*	ah pwan
well-done	*bien cuit*	bee-an kwee
very well-done	*très bien cuit*	treh bee-an kwee

sausage	*saucisse*	soh-sees
snails	*escargots*	ehs-kar-goh
steak	*onglet*	ohn-glay
veal	*veau*	voh

Meat, but...

These are the cheapest items on a menu for good reason.

brains	*cervelle*	sehr-vehl
calf pancreas	*ris de veau*	ree duh voh
horse meat	*viande de cheval*	vee-ahnd duh shuh-vahl
intestines	*andouillette*	ahn-doo-yeht
liver	*foie*	fwah
tongue	*langue*	lahng
tripe	*tripes*	treep

How Food is Prepared

assorted	*assiette, variés*	ahs-yeht, vah-ree-ay
baked	*cuit au four*	kweet oh foor

EATING

boiled	*bouilli*	boo-yee
braised	*braisé*	breh-zay
cold	*froid*	frwah
cooked	*cuit*	kwee
deep-fried	*frit*	free
fillet	*filet*	fee-lay
fresh	*frais*	fray
fried	*frit*	free
grilled, broiled	*grillé*	gree-yay
homemade	*fait à la maison*	fay ah lah may-zohn
hot	*chaud*	shoh
in cream sauce	*en crème*	ahn krehm
medium	*moyen*	moh-yahn
microwave	*four à micro-ondes*	foor ah mee-kroh-ohnd
mild	*doux*	doo
mixed	*mixte*	meekst
poached	*poché*	poh-shay
rare	*saignant*	sayn-yahn
raw	*cru*	krew
roasted	*rôti*	roh-tee
sautéed	*sauté*	soh-tay
smoked	*fumé*	few-may
sour	*aigre*	ay-gruh
spicy hot	*piquant*	pee-kahn
steamed	*à la vapeur*	ah lah vah-pur
stuffed	*farci*	far-see
sweet	*doux*	doo
topped with cheese	*gratinée*	grah-tee-nay
well-done	*bien cuit*	bee-an kwee
with rice	*avec du riz*	ah-vehk dew ree

EATING

Veggies

vegetables	*légumes*	lay-gewm
mixed vegetables	*légumes variés*	lay-gewm vah-ree-ay
with vegetables	*garni*	gar-nee
artichoke	*artichaut*	ar-tee-shoh

French Regional Specialties

Each region is followed by the name of a local city (in parentheses) and the region's specialties.

Alps (Chamonix): Try *raclette* (melted cheese over potatoes and meats) and *fondue Savoyarde* (cheese fondue).

Alsace (Colmar): Flavored by German heritage, Alsace is known for *choucroute* (sauerkraut and sausage), *tarte à l'oignon* (onion tart), *tarte flambée* (thin quiche), and *baeckeanoffe* (stew of onions, meat, and potatoes).

Burgundy (Beaune): This wine region excels in *coq au vin* (chicken with wine sauce), *boeuf bourgignon* (beef stew cooked with wine, bacon, onions, and mushrooms), *oeufs en meurette* (eggs poached in red wine), *escargots* (snails), and *jambon persillé* (ham with garlic and parsley).

Languedoc (Carcassonne): Try the hearty *cassoulet* (white bean, duck, and sausage stew), *canard* (duck), and *cargolade* (snail, lamb, and sausage stew).

Loire Valley (Amboise): Savor the fresh *truite* (trout), *veau* (veal), *rillettes* (cold minced pork paté), *fromage du chèvre*

asparagus	*asperges*	ah-spehrzh
beans	*haricots*	ah-ree-koh
beets	*betterave*	beh-teh-rahv
broccoli	*brocoli*	broh-koh-lee
cabbage	*chou*	shoo
carrots	*carottes*	kah-roht
cauliflower	*chou-fleur*	shoo-flur
corn	*maïs*	mah-ees
cucumber	*concombre*	koh<u>n</u>-koh<u>n</u>-bruh

EATING

(goat cheese), *aspèrges* (asparagus), and *champignons* (mushrooms).

Normandy (Bayeux): Munch some *moules* (mussels) and *escalope Normande* (veal in cream sauce). Swallow some *cidre* (apple cider) or *calvados* (apple brandy).

Périgord (Sarlat): The food is ducky. Try the *confit de canard* (duck cooked in its own juice), *pâté de foie gras* (goose liver paté), *salade périgourdine* (mixed green salad with foie gras, gizzards, and various duck parts), *pommes sarladaise* (potatoes fried in duck fat), *truffes* (truffles, earthy mushrooms), and anything with *noix* (walnuts).

Provence (Avignon): Sample the *soupe au pistou* (vegetable soup with garlic, cheese, and basil), *ratatouille* (casserole of eggplant, zucchini, tomatoes, onions, and green peppers), *brandade* (salted cod in garlic cream), and *tapenade* (a spread of pureed olives, garlic, and anchovies).

Riviera (Nice): Dive into *bouillabaisse* (seafood stew), *bourride* (creamy fish soup), *salade niçoise* (salad with potatoes, tomatoes, olives, tuna, and anchovies), and *pan bagna* (a salade niçoise on a bun).

EATING

eggplant	aubergine	oh-behr-zheen
garlic	ail	ah-ee
green beans	haricots verts	ah-ree-koh vehr
leeks	poireaux	pwah-roh
lentils	lentilles	lahn-teel
mushrooms	champignons	shahn-peen-yohn
olives	olives	oh-leev
onions	oignons	ohn-yohn
peas	pois	pwah

French Cooking Styles and Sauces

aïoli	*ah-ee-oh-lee*	garlic mayonnaise
à l'anglaise	*ah lahn-glehz*	boiled
au jus	*oh zhew*	in its natural juices
Béarnaise	*bayr-nehz*	sauce of egg yolks, butter, tarragon, white wine, and shallots
beurre blanc	*bur blahn*	sauce of butter, white wine, and shallots
Bourguignon	*boor-geen-yohn*	cooked in red wine
confit	*kohn-fee*	any meat cooked in its own fat
fines herbes	*feen ehrb*	with chopped fresh herbs
forestière	*foh-rehs-tee-yehr*	with mushrooms
gratinée	*grah-tee-nay*	topped with cheese, then broiled
Hollandaise	*oh-lahn-dayz*	sauce of butter and egg yolks
jardinière	*zhar-dan-yehr*	with vegetables
meunière	*muhn-yehr*	coated with flour and fried in butter
mornay	*mor-nay*	white sauce with grated gruyère cheese
Normande	*nor-mahnd*	cream sauce
nouvelle cuisine	*noo-vehl kwee-zeen*	fresh ingredients: appealing, low in fat, and expensive
Provençale	*proh-vahn-sahl*	with tomatoes, garlic, olive oil, and herbs

EATING

pepper...	*poivron...*	pwah-vrohn
...green / red / yellow	*...vert / rouge / jaune*	vehr / roozh / zhohn
pickles	*cornichons*	kor-nee-shohn
potato	*pomme de terre*	pohm duh tehr

radish	radis	rah-dee
rice	riz	ree
spaghetti	spaghetti	"spaghetti"
spinach	épinards	ay-pee-nar
tomatoes	tomates	toh-maht
truffles	truffes	trewf
zucchini	courgette	koor-zheht

Fruits

apple	pomme	pohm
apricot	abricot	ah-bree-koh
banana	banane	bah-nahn
berries	baies	bay
cherry	cerise	suh-reez
date	datte	daht
fig	figue	feeg
fruit	fruit	frwee
grapefruit	pamplemousse	pahn-pluh-moos
grapes	raisins	ray-zan
lemon	citron	see-trohn
melon	melon	muh-lohn
orange	orange	oh-rahnzh
peach	pêche	pehsh
pear	poire	pwar
pineapple	ananas	ah-nah-nah
plum	prune	prewn
prune	pruneau	prew-noh
raspberry	framboise	frahn-bwahz
strawberry	fraise	frehz
tangerine	mandarine	mahn-dah-reen
watermelon	pastèque	pah-stehk

Nuts

almond	amande	ah-mahnd
chestnut	marron, chataîgne	mah-rohn, shah-tayn
coconut	noix de coco	nwah duh koh-koh

hazelnut	*noisette*	nwah-zeht
peanut	*cacahuète*	kah-kah-weet
pistachio	*pistache*	pee-stahsh
walnut	*noix*	nwah

Just Desserts

dessert	*dessert*	duh-sehr
cake	*gâteau*	gah-toh
ice cream...	*glace...*	glahs
...scoop	*...boule*	bool
...cone	*...cornet*	kor-nay
...cup	*...bol*	bohl
...vanilla	*...vanille*	vah-nee
...chocolate	*...chocolat*	shoh-koh-lah
...strawberry	*...fraise*	frehz
sherbet	*sorbet*	sor-bay
fruit cup	*salade de fruits*	sah-lahd duh frwee
tart	*tartelette*	tar-tuh-leht
pie	*tarte*	tart
whipped cream	*crème chantilly*	krehm shahn-tee-yee
pastry	*pâtisserie*	pah-tee-suh-ree
fruit pastry	*chausson*	shoh-sohn
chocolate-filled pastry	*pain au chocolat*	pan oh shoh-koh-lah
buttery cake	*madeleine*	mah-duh-lehn
crêpes	*crêpes*	krehp
sweet crêpes	*crêpes sucrées*	krehp sew-kray
cookies	*petits gâteaux*	puh-tee gah-toh
candy	*bonbon*	bohn-bohn
low calorie	*bas en calories*	bah ahn kah-loh-ree
homemade	*fait à la maison*	fay ah lah may-zohn
We'll split one.	*Nous le partageons.*	noo luh par-tah-zhohn
Two forks / spoons, please.	*Deux fourchettes / cuillères, s'il vous plaît.*	duh foor-sheht / kwee-yehr see voo play
I shouldn't, but...	*Je ne devrais pas, mais...*	zhuh nuh duh-vray pah may

EATING

Magnificent!	*Magnifique!*	mahn-yee-feek
It's heavenly!	*C'est divin!*	say dee-van
Death by pleasure.	*C'est à mourrir de plaisir.*	say ah moo-reer duh play-zeer
Orgasmic.	*Orgasmique.*	or-gahz-meek
A moment on the lips, forever on the hips.	*Un moment sur les lèvres et pour toujours sur les hanches.*	uhn moh-mahn sewr lay lehv-ruh ay poor too-zhoor sewr lay ahnsh

Crème de la Crème

beignets	*bahn-yay*	fritters made with fruit (usually apples)
crème brulée	*krehm brew-lay*	rich caramelized custard
crème caramel	*krehm ka-ra-mehl*	custard with caramel sauce
crêpes suzette	*krehp soo-zeht*	crêpes flambéed with an orange brandy sauce
fromage blanc	*froh-mahzh blahn*	fresh white cheese eaten with sugar
gâteau	*gah-toh*	decorated sponge cake layered w/ pastry cream
île flottante	*eel floh-tahnt*	meringues floating in cream sauce
mille feuille ("thousand sheets")	*meel foy-ee*	light pastry
mousse au chocolat	*moos oh shoh-koh-lah*	ultra-light chocolate pudding
poires au vin rouge	*pwar oh van roozh*	pears poached in red wine and spices
profitterolle	*proh-fee-tuh-rohl*	cream puff filled with ice cream
soufflé au chocolat	*soo-flay oh shoh-koh-lah*	chocolate soufflé
tarte tatin	*tart tah-tan*	upside-down apple pie
tourteau fromager	*toor-toh froh-mah-zhay*	goat-cheese cake

EATING

DRINKING

Water, Milk, and Juice

mineral water...	*eau minérale...*	oh mee-nay-rahl
...carbonated	*...gazeuse*	gah-zuhz
...not carbonated	*...non gazeuse*	nohn gah-zuhz
tap water	*l'eau du robinet*	loh dew roh-bee-nay
whole milk	*lait entier*	lay ahnt-yay
skim milk	*lait écrémé*	lay ay-kray-may
fresh milk	*lait frais*	lay fray
chocolate milk	*lait au chocolat*	lay oh shoh-koh-lah
hot chocolate	*chocolat chaud*	shoh-koh-lah shoh
fruit juice	*jus de fruit*	zhew duh frwee
100% juice	*cent pour cent jus*	sahn poor sahn zhew
orange juice	*jus d'orange*	zhew doh-rahnzh
freshly squeezed	*pressé*	preh-say
apple juice	*jus de pomme*	zhew duh pohm
grapefruit juice	*jus de pamplemouse*	zhew duh pahn-pluh-moos
iced tea	*thé glacé*	tay glah-say
with / without...	*avec / sans...*	ah-vehk / sahn
...sugar	*...sucre*	sew-kruh
...ice	*...glaçons*	glah-sohn
glass / cup	*verre / tasse*	vehr / tahs
small / large	*petite / grande*	puh-teet / grahnd
bottle	*bouteille*	boo-teh-ee
Is the water safe to drink?	*L'eau est potable?*	loh ay poh-tah-bluh

To get free tap water at a restaurant, say, *"L'eau du robinet, s'il vous plaît."* The French typically order mineral water (and wine) with their meals. The half-liter plastic water bottles with screw tops are light and sturdy—great to pack along and reuse as you travel.

Coffee and Tea

coffee...	*café...*	kah-fay
...black	*...noir*	nwar

...with milk	*...crème*	krehm
...with lots of milk	*...au lait*	oh lay
...American-style	*...américain*	ah-may-ree-ka<u>n</u>
espresso	*express*	"express"
espresso with a touch of brandy	*café-calva*	kah-fay-kahl-vah
espresso with a touch of milk	*noisette*	nwah-zeht
instant coffee	*Nescafé*	"Nescafé"
decaffeinated / decaf	*décaféiné / déca*	day-kah-fay-nay / day-kah
sugar	*sucre*	sew-kruh
hot water	*l'eau chaude*	loh shohd
tea / lemon	*thé / citron*	tay / see-troh<u>n</u>
tea bag	*sachet de thé*	sah-shay duh tay
herbal tea	*tisane*	tee-zah<u>n</u>
lemon tea / orange tea	*thé au citron / thé à l'orange*	tay oh see-troh<u>n</u> / tay ah loh-rah<u>n</u>zh
peppermint tea / fruit tea	*thé à la menthe / thé de fruit*	tay ah lah mehnt / tay duh frwee
small / big	*petit / grand*	puh-tee / grah<u>n</u>
Another cup.	*Encore une tasse.*	ah<u>n</u>-kor ewn tahs
Is it the same price if I sit or stand?	*C'est le même prix au bar ou dans la salle?*	say luh mehm pree oh bar oo dah<u>n</u> lah sahl

Every *café* or *bar* has a complete price list posted. In bigger cities, prices go up when you sit down. It's cheapest to stand at the bar (*au bar* or *au comptoir*), more expensive to sit in the dining room (*la salle*), and most expensive to sit outside (*la terrasse*). Refills aren't free.

Wine

I would like...	*Je voudrais...*	zhuh voo-dray
We would like...	*Nous voudrions...*	noo voo-dree-oh<u>n</u>
...a glass...	*...un verre...*	uh<u>n</u> vehr
...a carafe...	*...une carafe...*	ewn kah-rahf
...a half bottle...	*...une demi-bouteille...*	ewn duh-mee-boo-teh-ee

...a bottle...	...une bouteille...	ewn boo-teh-ee
...a 5-liter jug...	...un bidon de cinq litres...	uhn bee-dohn duh sank lee-truh
...a barrel...	...un tonneau...	uhn toh-noh
...a vat...	...un fût...	uhn foewt
...of red wine.	...de vin rouge.	duh van roozh
...of white wine.	...de vin blanc.	duh van blahn
...of the region.	...de la région.	duh lah ray-zhee-ohn
...the wine list.	...la carte des vins.	lah kart day van

In France, wine is a work of art. Each wine-growing region and each vintage has its own distinct personality. I prefer drinking wine from the region I'm in. Ask for *vin de la région,* available at reasonable prices. As you explore France, look for the *dégustation* signs welcoming you in for a wine tasting. It's normally free or very cheap. To get a decent table wine in a region that doesn't produce wine (Normandy, Brittany, Paris/Ile de France), ask for *un Côtes du Rhône.*

Look for these regional specialties. **Alsace** specializes in white wines—try the *Reisling, Tokay,* and *Slyvaner.* **Bordeaux** offers elegant, expensive red wines, along with *Sauternes* (a sweet dessert wine) and *Graves* (a fine white).

Burgundy has the best *Chardonnay* in France. Its reds are

Key Phrases: Drinking

drink	verre	vehr
(mineral) water	eau (minérale)	oh (mee-nay-rahl)
tap water	l'eau du robinet	loh dew roh-bee-nay
milk	lait	lay
juice	jus	zhew
coffee	café	kah-fay
tea	thé	tay
wine	vin	van
beer	bière	bee-ehr
Cheers!	Santé!	sahn-tay

mostly *Pinot Noir*—to save money, try a *Gamay*. The people of **Brittany** are proud of their *Muscadet* (excellent with seafood). In **Périgord**, try the full-bodied red *Cahors*. The **Loire Valley** produces dry whites (*Sancerre* and *Pouilly Fumé*) and the sweet white *Vouvray* wines. Fruity reds rule **Provence**—look for *Côtes du Rhône* and *Chateauneuf du Pape*. Hilly **Champagne** pops the cork on the finest *Champagne* in the world.

Wine Words

wine	*vin*	va<u>n</u>
table wine	*vin de table*	va<u>n</u> duh tah-bluh
house wine (cheapest)	*vin ordinaire*	va<u>n</u> or-dee-nair
local	*du coin*	dew kwa<u>n</u>
of the region	*de la région*	duh lah ray-zhee-oh<u>n</u>
red	*rouge*	roozh
white	*blanc*	blah<u>n</u>
rosé	*rosé*	roh-zay
sparkling	*mousseux*	moo-suh
sweet	*doux*	doo
semi-dry	*demi-sec*	duh-mee-sehk
dry	*sec*	sehk
very dry	*brut*	brewt
full-bodied	*robuste*	roh-boost
fruity	*fruité*	frwee-tay
light	*léger*	lay-zhay
mature	*prêt à boire*	preh ah bwar
cork	*bouchon*	boo-shoh<u>n</u>
corkscrew	*tire-bouchon*	teer-boo-shoh<u>n</u>
vineyard	*vignoble*	veen-yoh-bluh
harvest	*vendange*	vah<u>n</u>-dah<u>n</u>zh
What is a good vintage?	*Quelles est un bon millésime?*	kehl ay uh<u>n</u> boh<u>n</u> mee-lay-zeem
What do you recommend?	*Qu'est-ce que vous recommandez?*	kehs kuh voo ruh-koh-mah<u>n</u>-day

Wine Labels

The information on a French wine label can give you a lot of details about the wine. Listed below are several terms to help you identify and choose a specific wine.

AOC (appellation d'origine contrôlée)	meets nationwide laws for production of the highest-quality French wines
VDQS (vin délimité de qualité supérieure)	quality standards for specific regional wines
vin de pays	local wine (medium quality)
vin de table	table wine (quality varies)
millésime	vintage
mis en bouteilles dans nos caves	bottled in our cellars
cru	superior growth
cépage	grape variety

Beer

beer	*bière*	bee-ehr
from the tap	*pression*	preh-see-oh<u>n</u>
bottle	*bouteille*	boo-teh-ee
light / dark	*blonde / brune*	bloh<u>n</u>d / brewn
local / imported	*régionale / importée*	ray-zhee-oh-nahl / a<u>n</u>-por-tay
a small beer	*un demi*	uh<u>n</u> duh-mee
a large beer	*une chope*	ewn shohp
low-calorie beer (hard to find)	*bière "light"*	bee-ehr "light"
alcohol-free	*sans alcool*	sah<u>n</u>z ahl-kohl
hard apple cider	*cidre*	see-druh
cold	*fraîche*	fraysh
colder	*plus fraîche*	plew fraysh

Bar Talk

Would you like to go out for a drink?	*Voulez-vous prendre un verre?*	voo-lay-vooz prah<u>n</u>-druh uh<u>n</u> vehr

EATING

I'll buy you a drink.	Je vous offre un verre.	zhuh voo oh-fruh uhn vehr
It's on me.	C'est moi qui paie.	say mwah kee pay
The next one's on me.	Le suivant est sur moi.	luh see-vahn tay sewr mwah
What would you like?	Qu'est-ce que vous prenez?	kehs kuh voo pruh-nay
I'll have a___	Je prends un___	zhuh prahn uhn
I don't drink alcohol.	Je ne bois pas d'alcool.	zhuh nuh bwah pah dahl-kohl
alcohol-free	sans alcool	sahnz ahl-kohl
What is the local specialty?	Quelle est la spécialité régionale?	kehl ay lah spay-see-ah-lee-tay ray-zhee-oh-nahl
What is a good drink for a man / a woman?	Quelle est une bonne boisson pour un homme / une dame?	kehl ay ewn buhn bwah-sohn poor uhn ohm / ewn dahm
Straight.	Sec.	sehk
With / Without...	Avec / Sans...	ah-vehk / sahn
...alcohol.	...alcool.	ahl-kohl
...ice.	...glaçons.	glah-sohn
One more.	Encore une.	ahn-kor ewn
Cheers!	Santé!	sahn-tay
To your health!	À votre santé!	ah voh-truh sahn-tay
Long live France!	Vive la France!	veev lah frahns
I'm feeling...	Je me sens...	zhuh muh sahn
...tipsy.	...éméché.	ay-may-shay
...a little drunk.	...un peu ivre.	uhn puh ee-vruh
...wasted. (m / f)	...ivre mort / ivre morte.	ee-vruh mor / ee-vruh mort
I'm hung over.	J'ai la gueule de bois.	zhay lah guhl duh bwah

An *apéritif* is served before dinner, and a *digestif* is served after dinner. Ask what's local.

Typical *apéritifs* are *Champagne, bière* (beer), *kir* (white wine and black currant liqueur), *kir royal* (champagne with cassis), *pastis* (anise-flavored—Pernod and Ricard are popular brands), *pineau* (cognac and grape juice), and *port.*

Common *digestifs* (for after the meal) are *cognac* (wine-distilled brandy from the Charentes region—well-known brands are Rémy Martin, Hennessy, and Martel), *armagnac* (cognac from a different region), *calvados* (apple brandy from Normandy), *eaux de vie* (fruit brandy, literally "waters of life"—Framboise, Poire William, and Kirsch are best known), and liqueurs such as *Cointreau* (orange-based), *Chartreuse* and *Benedictine* (two distinct, herb-based liqueurs, made by monks with secret formulas), *Grand Marnier* (orange brandy), *B&B* (brandy and Benedictine), *crème de menthe,* and *Chambord* (raspberry).

PICNICKING

At the Grocery

Is it self-service?	*C'est libre service?*	say lee-bruh sehr-vees
Ripe for today?	*Pour manger aujourd'hui?*	poor mahn-zhay oh-joord-wee
Does it need to be cooked?	*Il faut le faire cuire?*	eel foh luh fair kweer
Can I taste it?	*Je peux goûter?*	zhuh puh goo-tay
Fifty grams.	*Cinquante grammes.*	san-kahnt grahm
One hundred grams.	*Cent grammes.*	sahn grahm
More. / Less.	*Plus. / Moins.*	plew / mwan
A piece.	*Un morceau.*	uhn mor-soh
A slice.	*Une tranche.*	ewn trahnsh
Four slices.	*Quatre tranches.*	kah-truh trahnsh
Sliced.	*Tranché.*	trahn-shay
Half.	*La moitié.*	lah mwaht-yay
A few.	*Quelques.*	kehl-kuh
A handful.	*Une poignée.*	ewn pwahn-yay
A small bag.	*Un petit sachet.*	uhn puh-tee sah-shay
A bag, please.	*Un sachet, s'il vous plaît.*	uhn sah-shay see voo play

EATING

Can you make me...?	*Vous pouvez me faire...?*	voo poo-vay muh fair
Can you make us...?	*Vous pouvez nous faire...?*	voo poo-vay noo fair
...a sandwich	*...un sandwich*	uhn sahnd-weech
...two sandwiches	*...deux sandwichs*	duh sahnd-weech
To take out.	*Pour emporter.*	poor ahn-por-tay
Can I / Can we use...?	*Je peux / Nous pouvons utiliser...?*	zhuh puh / noo poo-vohn oo-tee-lee-zay
...the microwave	*...le micro-onde*	luh mee-kroh-ohnd
May I borrow a...?	*Je peux emprunter...?*	zhuh puh ahn-pruhn-tay
Do you have a...?	*Vous avez...?*	vooz ah-vay
Where can I buy / find a...?	*Où puis-je acheter / trouver un...?*	oo pwee-zhuh ah-shuh-tay / troo-vay uhn
...corkscrew	*...tire-bouchon*	teer-boo-shohn
...can opener	*...ouvre boîte*	oo-vruh bwaht
Is there a park nearby?	*Il y a un parc près d'ici?*	eel yah uhn park preh dee-see
Where is a good place to picnic?	*Il y a un coin sympa pour pique-niquer?*	eel yah uhn kwan sahn-pah poor peek-nee-kay
Is picnicking allowed here?	*On peut pique-niquer ici?*	ohn puh peek-nee-kay ee-see

Ask if there's a *marché* (open air market) nearby. These lively markets offer the best selection and ambience.

Tasty Picnic Words

open air market	*marché*	mar-shay
grocery store	*épicerie*	ay-pee-suh-ree
supermarket	*supermarché*	sew-pehr-mar-shay
super-duper market	*hypermarché*	ee-pehr-mar-shay
delicatessen	*charcuterie-traiteur*	shar-koo-tuh-ree-tray-tur

bakery	*boulangerie*	boo-lahn-zhuh-ree
pastry shop	*pâtisserie*	pah-tee-suh-ree
sweets shop	*confiserie*	kohn-fee-suh-ree
cheese shop	*fromagerie*	froh-mah-zhuh-ree
picnic	*pique-nique*	peek-neek
sandwich	*sandwich*	sahnd-weech
bread	*pain*	pan
roll	*petit pain*	puh-tee pan
ham	*jambon*	zhahn-bohn
sausage	*saucisse*	soh-sees
cheese	*fromage*	froh-mahzh
mustard...	*moutarde...*	moo-tard
mayonnaise...	*mayonnaise...*	mah-yuh-nehz
...in a tube	*...en tube*	ahn tewb
yogurt	*yaourt*	yah-oort
fruit	*fruit*	frwee
juice	*jus*	zhew
cold drinks	*boissons fraîches*	bwah-sohn frehsh
spoon / fork...	*cuillère / fourchette...*	kwee-yehr / foor-sheht
...made of plastic	*...en plastique*	ahn plah-steek
cup / plate...	*gobelet / assiette...*	gob-leh / ahs-yeht
...made of paper	*...en papier*	ahn pahp-yay

For convenience, you can assemble your picnic at a ***supermarché***
(supermarket)—but smaller shops or a ***marché*** (open-air market)
are more fun. Get bread for your sandwich at a ***boulangerie*** and
order meat and cheese by the gram at an ***épicerie.*** One hundred
grams is about a quarter pound, enough for two sandwiches. To
weigh and price your produce at more modern stores, put it on the
scale, push the photo or number (keyed to the bin it came from),
and then stick your sticker on the food. To get real juice, look for
100% or ***sans sucre*** on the label.

MENU DECODER

FRENCH/ENGLISH

This handy decoder won't list every word on the menu, but it'll help you get *riz et veau* (rice and veal) instead of *ris de veau* (calf pancreas).

à l'anglaise	boiled
à la carte	side dishes
à la vapeur	steamed
à point	medium (meat)
abricot	apricot
agneau	lamb
ail	garlic
aïoli	garlic mayonnaise
alcool	alcohol
amande	almond
amuse bouche	munchies
ananas	pineapple
anchois	anchovies
artichaut	artichoke
asperges	asparagus
assiette	plate
assiette d'enfant	children's plate
au jus	in its natural juices

auberge	country inn
aubergine	eggplant
avec	with
baguette	long loaf of bread
baies	berries
banane	banana
Béarnaise	sauce of egg and wine
beignets	fritters with fruit
betterave	beets
beurre	butter
beurre blanc	sauce of butter, white wine, and shallots
beurre de cacahuètes	peanut butter
bien cuit	well-done (meat)
bière	beer
bifteck	steak
biologique	organic
bisque	shellfish chowder
bistro	small, informal restaurant
blanc	white
bleu	blue (cheese); very rare (meat)
blonde	light (beer)
boeuf	beef
boissons	beverages
bon	good
bonbon	candy
bouchée à la reine	pastry shell with creamed sweetbreads
bouillabaisse	seafood stew
bouilli	boiled
bouillon	broth
boulangerie	bakery
boule	scoop
Bourguignon	cooked in red wine
bouteille	bottle
braisé	braised
brasserie	large café with simple food

brioche	sweet, flaky roll
brocoli	broccoli
brouillés	scrambled
brune	dark (beer)
brut	very dry (wine)
cabillaud	cod
cacahuète	peanut
café	coffee
café américain	American-style coffee
café au lait	coffee with lots of milk
café crème	coffee with milk
café noir	black coffee
café-calva	espresso with a touch of brandy
calamar	squid
canard	duck
carottes	carrots
carte	menu
carte des consommation	drink menu
carte des vins	wine list
cassoulet	bean and meat stew
cerise	cherry
cervelle	brains
champignons	mushrooms
charcuterie	delicatessen
chataîgne	chestnut
chaud	hot
chausson	fruit pastry
cheval	horse
chèvre	goat
chinois	Chinese
chocolat	chocolate
chope	large beer
chorizo	pepperoni
chou	cabbage
chou-fleur	cauliflower
cidre	hard apple cider
citron	lemon

complet	whole; full
compris	included
concombre	cucumber
confiserie	sweets shop
confit	cooked in its own fat
confiture	jelly
consommé	broth
copieux	filling
coq	rooster
coquilles	scallops
cornichon	pickle
costaud	full-bodied (wine)
côte de boeuf	T-bone
côtelette	cutlet
courgette	zucchini
couvert	cover charge
crabe	crab
crème	cream
crème (velouté) d'asperges	cream of asparagus soup
crème brulée	caramelized custard
crème caramel	custard with caramel sauce
crème chantilly	whipped cream
crêpe	crêpe
crêpes froment	buckwheat crêpes
crêpes sucrées	sweet crêpes
crêpes suzette	crêpes flambéed with orange brandy sauce
crevettes	shrimp
croissant	crescent roll
croque madame	ham, cheese, and egg sandwich
croque monsieur	ham and cheese sandwich
croûte au fromage	cheese pastry
cru	raw
crudités	raw vegetables
cuisses de grenouilles	frog legs
cuit	cooked
cuit au four	baked

cure-dent	toothpick
datte	date
déjeuner	lunch
demi	half; small beer
demi-bouteille	half bottle
demi-sec	semi-dry (wine)
dinde	turkey
dîner	dinner
doux	mild, sweet (wine)
eau	water
édulcorant	artificial sweetener
emmenthal	Swiss cheese
entier	whole
entrecôte	rib steak
entrée	first course
épicée	spicy
épinards	spinach
escargots	snails
et	and
express	espresso
fait à la maison	homemade
farci	stuffed
faux-filet	flank steak
figue	fig
filet	fillet
fines herbes	chopped fresh herbs
flambée	flaming
foie	liver
forestière	with mushrooms
fort	sharp (cheese)
fougasse	lace-like bread
frais	fresh
fraise	strawberry
framboise	raspberry
frit	fried
froid	cold
fromage	cheese

fromage à la crème	cream cheese
fromage aux herbes	cheese with herbs
fromage blanc	fresh white cheese eaten with sugar
fromage bleu	bleu cheese
fromage chèvre	goat cheese
fromage de la région	cheese of the region
fromage doux	mild cheese
fromage fort	sharp cheese
fromagerie	cheese shop
froment	wheat
fruit	fruit
fruité	fruity (wine)
fruits de mer	seafood
fumé	smoked
galette	buckwheat crêpe
garni	with vegetables
gâteau	cake
gazeuse	carbonated
glace	ice cream
glaçons	ice
grand	large
gras	fat
gratinée	topped with cheese
grenouille	frog
grillades	mixed grill
grillé	grilled
gruyère	Swiss cheese
hareng	herring
haricots	beans
Hollandaise	sauce of egg and butter
homard	lobster
hors d'oeuvre	appetizers
huile	oil
huîtres	oysters
île flottante	meringues floating in cream sauce
importée	imported

jambon	ham
jardinière	with vegetables
jus	juice
kasher	kosher
La vache qui rit	Laughing Cow (brand of cheese)
lait	milk
laitue	lettuce
langue	tongue
lapin	rabbit
léger	light (not heavy)
légumes	vegetables
lentilles	lentils
light	light (low-calorie)
madeleine	buttery cake
maïs	corn
maison	house
mandarine	tangerine
marron	chestnut
médaillon	tenderloin
melon	canteloupe
menu du jour	menu of the day
meunière	fried in butter
micro-onde	microwave
miel	honey
mille feuille	light pastry
millésime	vintage date (wine)
mixte	mixed
morceau	piece
mornay	white sauce with gruyère
morue	salty cod
moules	mussels
mousseux	sparkling
moutarde	mustard
Nescafé	instant coffee
noir	black
noisette	hazelnut
noix	walnut

noix de coco	coconut
Normande	cream sauce
nouvelle	new
oeufs	eggs
oeufs à la coque	boiled eggs
(mollet / dur)	(soft / hard)
oeufs au plat	fried eggs
oeufs brouillés	scrambled eggs
oignon	onion
olives	olives
onglet	steak
ou	or
pain	bread
pain bisse	dark-grain bread
pain complet	
pain de seigle	dark bread
palourdes	clams
pamplemousse	grapefruit
pas	not
pastèque	watermelon
pâtes	pasta
pâtisserie	pastry; pastry shop
pêche	peach
petit	small
petit déjeuner	breakfast
petits gâteaux	cookies
petits pois	peas
piquant	spicy hot
pissaladière	onion and anchovy pizza
pistache	pistachio
plat du jour	special of the day
plat principal	main course
plâteau	platter
plâteau de fromages	cheese platter
poché	poached
poire	pear
poireaux	leeks

poires au vin rouge	pears poached in red wine and spices
pois	peas
poisson	fish
poivre	pepper
poivron	bell pepper
pomme	apple
pomme de terre	potato
pommes frites	French fries
porc	pork
potage	soup
potage de légumes	thick vegetable soup
poulet	chicken
pour emporter	to go
pression	draft (beer)
prix fixe	fixed price
profitterole	cream puff with ice cream
Provençale	with garlic and tomatoes
prune	plum
pruneau	prune
quenelles	meat or fish dumplings
quiche	quiche
quiche au fromage	quiche with cheese
quiche au jambon	quiche with ham
quiche aux champignons	quiche with mushrooms
quiche lorraine	quiche with bacon, cheese, and onions
radis	radish
ragoût	meat stew
raisins	grapes
ratatouille	eggplant casserole
régionale	local
rillettes	cold, minced pork
ris de veau	sweetbreads
riz	rice
robuste	full-bodied (wine)
rosbif	roast beef
rosé	rosé (wine)
rôti	roasted

rouge	red
routier	truck stop with simple food
saignant	rare (meat)
salade	salad
sans	without
saucisse	sausage
saucisse-frites	hot dog and fries
saumon	salmon
scampi	prawns
sec	dry
sel	salt
service compris	service included
service non compris	service not included
sorbet	sherbet
soufflé	soufflé (light, fluffy eggs baked with savory fillings)
soufflé au chocolat	chocolate soufflé
soupe	soup
soupe à l'oignon	onion soup
soupe au pistou	Provençal vegetable soup
spécialité	specialty
steak tartare	raw hamburger
sucre	sugar
tapenade	olive, anchovy paste
tartare	raw
tarte	pie
tarte à l'oignon	onion tart
tarte au fromage	cheese tart
tarte tatin	upside-down apple pie
tartelette	tart
tasse	cup
terrine	pâté
thé	tea
thon	tuna
tire-bouchon	corkscrew
tisane	herbal tea
tournedos	tenderloin of T-bone

tourteau fromager	goat-cheese cake
tranche	slice
tranché	sliced
très bien cuit	very well-done (meat)
tripes	tripe
truffes	truffles (earthy mushrooms)
truite	trout
vapeur	steamed
variés	assorted
veau	veal
végétarien	vegetarian
vendange	harvest (wine)
verre	glass
vert	green
viande	meat
vichyssoise	potato, leek soup
vignoble	vineyard
vin	wine
vin de table	table wine
vin ordinaire	house wine
vinaigre	vinegar
volaille	poultry
yaourt	yogurt

ENGLISH/FRENCH

alcohol	alcool
almond	amande
anchovies	anchois
and	et
appetizers	hors d'oeuvre
apple	pomme
apple cider, hard	cidre
apple pie, upside-down	tarte tatin
apricot	abricot
artichoke	artichaut
artificial sweetener	édulcorant
asparagus	asperges
assorted	variées
baked	cuit au four
bakery	boulangerie
banana	banane
beans	haricots
beef	boeuf
beef steak	bifteck
beer	bière
beer, draft	pression
beer, large	chope
beer, small (half)	demi
beets	betterave
bell pepper	poivron
berries	baies
beverages	boissons
black	noir
blue cheese	fromage bleu
boiled	à l'anglaise, bouilli
boiled egg	oeuf à la coque
(soft / hard)	(mollet / dur)
bottle	bouteille
brains	cervelle

braised	braisé
bread	pain, baguette
bread, dark-grain	pain bisse, pain de seigle
bread, lace-like	fougasse
bread, whole-grain	pain complet
breakfast	petit déjeuner
broccoli	brocoli
broth	bouillon, consommé
buckwheat crêpe	galette, crêpe froment
butter	beurre
cabbage	chou
cake	gâteau
candy	bonbon
canteloupe	melon
carafe	carafe
caramelized custard	crème brulée
carbonated	gazeuse
carrots	carottes
cauliflower	chou-fleur
cheese	fromage
cheese of the region	fromage de la région
cheese pastry	croûte au fromage
cheese platter	plâteau de fromages
cheese shop	fromagerie
cheese tart	tarte au fromage
cheese with herbs	fromage aux herbes
cheese, blue	fromage bleu
cheese, cream	fromage à la crème
cheese, Laughing Cow	La vache qui rit
cheese, Swiss	gruyère, emmenthal
cheese, topped with	gratinée
cheese, white	fromage blanc
cherry	cerise
chestnut	châtaigne, marron
chicken	poulet
children's plate	assiette d'enfant
Chinese	chinois

chocolate	chocolat
chocolate soufflé	soufflé au chocolat
clams	palourdes
coconut	noix de coco
cod	cabillaud
cod, salty	morue
coffee	café
coffee, American-style	café américain
coffee, black	café noir
coffee, instant	Nescafé
coffee with lots of milk	café au lait
coffee with some milk	café crème
cold	froid
cooked	cuit
cooked in its own fat	confit
cooked in red wine	Bourguignon
cookies	petits gâteaux
corkscrew	tire-bouchon
corn	maïs
country inn	auberge
course, first	entrée
course, main	plat principal
cover charge	couvert
crab	crabe
cream	crème
cream cheese	fromage à la crème
cream puff (with ice cream)	profitterole
cream sauce	Normande
crêpe	crêpe
crêpe, buckwheat	galette, crêpe froment
crêpes flambéed with orange brandy sauce	crêpes suzette
crêpes, sweet	crêpes sucrées
crescent roll	croissant
cucumber	concombre
cup	tasse
custard with caramel sauce	crème caramel

custard, caramelized	crème brulée
cutlet	côtelette
dark (beer)	brune
dark-grain bread	pain bisse, pain de seigle
date	datte
delicatessen	charcuterie
dinner	diner
draft (beer)	pression
drink menu	carte des consommation
dry	sec
dry, very (wine)	brut
duck	canard
dumplings, meat or fish	quenelles
eggplant	aubergine
eggplant casserole	ratatouille
eggs	oeufs
eggs, boiled	oeuf à la coque
(soft / hard)	(mollet / dur)
eggs, fried	oeufs au plat
eggs, scrambled	oeufs brouillés
espresso	express
espresso with brandy	café-calva
fat	gras
fig	figue
fillet	filet
filling	copieux
first course	entrée
fish	poisson
fixed price	prix fixe
flaming	flambée
flank steak	faux-filet
French fries	pommes frites
fresh	frais
fried	frit
fried eggs	oeufs au plat
fried in butter	meunière
fritters	beignets

frog	grenouille
frog legs	cuisses de grenouilles
fruit	fruit
fruit pastry	chausson
fruity (wine)	fruité
full-bodied (wine)	robuste, costaud
garlic	ail
garlic and tomatoes, with	Provençale
garlic mayonnaise	aïoli
glass	verre
goat	chèvre
goat cheese	fromage chèvre
good	bon
grapefruit	pamplemousse
grapes	raisins
green	vert
grill, mixed	grillades
grilled	grillé
half bottle	demi-bouteille
half, small beer	demi
ham	jambon
ham and cheese sandwich	croque monsieur
ham and egg sandwich	croque madame
hard apple cider	cidre
harvest (wine)	vendange
hazelnut	noisette
herbal tea	tisane
herring	hareng
homemade	fait à la maison
honey	miel
horse	cheval
hot	chaud
hot dog and fries	saucisse-frites
house	maison
house wine	vin ordinaire
ice	glaçons
ice cream	glace

imported	importée
included	compris
jelly	confiture
juice	jus
kosher	kasher
lamb	agneau
large	grand
large beer	chope
Laughing Cow cheese	La vache qui rit
leeks	poireaux
lemon	citron
lentils	lentilles
lettuce	laitue
light (beer)	blonde
light (not heavy)	léger
liver	foie
lobster	homard
local	régionale
lunch	déjeuner
main course	plat principal
mayonnaise, garlic	aïoli
meat	viande
meat stew	ragoût
medium (meat)	à point
medium (wine)	demi-sec
menu	carte
menu of the day	menu du jour
menu, drink	carte des consommation
menu, wine	carte des vins
microwave	micro-onde
mild (cheese)	doux
mild, sweet (wine)	doux
milk	lait
mixed	mixte
mixed grill	grillades
munchies	amuse bouche
mushrooms	champignons

mushrooms, with	forestière
mussels	moules
mustard	moutarde
new	nouvelle
not	pas
oil	huile
olives	olives
onion	oignon
onion tart	tarte à l'oignon
or	ou
orange	orange
organic	biologique
oysters	huîtres
pasta	pâtes
pastry, pastry shop	pâtisserie
pâté	pâté, terrine
peach	pêche
peanut	cacahuète
peanut butter	beurre de cacahuètes
pear	poire
peas	pois
pepper	poivre
pepper (bell)	poivron
pepperoni	chorizo
pickle	cornichon
pie	tarte
piece	morceau
pineapple	ananas
pistachio	pistache
plate	assiette
platter	plâteau
plum	prune
poached	poché
pork	porc
potato	pomme de terre
poultry	volaille
prawns	scampi

prune	pruneau
quiche	quiche
quiche with bacon, cheese, and onions	quiche lorraine
quiche with cheese	quiche au fromage
quiche with ham	quiche au jambon
quiche with mushrooms	quiche aux champignons
rabbit	lapin
radish	radis
rare (meat)	saignant
rare, very (meat)	bleu
raspberry	framboise
raw	cru, tartare
raw hamburger	steak tartare
raw vegetables	crudités
red	rouge
rib steak	entrecôte
rice	riz
roast beef	rosbif
roasted	rôti
rooster	coq
rosé (wine)	rosé
salad	salade
salmon	saumon
salt	sel
sandwich, ham and cheese	croque monsieur
sandwich, ham and egg	croque madame
sauce	sauce
sauce of butter, white wine, and shallots	beurre blanc
sauce of egg and butter	Hollandaise
sauce of egg and wine	Béarnaise
sauce, cream	Normande
sauce, white, with gruyère	mornay
sausage	saucisse
scallops	coquilles
scoop	boule

scrambled	brouillés
scrambled eggs	oeufs brouillés
seafood	fruits de mer
seafood stew	bouillabaisse
semi-dry (wine)	demi-sec
service included	service compris
service not included	service non compris
sharp (cheese)	fort
shellfish chowder	bisque
sherbet	sorbet
shrimp	crevettes
side dishes	à la carte
slice	tranche
sliced	tranché
small	petit
smoked	fumé
snacks	amuse bouche
snails	escargots
soufflé	soufflé
soufflé, chocolate	soufflé au chocolat
soup	soupe, potage
soup, cream of asparagus	crème (velouté) d'asperges
soup, onion	soupe à l'oignon
soup, potato and leek	vichyssoise
soup, Provençal vegetable	soupe au pistou
soup, thick vegetable	potage de légumes
sparkling	mousseux
special of the day	plat du jour
specialty	spécialité
spicy	épicée, piquant
spinach	épinards
squid	calamar
steak	onglet, bifteck
steamed	à la vapeur
stew, bean and meat	cassoulet
stew, seafood	bouillabaisse
strawberry	fraise

stuffed	farci
sugar	sucre
sweet, mild (wine)	doux
sweetbreads	ris de veau
sweetener, artificial	édulcorant
sweets shop	confiserie
Swiss cheese	gruyère, emmenthal
table wine	vin de table
tangerine	mandarine
tart	tartelette
tart, cheese	tarte au fromage
tart, onion	tarte à l'oignon
T-bone	côte de boeuf
tea	thé
tenderloin	médaillon, tournedos
to go	pour emporter
tomatoes and garlic, with	Provençale
tongue	langue
toothpick	cure-dent
tripe	tripes
trout	truite
truffles	truffes
tuna	thon
turkey	dinde
veal	veau
vegetables	légumes
vegetables, raw	crudités
vegetables, with	jardinière, garni
vegetarian	végétarien
very dry (wine)	brut
very rare (meat)	bleu
very well-done (meat)	très bien cuit
vinegar	vinaigre
vineyard	vignoble
vintage date (wine)	millésime
walnut	noix
water	eau

English / French

MENU DECODER

watermelon	pastèque
well-done (meat)	bien cuit
well-done, very (meat)	très bien cuit
wheat	froment
whipped cream	crème chantilly
white	blanc
whole (entire)	entier
whole (full)	complet
whole-grain bread	pain complet
wine	vin
dry	sec
fruity	fruité
full-bodied	robuste, costaud
medium dry	demi-sec
mild, sweet	doux
semi-dry	demi-sec
very dry	brut
wine list	carte des vins
wine, house	vin ordinaire
wine, table	vin de table
with	avec
without	sans
yogurt	yaourt
zucchini	courgette

ACTIVITIES

SIGHTSEEING

Where?

Where is...?	Où est...?	oo ay
...the tourist information office	...l'office du tourisme	loh-fees dew too-reez-muh
...the best view	...la meilleure vue	lah meh-yur vew
...the main square	...la place principale	lah plahs pra<u>n</u>-see-pahl
...the old town center	...la vieille ville	lah vee-yay-ee veel
...the museum	...le musée	luh mew-zay
...the castle	...le château	luh shah-toh
...the palace	...le palais	luh pah-lay
...an amusement park	...un parc d'amusement	uh<u>n</u> park dah-mooz-mah<u>n</u>
...the entrance / exit	...l'entrée / la sortie	lah<u>n</u>-tray / lah sor-tee
Where are...?	Où sont...?	oo soh<u>n</u>
...the toilets	...les toilettes	lay twah-leht
...the ruins	...les ruines	lay rween
Is there a festival nearby?	Il y a un festival dans la région?	eel yah uh<u>n</u> fehs-tee-vahl dah<u>n</u> lah ray-zhee-oh<u>n</u>

Key Phrases: Sightseeing

Where is...?	*Où est...?*	oo ay
How much is it?	*C'est combien?*	say kohn-bee-an
At what time does this open / close?	*À quelle heuere c'est ouvert / fermé?*	ah kehl ur say oo-vehr / fehr-may
Do you have a guided tour?	*Vous avez une visite guidée?*	vooz ah-vay ewn vee-zeet gee-day
When is the next tour in English?	*La prochaine visite en anglais est à quelle heure?*	lah proh-shehn vee-zeet ahn ahn-glay ay ah kehl ur

At the Sight

Do you have...?	*Vous avez...?*	vooz ah-vay
...information...	*...des renseignements...*	day rahn-sehn-yuh-mahn
...a guidebook...	*...un guide...*	uhn geed
...in English	*...en anglais*	ahn ahn-glay
Is it free?	*C'est gratuit?*	say grah-twee
How much is it?	*C'est combien?*	say kohn-bee-an
Is the ticket good all day?	*Le billet est valable toute la journée?*	luh bee-yay ay vah-lah-bluh toot lah zhoor-nay
Can I get back in?	*Je peux rentrer?*	zhuh puh rahn-tray
At what time does this open / close?	*À quelle heuere c'est ouvert / fermé?*	ah kehl ur say oo-vehr / fehr-may
What time is the last entry?	*La dernière entrée est à quelle heure?*	lah dehrn-yehr ahn-tray ay ah kehl ur

Please

PLEASE let me in.	*S'IL VOUS PLAÎT, laissez-moi entrer.*	see voo play lay-say-mwah ahn-tray
PLEASE let us in.	*S'IL VOUS PLAÎT, laissez-nous entrer.*	see voo play lay-say-nooz ahn-tray

ACTIVITIES

I've traveled all the way from ___.	*Je suis venu de ___.*	zhuh swee vuh-new duh
We've traveled all the way from ___.	*Nous sommes venus de ___.*	noo suhm vuh-new duh
I must leave tomorrow.	*Je dois partir demain.*	zhuh dwah par-teer duh-man
We must leave tomorrow.	*Nous devons partir demain.*	noo duh-vohn par-teer duh-man
I promise I'll be fast.	*Je promets d'aller vite.*	zhuh proh-may dah-lay veet
We promise we'll be fast.	*Nous promettons d'aller vite.*	noo proh-meh-tohn dah-lay veet
It was my mother's dying wish that I see this.	*C'était le dernier souhait de ma mère que je voies ça.*	say-tay luh dehrn-yay soo-ay duh mah mehr kuh zhuh vwah sah
I've always wanted to see this.	*J'ai toujours voulu voir ça.*	zhay too-zhoor voo-lew vwar sah

Tours

Do you have...?	*Vous avez...?*	vooz ah-vay
...an audioguide	*...un guide audio*	uhn geed oh-dee-oh
...a guided tour	*...une visite guidée*	ewn vee-zeet gee-day
...a city walking tour	*...une promenade guidée de la ville*	ewn proh-muh-nahd gee-day duh lah veel
...in English	*...en anglais*	ahn ahn-glay
When is the next tour in English?	*La prochaine visite en anglais est à quelle heure?*	lah proh-shehn vee-zeet ahn ahn-glay ay ah kehl ur
Is it free?	*C'est gratuit?*	say grah-twee
How much is it?	*C'est combien?*	say kohn-bee-an
How long does it last?	*Ça dure combien de temps?*	sah door kohn-bee-an duh tahn
Can I / Can we join a tour in progress?	*Je peux / Nous pouvons joindre une visite qui a commencé?*	zhuh puh / noo poo-vohn zhwahn-druh ewn vee-zeet kee ah koh-mahn-say

Entrance Signs

adultes	the price you'll pay
dernière entrée	last admission before sight closes
exposition	special exhibit
ticket global	combination ticket with another sight
visite guidée	guided tour
vous êtes ici	you are here (on map)

Discounts

You may be eligible for a discount at tourist sights, hotels, or on buses and trains—ask.

Is there a discount for...?	*Il y a une réduction pour...?*	eel yah ewn ray-dewk-see-ohn poor
...youth	*...les jeunes*	lay juh-nehs
...students	*...les étudiants*	layz ay-tew-dee-ahn
...families	*...les familles*	lay fah-meel
...seniors	*...les gens âgés*	lay zhahn ah-zhay
...groups	*...les groupes*	lay groop
I am...	*J'ai...*	zhay
He / She is...	*Il / Elle a...*	eel / ehl ah
...___ years old.	*...___ans.*	___ahn
...extremely old.	*...très âgé.*	treh ah-zhay

In the Museum

Where is...?	*Où est...?*	oo ay
I'd like to see...	*Je voudrais voir...*	zhuh voo-dray vwar
We'd like to see...	*Nous voudrions voir...*	noo voo-dree-ohn vwar
Photo / Video O.K.?	*Photo / Vidéo O.K.?*	foh-toh / vee-day-oh "O.K."
No flash / tripod.	*Pas de flash / trépied.*	pah duh flahsh / tray-pee-yay
I like it.	*Ça me plaît.*	sah muh play
It's so...	*C'est si...*	say see
...beautiful.	*...beau.*	boh

...ugly.	...laid.	lay
...strange.	...bizarre.	bee-zar
...boring.	...ennuyeux.	ahn-new-yuh
...interesting.	...intéressant.	an-tay-reh-sahn
...pretentious.	...prétentieux.	pray-tahn-see-uh
...thought-provoking.	...provocateur.	proh-voh-kah-tur
...B.S.	...con.	kohn
I don't get it.	Je n'y comprends rien.	zhuhn yuh kohn-prahn ree-an
Is it upside down?	C'est à l'envers?	say ah lahn-vehr
Who did this?	Qui a fait ça?	kee ah fay sah
How old is this?	C'est vieux?	say vee-uh
Wow!	Sensass!	sahn-sahs
My feet hurt!	J'ai mal aux pieds!	zhay mahl oh pee-yay
I'm exhausted!	Je suis épuisé!	zhuh sweez ay-pwee-zay
We're exhausted!	Nous sommes épuisé!	noo suhmz ay-pwee-zay

France's national museums close on Tuesdays. For efficient sightseeing in Paris, buy a Museum Pass. It'll save you money and time (because you're entitled to slip right into museums, bypassing the notorious lines).

Art and Architecture

art	art	ar
artist	artiste	ar-teest
painting	tableau	tah-bloh
self-portrait	autoportrait	oh-toh-por-tray
sculptor	sculpteur	skewlp-tur
sculpture	sculpture	skewlp-tewr
architect	architecte	ar-shee-tehkt
architecture	architecture	ar-shee-tehk-tewr
original	original	oh-ree-zhee-nahl
restored	restauré	rehs-toh-ray
B.C.	avant J.-C.	ah-vahn zhay-zew-kree
A.D.	après J.-C.	ah-preh zhay-zew-kree
century	siècle	see-eh-kluh

style	*style*	steel
after the style of __	*de l'époque __*	duh lay-pohk
copy by __	*reproduction de __*	ray-proh-dook-see-ohn duh
from the school of __	*de l'école de __*	duh lay-kohl duh
abstract	*abstrait*	ahb-stray
ancient	*ancien*	ahn-see-an
Art Nouveau	*art nouveau*	ar noo-voh
Baroque	*baroque*	bah-rohk
classical	*classique*	klahs-seek
Gothic	*gothique*	goh-teek
Impressionist	*impressionniste*	an-preh-see-uh-neest
medieval	*médiéval*	mayd-yay-vahl
modern	*moderne*	moh-dehrn
Neoclassical	*néoclassique*	nay-oh-klah-seek
Renaissance	*renaissance*	ruh-nay-sahns
Romanesque	*romanesque*	roh-mah-nehsk
Romantic	*romantique*	roh-mahn-teek

Castles and Palaces

castle	*château*	shah-toh
fortified castle	*château-fort*	shah-toh-for
palace	*palais*	pah-lay
hall	*grande salle*	grahnd sahl
kitchen	*cuisine*	kwee-zeen
cellar	*cave*	kahv
dungeon	*cachot*	kah-shoh
castle keep	*donjon*	dohn-zhohn
moat	*fossé*	foh-say
fortified walls	*remparts*	rahn-par
tower	*tour*	toor
fountain	*fontaine*	fohn-tehn
garden	*jardin*	zhar-dan
king	*roi*	rwah
queen	*reine*	rehn
knight	*chevalier*	shuh-vahl-yay

ACTIVITIES

Religious Words

cathedral	*cathédrale*	kah-tay-drahl
church	*église*	ay-gleez
monastery	*monastère*	moh-nah-stehr
mosque	*mosquée*	mohs-kay
synagogue	*synagogue*	see-nah-gohg
chapel	*chapelle*	shah-pehl
altar	*autel*	oh-tehl
bells	*cloches*	klohsh
choir	*choeur*	kur
cloister	*cloître*	klwah-truh
cross	*croix*	krwah
crypt	*crypte*	kreept
dome	*dôme*	dohm
organ	*orgue*	org
pulpit	*chaire*	shair
relic	*relique*	ruh-leek
treasury	*trésorerie*	tray-zoh-ree
saint (m /f)	*saint / sainte*	sahn / sahnt
God	*Dieu*	dee-uh
Christian	*chrétien*	kray-tee-an
Protestant	*protestant*	proh-tehs-tahn
Catholic	*catholique*	kah-toh-leek
Jew	*juif*	zhweef
Muslim	*musulman*	mew-zewl-mahn
agnostic	*agnostique*	ahn-yoh-steek
atheist	*athée*	ah-tay
When is the service?	*La messe est quand?*	lah mehs ay kahn
Are there church concerts?	*Il y a des concerts à l'église?*	eel yah day kohn-sehr ah lay-gleez

SHOPPING

French Shops

Where is a...?	*Où est un...?*	oo ay uhn
antique shop	*magasin d'antiquités*	mah-gah-zan dahn-tee-kee-tay

Key Phrases: Shopping

Where can I buy___?	*Où puis-je acheter___?*	oo pwee-zhuh ah-shuh-tay
Where is...?	*Où est...?*	oo ay
...a grocery store	*...une épicerie*	ewn ay-pee-suh-ree
...a department store	*...un grand magasin*	uhn grahn mah-gah-zan
...an Internet café	*...un café internet*	uhn kah-fay an-tehr-neht
...a launderette	*...une laverie*	ewn lah-vuh-ree
...a pharmacy	*...une pharmacie*	ewn far-mah-see
How much is it?	*C'est combien?*	say kohn-bee-an
I'm just browsing.	*Je regarde.*	zhuh ruh-gard

art gallery	*gallerie d'art*	gah-luh-ree dar
bakery	*boulangerie*	boo-lahn-zhuh-ree
barber shop	*coiffeur*	kwah-fur
beauty salon	*coiffeur pour dames*	kwah-fur poor dahm
book shop	*librairie*	lee-bray-ree
camera shop	*magasin de photo*	mah-gah-zan duh foh-toh
cell phone shop	*magasin de portables*	mah-gah-zan duh por-tah-bluh
cheese shop	*fromagerie*	froh-mah-zhuh-ree
clothing boutique	*boutique, magasin de vêtements*	boo-teek, mah-gah-zan duh veht-mahn
coffee shop	*café*	kah-fay
delicatessen	*charcuterie-traiteur*	shar-koo-tuh-ree-tray-tur
department store	*grand magasin*	grahn mah-gah-zan
flea market	*marché aux puces*	mar-shay oh pews
flower market	*marché aux fleurs*	mar-shay oh flur
grocery store	*épicerie*	ay-pee-suh-ree
hardware store	*quincaillerie*	kan-kay-yay-ree
Internet café	*café internet*	kah-fay an-tehr-neht

ACTIVITIES

jewelry shop	bijouterie	bee-zhoo-tuh-ree
launderette	laverie	lah-vuh-ree
newsstand	maison de la presse	meh-zohn duh lah prehs
office supplies	papeterie	pah-pay-tuh-ree
open-air market	marché en plein air	mar-shay ahn plan air
optician	opticien	ohp-tee-see-an
pastry shop	pâtisserie	pah-tee-suh-ree
pharmacy	pharmacie	far-mah-see
photocopy shop	magasin de photocopie	mah-gah-zan duh foh-toh-koh-pee
shopping mall	centre commercial	sahn-truh koh-mehr-see-ahl
souvenir shop	boutique de souvenirs	boo-teek duh soo-vuh-neer
supermarket	supermarché	sew-pehr-mar-shay
sweets shop	confiserie	kohn-fee-suh-ree
toy store	magasin de jouets	mah-gah-zan duh zhway
travel agency	agence de voyages	ah-zhahns duh voy-yahzh
used bookstore...	boutique de livres d'occasion...	boo-teek duh lee-vruh doh-kah-zee-ohn
...with books in English	...avec des livres en anglais	ah-vehk day lee-vruh ahn ahn-glay
wine shop	marchand de vin	mar-shahn duh van

In France, most shops close for a long lunch (noon until about 2 P.M.), and all day on Sundays and Mondays. Grocery stores are often open on Sunday mornings.

Shop Till You Drop

opening hours	les heures d'ouverture	layz ur doo-vehr-tewr
sale	solde	sohld
I'd like...	Je voudrais...	zhuh voo-dray
We'd like...	Nous voudrions...	noo voo-dree-ohn
Where can I buy...?	Où puis-je acheter...?	oo pwee-zhuh ah-shuh-tay

Where can we buy...?	Où pouvons-nous acheter...?	oo poo-vohn-noo ah-shuh-tay
How much is it?	C'est combien?	say kohn-bee-an
I'm just browsing.	Je regarde.	zhuh ruh-gard
We're just browsing.	Nous regardons.	noo ruh-gar-dohn
Do you have...?	Vous avez...?	vooz ah-vay
...more	...plus	plew
...something cheaper	...quelque chose de moins cher	kehl-kuh shohz duh mwan shehr
Better quality, please.	De meilleure qualité, s'il vous plaît.	duh meh-yur kah-lee-tay see voo play
genuine / imitation	authentique / imitation	oh-tahn-teek / ee-mee-tah-see-ohn
Can I / Can we see more?	Je peux / Nous pouvons en voir d'autres?	zhuh puh / noo poo-vohn ahn vwar doh-truh
This one.	Celui ci.	suh-lwee see
Can I try it on?	Je peux l'essayer?	zhuh puh leh-say-yay
A mirror?	Un miroir?	uhn meer-war
Too...	Trop...	troh
...big.	...grand.	grahn
...small.	...petit.	puh-tee
...expensive.	...cher.	shehr
It's too...	C'est trop...	say troh
...short / long.	...court / long.	koor / lohn
...tight / loose.	...serré / grand.	suh-ray / grahn
...dark / light.	...foncé / clair.	fohn-say / klair
What is it made out of?	De quoi c'est fait?	duh kwah say fay
Is it machine washable?	C'est lavable en machine?	say lah-vah-bluh ahn mah-sheen
Will it shrink?	Ça va rétrécir?	sah vah ray-tray-seer
Will it fade in the wash?	Ça va déteindre au lavage?	sah vah day-tan-druh oh lah-vahzh
Credit card O.K.?	Carte de crédit O.K.?	kart duh kray-dee "O.K."
Can you ship this?	Vous pouvez l'envoyer?	voo poo-vay lahn-voy-ay

Tax-free?	*Hors taxe?*	or tahks
I'll think about it.	*Je vais y penser.*	zhuh vay zee pahn-say
What time do you close?	*Vous fermez à quelle heure?*	voo fehr-may ah kehl ur
What time do you open tomorrow?	*Vous allez ouvrir à quelle heure demain?*	vooz ah-lay oo-vreer ah kehl ur duh-man

The French definition of customer service is different from ours. At department stores, be prepared to be treated as if you're intruding on the clerk's privacy. Exchanges are possible with receipts. Refunds are difficult. Buy to keep.

Street Markets

Did you make this?	*C'est vous qui l'avez fait?*	say voo kee lah-vay fay
Is that your lowest price?	*C'est votre prix le plus bas?*	say voh-truh pree luh plew bah
Cheaper?	*Moins cher?*	mwan shehr
My last offer.	*Ma dernière offre.*	mah dehrn-yehr oh-fruh
Good price.	*C'est bon marché.*	say bohn mar-shay
I'll take it.	*Je le prends.*	zhuh luh prahn
We'll take it.	*Nous le prenons.*	noo luh prahn-nohn
I'm nearly broke.	*Je suis presque fauché.*	zhuh swee prehsk foh-shay
We're nearly broke.	*Nous sommes presque fauché.*	noo suhm prehsk foh-shay
My friend...	*Mon ami...*	mohn ah-mee
My husband...	*Mon mari...*	mohn mah-ree
My wife...	*Ma femme...*	mah fahm
...has the money.	*...a l'argent.*	ah lar-zhahn

Clothes

For...	*Pour...*	poor
...a male baby / a female baby.	*...un bébé garçon / un bébé fille.*	uhn bay-bay gar-sohn / uhn bay-bay fee
...a male child / a female child.	*...un petit garçon / une petite fille.*	uhn puh-tee gar-sohn / ewn puh-tee fee

...a male teenager	*...un adolescent /*	uhn ah-doh-luh-sahn /
a female teenager.	*une adolescente.*	ewn ah-doh-luh-sahnt
...a man.	*...un homme.*	uhn ohm
...a woman.	*...une femme.*	ewn fahm
bathrobe	*peignoir de bain*	peh-nwar duh ban
bib	*bavoir*	bah-vwar
belt	*ceinture*	san-tewr
bra	*soutien gorge*	soo-tee-an gorzh
clothing	*vêtement*	veht-mahn
dress	*robe*	rohb
flip-flops	*tongues*	tohn-guh
gloves	*gants*	gahn
hat	*chapeau*	shah-poh
jacket	*veste*	vehst
jeans	*jeans*	"jeans"
nightgown	*chemise de nuit*	shuh-meez duh nwee
nylons	*collants*	koh-lahn
pajamas	*pyjama*	pee-zhah-mah
pants	*pantalons*	pahn-tah-lohn
raincoat	*imperméable*	an-pehr-may-ah-bluh
sandals	*sandales*	sahn-dahl
scarf	*foulard*	foo-lar
shirt...	*chemise...*	shuh-meez
...long-sleeved	*...à manches longues*	ah mahnsh lohn-guh
...short-sleeved	*...à manches courtes*	ah mahnsh koort
...sleeveless	*...sans manche*	sahn mahnsh
shoelaces	*lacets*	lah-say
shoes	*chaussures*	shoh-sewr
shorts	*shorts*	short
skirt	*jupe*	zhoop
slip	*jupon*	zhoo-pohn
slippers	*chaussons*	shoh-sohn
socks	*chaussettes*	shoh-seht
sweater	*pull*	pool
swimsuit	*maillot de bain*	mī-yoh duh ban
tennis shoes	*baskettes*	bahs-keht
T-shirt	*T-shirt*	"T-shirt"

| underwear | *sous vêtements* | soo veht-mah<u>n</u> |
| vest | *gilet sans manche* | gee-lay sah<u>n</u> mah<u>n</u>sh |

Colors

black	*noir*	nwar
blue	*bleu*	bluh
brown	*marron*	mah-roh<u>n</u>
gray	*gris*	gree
green	*vert*	vehr
orange	*orange*	oh-rah<u>n</u>zh
pink	*rose*	rohz
purple	*violet*	vee-oh-lay
red	*rouge*	roozh
white	*blanc*	blah<u>n</u>
yellow	*jaune*	zhoh<u>n</u>
dark / light	*foncé / clair*	foh<u>n</u>-say / klair
A shade...	*Un teint...*	uh<u>n</u> ta<u>n</u>
...lighter.	*...plus clair.*	plew klair
...brighter.	*...plus coloré.*	plew koh-loh-ray
...darker.	*...plus foncé.*	plew foh<u>n</u>-say

Materials

brass	*cuivre jaune*	kwee-vruh zhoh<u>n</u>
bronze	*bronze*	broh<u>n</u>z
ceramic	*céramique*	say-rah-meek
copper	*cuivre*	kwee-vruh
cotton	*cotton*	koh-toh<u>n</u>
glass	*verre*	vehr
gold	*or*	or
lace	*dentelle*	dah<u>n</u>-tehl
leather	*cuir*	kweer
linen	*lin*	leen
marble	*marbre*	mar-bruh
metal	*métal*	may-tahl
nylon	*nylon*	nee-loh<u>n</u>
paper	*papier*	pahp-yay

ACTIVITIES

pewter	laiton	lay-tohn
plastic	plastique	plah-steek
polyester	polyester	poh-lee-ehs-tehr
porcelain	porcelaine	por-suh-lehn
silk	soie	swah
silver	argent	ar-zhahn
velvet	velours	veh-loor
wood	bois	bwah
wool	laine	lehn

Jewelry

bracelet	bracelet	brah-suh-lay
brooch	broche	brohsh
earrings	boucles d'oreille	boo-kluh doh-ray
jewelry	bijoux	bee-zhoo
necklace	collier	kohl-yay
ring	bague	bahg
Is this...?	C'est...?	say
...sterling silver	...de l'argent	duh lar-zhahn
...real gold	...de l'or véritable	duh lor vay-ree-tah-bluh
...stolen	...volé	voh-lay

SPORTS

ACTIVITIES

Bicycling

bicycle / bike	bicyclette / vélo	bee-see-kleht / vay-loh
mountain bike	VTT	vay-tay-tay
I'd like to rent a bike.	Je voudrais louer un vélo.	zhuh voo-dray loo-ay uhn vay-loh
We'd like to rent two bikes.	Nous voudrions louer deux vélos.	noo voo-dree-ohn loo-ay duh vay-loh
How much per...?	C'est combien par...?	say kohn-bee-an par
...hour	...heure	ur
...half day	...demie-journée	duh-mee-zhoor-nay
...day	...jour	zhoor
Is a deposit required?	Une caution est obligatoire?	ewn koh-see-ohn ay oh-blee-gah-twar

deposit	*caution*	koh-see-ohn
helmet	*casque*	kahsk
lock	*antivol*	ahn-tee-vohl
air / no air	*air / pas d'air*	air / pah dair
tire	*pneu*	puh-nuh
pump	*pompe*	pohmp
map	*carte*	kart
How many gears?	*Combien vitesses?*	kohn-bee-an vee-tehs
What is a...	*Quel est un...*	kehl ay uhn...
route of about	*circuit de ___*	seer-kwee duh ___
___ kilometers?	*kilometers?*	kee-loh-meh-truh
...good	*...bon*	bohn
...scenic	*...panoramique, beau*	pah-noh-rah-meek, boh
...interesting	*...intéressante*	an-tay-reh-sahn
...easy	*...facile*	fah-seel
How many	*Combien*	kohn-bee-an
minutes / hours	*de minutes /*	duh mee-newt /
by bicycle?	*d'heures à vélo?*	dur ah vay-loh
I like hills.	*J'aime les côtes.*	zhehm lay koht
I don't like hills.	*Je n'aime pas les côtes.*	zhuh nehm pah lay koht
I brake for bakeries.	*Je m'arrête à chaque boulangerie.*	zhuh mah-reht ah shahk boo-lahn-zhuh-ree

Swimming and Boating

Where can I / can we rent a...?	*Où puis-je / pouvons-nous louer...?*	oo pwee-zhuh / poo-vohn-noo loo-ay
...paddleboat	*...pédalo*	pay-dah-loh
...rowboat	*...barque*	bark
...boat	*...bâteau*	bah-toh
...sailboat	*...voilier*	vwah-lee-ay
How much per...?	*C'est combien par...?*	say kohn-bee-an par
...hour	*...heure*	ur
...half day	*...demie-journée*	duh-mee-zhoor-nay
...day	*...jour*	zhoor
beach	*plage*	plahg

nude beach (topless)	plage naturiste (monokini)	plahg nah-toor-eest (moh-noh-kee-nee)
Where's a good beach?	Où est une belle plage?	oo ay ewn behl plahg
Is it safe for swimming?	On peut nager en sécurité?	ohn puh nah-zhay ahn say-kew-ree-tay
flip-flops	tongues	tohn-guh
pool	piscine	pee-seen
snorkel and mask	tuba et masque	too-bah ay mahsk
sunglasses	lunettes de soleil	loo-neht duh soh-lay
sunscreen	crème solaire	krehm soh-lair
surfboard	planche de surf	plahnsh duh surf
surfer	surfeur	surf-ur
swimsuit	maillot de bain	mī-yoh duh ban
towel	serviette	sehrv-yeht
waterskiing	ski nautique	skee noh-teek
windsurfing	planche à voile	plahnsh ah vwahl

In France, nearly any beach is topless. For a nude beach, look for a *naturiste plage*.

Sports Talk

sports	sport	spor
game	match	"match"
team	équipe	ay-keep
championship	championnat	shah-pee-oh-nah
soccer	football	foot-bahl
basketball	basket	bah-skeht
hockey	hockey	oh-kay
American football	football américain	foot-bahl ah-may-ree-kan
baseball	baseball	bahz-bahl
tennis	tennis	teh-nees
golf	golf	"golf"
skiing	ski	"ski"
gymnastics	gymnastique	zheem-nah-steek
jogging	jogging	zhoh-geeng

Olympics	Olympiques	oh-leem-peek
medal...	médaille	meh-dī
...gold / silver / bronze	d'or / d'argent / du bronze	dor / dar-zhah<u>n</u> / duh broh<u>n</u>z
What sport / athlete / team is your favorite?	Quel sport / jouer / équipe est votre préferé?	kehl spor / zhoo-ay / ay-keep ay voh-truh pray-fuh-ray
Where can I see a game?	Où puis-je voir un match?	oo pwee-zhuh vwar uh<u>n</u> "match"
Where's a good place to jog?	Où puis-je faire du jogging?	oo pwee-zhuh fair duh zhoh-geeng

ENTERTAINMENT

What's happening tonight?	Qu'est-ce qui ce passe ce soir?	kehs kee suh pahs suh swar
What do you recommend?	Qu'est-ce que vous recommandez?	kehs kuh voo ruh-koh-mah<u>n</u>-day
Where is it?	C'est où?	say oo
How to get there?	Comment le trouver?	koh-mah<u>n</u> luh troo-vay
Is it free?	C'est gratuit?	say grah-twee
Are there seats available?	Il y a des places disponible?	eel yah day plahs dee-spoh-nee-bluh
Where can I buy a ticket?	Où puis-je acheter un billet?	oo pwee-zhuh ah-shuh-tay uh<u>n</u> bee-yay
Do you have tickets for today / tonight?	Avez-vous des billets pour aujourd'hui / ce soir?	ah-vay-voo day bee-yay poor oh-zhoor-dwee / suh swar
When does it start?	Ça commence à quelle heure?	sah koh-mah<u>n</u>s ah kehl ur
When does it end?	Ça se termine à quelle heure?	sah suh tehr-meen ah kehl ur
The best place to dance nearby?	Le meilleur dancing dans le coin?	luh meh-yur dah<u>n</u>-seeng dah<u>n</u> luh kwa<u>n</u>
Where do people stroll?	Les gens se balladent où?	lay zhah<u>n</u> suh bah-lah-dah<u>n</u> oo

ACTIVITIES

Entertaining Words

movie...	film...	feelm
...original version	...version originale (V.O.)	vehr-see-ohn oh-ree-zhee-nahl
...in English	...en anglais	ahn ahn-glay
...with subtitles	...avec sous-titres	ah-vehk soo-tee-truh
...dubbed	...doublé	doo-blay
music...	musique...	mew-zeek
...live	...en directe	ahn dee-rehkt
...classical	...classique	klahs-seek
...folk	...folklorique	fohk-loh-reek
...opera	...d'opéra	doh-pay-rah
...symphony	...symphonique	seem-foh-neek
...choir	...de choeur	duh koh-ur
...traditional	...traditionnelle	trah-dee-see-oh-nehl
rock / jazz / blues	rock / jazz / blues	rohk / zhahz / "blues"
male singer	chanteur	shahn-tur
female singer	chanteuse	shahn-tuhz
concert	concert	kohn-sehr
show	spectacle	spehk-tahk-luh
sound and light show	son et lumière	sohn ay lew-mee-ehr
dancing	danse	dahns
folk dancing	danse folklorique	dahns fohk-loh-reek
disco	disco	dee-skoh
bar with live music	bar avec un groupe musical	bar ah-vehk uhn groop mew-zee-kahl
nightclub	boîte	bwaht
(no) cover charge	(pas de) admission	(pah duh) ahd-mee-see-ohn
sold out	complet	kohn-play

For concerts and special events, ask at the local tourist office. Cafés, very much a part of the French social scene, are places for friends to spend the evening together. To meet new friends, the French look for *pubs* or *bars américains*.

Paris has a great cinema scene, especially on the Champs-Élysées. Pick up a *Pariscope,* the periodical entertainment guide, and choose from hundreds of films (often discounted on Mondays). Those listed V.O. (rather than V.F.) are in their original language.

CONNECT

PHONING

I'd like to buy a...	*Je voudrais acheter une...*	zhuh voo-dray ah-shuh-tay oon
...telephone card.	*...carte téléphonique.*	kart tay-lay-foh-neek
...cheap international telephone card.	*...carte téléphonique à code internationale.*	kart tay-lay-foh-neek ah kohd an-tehr-nah-see-oh-nahl
The nearest phone?	*Le téléphone le plus proche?*	luh tay-lay-fohn luh plew prohsh
It doesn't work.	*Ça ne marche pas.*	sah nuh marsh pah
May I use your phone?	*Je peux téléphoner?*	zhuh puh tay-lay-foh-nay
Can you talk for me?	*Vous pouvez parler pour moi?*	voo poo-vay par-lay poor mwah
It's busy.	*C'est occupé.*	say oh-kew-pay
Will you try again?	*Essayez de nouveau?*	eh-say-yay duh noo-voh
Hello. (on the phone)	*Âllo.*	ah-loh
My name is ___.	*Je m'appelle ___.*	zhuh mah-pehl
Sorry, I speak only a little French.	*Désolé, je parle seulement un petit peu de français.*	day-zoh-lay zhuh parl suhl-mahn uhn puh-tee puh duh frahn-say
Speak slowly and clearly.	*Parlez lentement et clairement.*	par-lay lahn-tuh-mahn ay klair-mahn
Wait a moment.	*Un moment.*	uhn moh-mahn

148

In this book, you'll find phrases to reserve a hotel room (page 53) or a table at a restaurant (page 71). To spell your name on the phone, refer to the code alphabet (page 55).

Make your calls using a handy phone card (*carte téléphonique*), sold at post offices, train stations, and tobacco (*tabac*) shops. There are two kinds of phone cards: an insertable card that you slide into a phone in a phone booth, and a cheaper-per-minute international telephone card (with a scratch-off PIN code) that you can use from any phone, even your hotel room. Post offices often have easy-to-use metered phones.

At phone booths, you'll encounter these words: *inserer votre carte* (insert your card) and *composer votre numéro* (dial your number); it will also tell you how many *unités* are left on your card. If the number you're calling is out of service, you'll hear the dreaded recording: *"Le numéro que vous demandez n'est pas attribué."* For more tips, see "Let's Talk Telephones" in the appendix (page 257).

Telephone Words

telephone	téléphone	tay-lay-fohn
telephone card	carte téléphonique	kart tay-lay-foh-neek
cheap international telephone card	carte téléphonique à code internationale	kart tay-lay-foh-neek ah kohd an-tehr-nah-see-oh-nahl
PIN code	code	kohd
phone booth	cabine téléphonique	kah-been tay-lay-foh-neek
out of service	hors service	or sehr-vees
post office	Poste	pohst
operator	standardiste	stahn-dar-deest
international assistance	renseignements internationaux	rahn-sehn-yuh-mahn an-tehr-nah-see-oh-noh
international call	appel international	ah-pehl an-tehr-nah-see-oh-nahl
collect call	appel en PCV	ah-pehl ahn pay-say-vay
credit card call	appel avec une carte de crédit	ah-pehl ah-vehk ewn kart duh kray-dee

toll-free	gratuit	grah-twee
fax	fax	fahks
country code	code international	kohd an-tehr-nah-see-oh-nahl
area code	code régional	kohd ray-zhee-oh-nahl
extension	poste	pohst
telephone book	bottin, annuaire	boh-tan, ahn-new-air
yellow pages	pages jaunes	pahzh zhohn

Cell Phones

Where is a cell phone shop?	Où est un magasin de portables?	oo ay uhn mah-gah-zan duh por-tah-bluh
I'd like...	Je voudrais...	zhuh voo-dray
We'd like...	Nous voudrions...	noo voo-dree-ohn
...a cell phone.	...un portable.	uhn por-tah-bluh
...a chip.	...une puce.	ewn pews
...to buy more time.	...acheter plus de temps.	ah-shuh-tay plew duh tahn
How do you...?	Comment vous...?	koh-mahn voo
...make calls	...appelez	ah-puh-lay
...receive calls	...recevez les appels	ruh-suh-vay layz ah-pehl
Will this work outside this country?	Ça marche en dehors de ce pays?	sah marsh ahn duh-or duh suh peh-ee
Where can I buy more time for this phone?	Où puis-je acheter une recharge pour ce portable?	oo pwee-zhuh ah-shuh-tay ewn reh-sharzh poor suh por-tah-bluh

Many travelers now buy cell phones in Europe to make both local and international calls. You'll pay under €100 for a "locked" phone that works only in the country you buy it in (includes about €20 worth of calls). You can buy additional time at a newsstand or cell phone shop. An "unlocked" phone is more expensive, but it works all over Europe: when you cross a border, buy a SIM card at a cell phone shop and insert the pop-out chip, which comes with a new phone number. Pricier tri-band phones (*tribande*) also work in North America.

EMAIL AND THE WEB

Email

My email address is ___.	*Mon adresse email est ___.*	mohn ah-drehs ee-mayl ay
What's your email address?	*Quelle est votre adresse email?*	kehl ay voh-truh ah-drehs ee-mayl
Can I use this computer to check my email?	*Je peux utiliser cet ordinateur pour regarder mon email?*	zhuh puh oo-tee-lee-zay seht or-dee-nah-tur poor ruh-gar-day mohn ee-mayl
Where can I get get access to the Internet?	*Où est-ce que je peux accéder à l'internet?*	oo ehs kuh zhuh puh ahk-say-day ah lan-tehr-neht
Where is an Internet café?	*Où se trouve un café internet?*	oo suh troov uhn kah-fay an-tehr-neht
How much for... minutes?	*C'est combien pour... minutes?*	say kohn-bee-an poor... mee-newt
...10	*...dix*	dees
...15	*...quinze*	kanz
...30	*...trente*	trahnt
...60	*...soixante*	swah-sahnt
Help me, please.	*Aidez-moi, s'il vous plaît.*	ay-day-mwah see voo play

Key Phrases: Email and the Web

email	*email*	ee-mayl
Internet	*internet*	an-tehr-neht
Where is the nearest Internet café?	*Où se trouve le café internet le plus prôche?*	oo suh troov luh kah-fay an-tehr-neht luh plew prohsh
I'd like to check my email.	*Je voudrais regarder mon email.*	zhuh voo-dray ruh-gar-day mohn ee-mayl

How...	Comment...	koh-mah<u>n</u>
...do I start this?	... je démarre ça?	zhuh day-mar sah
...do I send a file?	...j'envoie un fichier?	zhah<u>n</u>-vwah uh<u>n</u> fee-shee-ay
...do I print out a file?	...j'imprime le fichier?	zhan-preem luh fee-shee-ay
...do I make this symbol?	...je fais ce symbole?	zhuh fay suh seem-bohl
...do I type @?	...je tape arobase?	zhuh tahp ah-roh-bahs
This doesn't work.	Ça ne marche pas.	sah nuh marsh pah

Web Words

website	site web	seet wehb
Internet	internet	a<u>n</u>-tehr-neht
surf the Web	surfer le web	surf-ay luh wehb
download	télécharge	tay-lay-sharzh
@ sign	signe arobase	seen ah-roh-bahs
dot	point	pwa<u>n</u>
hyphen (-)	tiret	tee-ray
underscore (_)	souligne	soo-leen
modem	modem	moh-dehm

On Screen

delete	annuler	message	message
send	envoyer	save	sauver
file	fichier	open	ouvrir
print	imprimer		

CONNECT

MAILING

Where is the post office?	Où est la Poste?	oo ay lah pohst
Which window for...?	Quel guichet pour...?	kehl gee-shay poor
Is this the line for...?	C'est la file pour...?	say lah feel poor
...stamps	...les timbres	lay ta<u>n</u>-bruh
...packages	...les colis	lay koh-lee

Key Phrases: Mailing

post office	la Poste	lah pohst
stamp	timbre	tan-bruh
postcard	carte postale	kart poh-stahl
letter	lettre	leht-ruh
air mail	par avion	par ah-vee-ohn
Where is the post office?	Où est la Poste?	oo ay lah pohst
I'd like to buy stamps for ___ postcards / letters to send to America.	Je voudrais acheter timbres pour ___ cartes postales / lettres d'envoyer pour l'Amérique.	zhuh voo-dray ah-shuh-tay tan-bruh poor ___ kart poh-stahl / leht-ruh dahn-voh-yay poor lah-may-reek

To the United States...	Aux Etats-Unis...	ohz ay-tah-zew-nee
...by air mail.	...par avion.	par ah-vee-ohn
...by surface mail.	...par surface.	par sewr-fahs
How much is it?	C'est combien?	say kohn-bee-an
How much to send a letter / postcard to ___?	Combien pour envoyer une lettre / carte postale pour___?	kohn-bee-an poor ahn-voh-yay ewn leht-ruh / kart poh-stahl poor
I need stamps for ___ postcards to...	J'ai besoin de timbres pour ___ cartes postales pour...	zhay buh-swan duh tan-bruh poor ___ kart poh-stahl poor
...America / Canada.	...l'Amérique / le Canada.	lah-may-reek / luh kah-nah-dah
Pretty stamps, please.	De jolis timbres, s'il vous plaît.	duh zhoh-lee tan-bruh see voo play
I always choose the slowest line.	Je choisis toujours la file la plus lente.	zhuh shwah-see too-zhoor lah feel lah plew lahnt
How many days will it take?	Ça va prendre combien de jours?	sah vah prahn-druh kohn-bee-an duh zhoor

You can also buy stamps at *tabac* shops—very handy, so long as you know in advance the amount of postage you need.

Licking the Postal Code

post office	*la Poste*	lah pohst
stamp	*timbre*	tan-bruh
postcard	*carte postale*	kart poh-stahl
letter	*lettre*	leht-ruh
envelope	*enveloppe*	ahn-vuh-lohp
package	*colis*	koh-lee
box	*boîte en carton*	bwaht ahn kar-tohn
string	*ficelle*	fee-sehl
tape	*scotch*	skotch
mailbox	*boîte aux lettres*	bwaht oh leht-truh
air mail	*par avion*	par ah-vee-ohn
express	*par express*	par ehk-sprehs
surface	*surface*	sewr-fahs
(slow and cheap)	*(lent et pas cher)*	(lahn ay pah shehr)
book rate	*tarif-livres*	tah-reef-lee-vruh
weight limit	*poids limite*	pwah lee-meet
registered	*enregistré*	ahn-ruh-zhee-stray
insured	*assuré*	ah-sew-ray
fragile	*fragile*	frah-zheel
contents	*contenu*	kohn-tuh-new
customs	*douane*	doo-ahn
to / from	*à / de*	ah / duh
address	*adresse*	ah-drehs
zip code	*code postal*	kohd poh-stahl
general delivery	*poste restante*	pohst rehs-tahnt

HELP!

Help!	Au secours!	oh suh-koor
Help me!	À l'aide!	ah layd
Call a doctor!	Appelez un docteur!	ah-puh-lay uhn dohk-tur
Call...	Appelez...	ah-puh-lay
...the police.	...la police.	lah poh-lees
...an ambulance.	...une ambulance.	ewn ahn-bew-lahns
...the fire department.	...les pompiers.	lay pohn-pee-yay
I'm lost.	Je suis perdu.	zhuh swee pehr-dew
We're lost.	Nous sommes perdus.	noo suhm pehr-dew
Thank you for your help.	Merci pour votre aide.	mehr-see poor voh-truh ayd
You are very kind.	Vous êtes très gentil.	vooz eht treh zhahn-tee

France's medical emergency phone number is 15. *SOS médecins* are doctors who make emergency house calls. If you need help, someone will call an *SOS médecin* for you.

Theft and Loss

Stop, thief!	Arrêtez, au voleur!	ah-reh-tay oh voh-lur
I have been / We have been robbed.	On m'a / Nous a volé.	ohn mah / nooz ah voh-lay
A thief took...	Un voleur à pris...	uhn voh-lur ah pree

HELP!

Key Phrases: Help!

accident	*accident*	ahk-see-dahn
emergency	*urgence*	ewr-zhahns
police	*police*	poh-lees
Help!	*Au secours!*	oh suh-koor
Call a doctor /	*Appelez un docteur /*	ah-puh-lay uhn dohk-tur /
the police!	*la police!*	lah poh-lees
Stop, thief!	*Arrêtez, au voleur!*	ah-reh-tay oh voh-lur

Thieves took...	*Des voleurs ont pris...*	day voh-lur ohn pree
I've lost...	*J'ai perdu...*	zhay pehr-dew
...my money.	*...mon argent.*	mohn ar-zhahn
...my passport.	*...mon passeport.*	mohn pah-spor
...my ticket.	*...mon billet.*	mohn bee-yay
...my baggage.	*...mes bagages.*	may bah-gahzh
...my purse.	*...mon sac.*	mohn sahk
...my wallet.	*...mon portefeuille.*	mohn por-tuh-fuh-ee
...my faith in	*...ma foi en*	mah fwah ahn
humankind.	*l'humanité.*	lew-mah-nee-tay
We've lost our...	*Nous avons*	nooz ah-vohn
	perdu nos...	pehr-dew noh
...passports.	*...passeports.*	pah-spor
...tickets.	*...billets.*	bee-yay
...bags.	*...bagages.*	bah-gahzh
I want to contact	*Je veux contacter*	zhuh vuh kohn-tahk-tay
my embassy.	*mon ambassade.*	mohn ahm-bah-sahd
I need to file a	*Je veux porter plainte*	zhuh vuh por-tay plant
police report for	*à la police pour*	ah lah poh-lees poor
my insurance.	*mon assurance.*	mohn ah-sewr-rahns

See page 258 in the appendix for contact information on the US and Canadian embassies in Paris.

Helpful Words

ambulance	*ambulance*	ahn-bew-lahns
accident	*accident*	ahk-see-dahn
injured	*blessé*	bleh-say
emergency	*urgence*	ewr-zhahns
emergency room	*aux urgences*	ohz ewr-zhahns
fire	*feu*	fuh
police	*police*	poh-lees
smoke	*fumée*	foo-may
thief	*voleur*	voh-lur
pickpocket	*pickpocket*	peek-poh-keht

Help for Women

Leave me alone.	*Laissez-moi tranquille.*	lay-say-mwah trahn-keel
I want to be alone.	*Je veux être seule.*	zhuh vuh eh-truh suhl
I'm not interested.	*Ça ne m'intéresse pas.*	sah nuh man-tay-rehs pah
I'm married.	*Je suis mariée.*	zhuh swee mah-ree-ay
I'm a lesbian.	*Je suis lesbienne.*	zhuh swee lehz-bee-ehn
I have a contagious disease.	*J'ai une maladie contagieuse.*	zhay ewn mah-lah-dee kohn-tah-zhuhz
You are bothering me.	*Vous m'embêtez.*	voo mahn-beh-tay
He is bothering me.	*Il m'embête.*	eel mahn-beht
Don't touch me.	*Ne me touchez pas.*	nuh muh too-shay pah
You're disgusting.	*Vous êtes dégoutant.*	vooz eht day-goo-tahn
Stop following me.	*Arrêtez de me suivre.*	ah-reh-tay duh muh swee-vruh
Stop it!	*Arrêtez!*	ah-reh-tay
Enough!	*Ça suffit!*	sah sew-fee
Get lost!	*Dégagez!*	day-gah-zhay
Drop dead!	*Foutez-moi la paix!*	foo-tay-mwah lah pay
I'll call the police.	*J'appelle la police.*	zhah-pehl lah poh-lees

SERVICES

Laundry

Is a... nearby?	Il y a une... près d'ici?	eel-yah ewn... preh dee-see
...self-service laundry	...laverie automatique	lah-vah-ree oh-toh-mah-teek
...full service laundry	...blanchisserie	blahn-shee-suh-ree
Help me, please.	Aidez-moi, s'il vous plaît.	ay-day-mwah see voo play
How does this work?	Ça marche comment?	sah marsh koh-mahn
Where is the soap?	Où se trouve la lessive?	oo suh troov lah luh-seev
Are these yours?	C'est à vous?	say ah voo
This stinks.	Ça pue.	sah pew
This smells like...	Ça sent comme...	sah sahn kohm
...spring time.	...le printemps.	luh pran-tahn
...a locker room.	...un vestiare.	ewn vehs-tee-ar
...cheese.	...le fromage.	luh froh-mahzh
I need change.	J'ai besoin de monnaie.	zhay buh-swan duh moh-nay
Same-day service?	Lavé le même jour?	lah-vay luh mehm zhoor
By when do I need to drop off my clothes?	Je dois déposer mon linge quand?	zhuh dwah day-poh-zay mohn lanzh kahn

158

When will my clothes be ready?	*Mon linge sera prêt quand?*	mohn lanzh suh-rah preh kahn
Dried?	*Séché?*	say-shay
Folded?	*Plié?*	plee-ay
Ironed?	*Repassé?*	ray-pah-say
Hey there, what's spinning?	*Pardon, qu'est-ce qui tourne?*	par-dohn, kehs kee toorn

Clean Words

full-service laundry	*blanchisserie*	blahn-shee-suh-ree
self-service laundry	*laverie automatique*	lah-vah-ree oh-toh-mah-teek
wash / dry	*laver / sécher*	lah-vay / say-shay
washer / dryer	*machine à laver / machine à sécher*	mah-sheen ah lah-vay / mah-sheen ah say-shay
detergent	*lessive*	luh-seev
token	*jeton*	zhuh-tohn
whites	*blancs*	blahn
colors	*couleurs*	koh-lur
delicates	*délicats*	day-lee-kah
handwash	*laver à la main*	lah-vay a lah man

Haircuts

Where is a barber / hair salon?	*Où se trouve un salon de coiffure hommes / femmes?*	oo suh troov uhn sah-lohn duh kwah-fur ohm / fahm
I'd like...	*J'aimerais...*	zhehm-uh-ray
...a haircut.	*...une coupe.*	ewn koop
...a permanent.	*...une permanente.*	ewn pehr-mah-nahnt
...just a trim.	*...juste raffraîchir.*	zhoost rah-freh-sheer
Cut about this much off.	*Coupez ça à peu près.*	koo-pay sah ah puh preh
Cut my bangs here.	*Coupez ma frange ici.*	koo-pay mah frahnzh ee-see
Longer / Shorter here.	*Plus long / Plus court ici.*	plew lohn / plew koort ee-see

I'd like my hair...	J'aimerais mes cheveux...	zhehm-uh-ray may shuh-vuh
...short.	...courts.	koort
...colored.	...colorés.	koh-loh-ray
...shampooed.	...lavés.	lah-vay
...blow dried.	...séchés.	say-shay
It looks good.	C'est bien.	say bee-an

SERVICES

Repair

These handy lines can apply to any repair, whether it's a ripped rucksack, bad haircut, or crabby camera.

This is broken.	C'est cassé.	say kah-say
Can you fix it?	Vous pouvez le réparer?	voo poo-vay luh ray-pah-ray
Just do the essentials.	Ne faites que le minimum.	nuh fayt kuh luh mee-nee-muhm
How much will it cost?	Ça coutera combien?	sah koo-teh-rah kohn-bee-an
When will it be ready?	Ce sera prêt quand?	suh suh-rah preh kahn
I need it by ___.	Il me le faut avant ___.	eel muh luh foh ah-vahn
We need it by ___.	Il nous le faut avant ___.	eel noo luh foh ah-vahn
Without it, I'm...	Sans, je suis...	sahn zhuh swee
...lost.	...perdu.	pehr-dew
...toast.	...grillé.	gree-yay
...dead in the water.	...une épave. ("a shipwreck")	ewn ay-pahv

Filling Out Forms

Monsieur	Mr.
Madame	Mrs.
Mademoiselle	Miss
prénom	first name
nom	name
adresse	address
lieu de domicile	address
rue	street
ville	city
état	state
pays	country
nationalité	nationality
originaire de	origin
destination	destination
âge	age
date de naissance	date of birth
lieu de naissance	place of birth
sexe	sex
mâle / femelle	male / female
marié / célibataire	married / single
profession	profession
adulte	adult
enfant / garçon / fille	child / boy / girl
enfants	children
famille	family
signature	signature

When filling out dates, do it European-style: day/month/year.

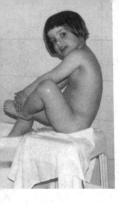

HEALTH

I am sick.	*Je suis malade.*	zhuh swee mah-lahd
I feel (very) sick.	*Je me sens*	zhuh muh sah<u>n</u>
	(très) malade.	(treh) mah-lahd
My husband /	*Mon mari /*	moh<u>n</u> mah-ree /
My wife...	*Ma femme...*	mah fahm
My son /	*Mon fils / Ma fille...*	moh<u>n</u> fees / mah fee
My daughter...		
My male friend /	*Mon ami /*	moh<u>n</u> ah-mee /
My female friend...	*Mon amie...*	mah ah-mee
...feels (very) sick.	*...se sent*	suh sah<u>n</u>
	(très) malade.	(treh) mah-lahd

Key Phrases: Health

doctor	*docteur*	dohk-tur
hospital	*hôpital*	oh-pee-tahl
pharmacy	*pharmacie*	far-mah-see
medicine	*médicament*	may-dee-kah-mah<u>n</u>
I am sick.	*Je suis malade.*	zhuh swee mah-lahd
I need a doctor	*J'ai besoin d'un*	zhay buh-swa<u>n</u> duh<u>n</u>
(who speaks	*docteur (qui*	dohk-tur (kee
English).	*parle anglais).*	parl ah<u>n</u>-glay)
It hurts here.	*J'ai mal ici.*	zhay mahl ee-see

162

It's urgent.	C'est urgent.	say ewr-zhah<u>n</u>
I need a doctor...	J'ai besoin d'un docteur...	zhay buh-swa<u>n</u> duh<u>n</u> dohk-tur
We need a doctor...	Nous avons besoin d'un docteur...	nooz ah-voh<u>n</u> buh-swa<u>n</u> duh<u>n</u> dohk-tur
...who speaks English.	...qui parle anglais.	kee parl ah<u>n</u>-glay see voo play
Please call a doctor.	S'il vous plaît appelez un docteur.	ah-puh-lay uh<u>n</u> dohk-tur
Could a doctor come here?	Un docteur pourrait venir?	uh<u>n</u> dohk-tur poo-ray vuh-neer
I am...	Je suis...	zhuh swee
He / She is...	Il / Elle est...	eel / ehl ay
...allergic to penicillin / sulfa.	...allergique à la pénicilline / les sulfamides.	ah-lehr-zheek ah lah pay-nee-see-leen / lay sool-fah-meed
I am diabetic.	Je suis diabétique.	zhuh swee dee-ah-bay-teek
I have cancer.	J'ai le cancer.	zhay luh kah<u>n</u>-say
I had a heart attack ___ years ago.	J'ai eu une crise cardiaque il y a ___ ans.	zhay uh ewn kreez kar-dee-ahk eel yah ___ ah<u>n</u>
It hurts here.	J'ai mal ici.	zhay mahl ee-see
I feel faint.	Je me sens faible.	zhuh muh sah<u>n</u> fay-bluh
It hurts to urinate.	Uriner me fait mal.	ew-ree-nay muh fay mahl
I have body odor.	Je sens mauvais.	zhuh sah<u>n</u> moh-vay
I'm going bald.	Je deviens chauve.	zhuh duh-vee-ah<u>n</u> shohv
Is it serious?	C'est sérieux?	say say-ree-uh
Is it contagious?	C'est contagieux?	say koh<u>n</u>-tah-zhee-uh
Aging sucks.	Vieillir c'est la poisse.	ve-yay-yeer say lah pwahs
Take one pill every ___ hours for ___ days before / with meals.	Prendre un comprimé toutes les ___ heures pendant ___ jours avant / durant les repas.	prah<u>n</u>-druh uh<u>n</u> koh<u>n</u>-pree-may toot lay ___ ur pah<u>n</u>-dah<u>n</u> ___ zhoor ah-vah<u>n</u> / doo-rah<u>n</u> lay ruh-pah
I need a receipt for my insurance.	J'ai besoin d'un reçu pour mon assurance.	zhay buh-swa<u>n</u> duh<u>n</u> ruh-sew poor moh<u>n</u> ah-sew-rah<u>n</u>s

HEALTH

Ailments

I have...	J'ai...	zhay
He / She has...	Il / Elle a...	eel / ehl ah
I need / We need	J'ai / Nous avons	zhay / nooz ah-vohn
medication for...	besoin d'un	buh-swan duhn
	médicament pour...	may-dee-kah-mahn poor
...arthritis.	...l'arthrite.	lar-treet
...asthma.	...l'asthme.	lahz-muh
...athlete's foot.	...la mycose.	lah mee-kohz
...bad breath.	...mauvaise haleine.	moh-vehz ah-leen
...blisters.	...des ampoules.	dayz ahm-pool
...bug bites.	...des piqures	day peek-ruh
	d'insectes.	dan-sehkt
...a burn.	...une brûlure.	ewn brew-lewr
...chest pains.	...maux de poitrine.	mahl duh pwah-treen
...chills.	...des frissons.	day free-sohn
...a cold.	...un rhume.	uhn rewm
...congestion.	...la congestion.	lah kohn-zhehs-tee-ohn
...constipation.	...la constipation.	lah kohn-stee-pah-see-ohn
...a cough.	...la toux.	lah too
...cramps.	...des crampes.	day krahmp
...diabetes.	...du diabète.	doo dee-ah-beht
...diarrhea.	...la diarrhée.	lah dee-ah-ray
...dizziness.	...le vertige.	luh vehr-teezh
...earache.	...mal aux oreilles.	mahl ohz oh-ray
...epilepsy.	...l'épilepsie.	lay-pee-lehp-see
...a fever.	...une fièvre.	ewn fee-eh-vruh
...the flu.	...la grippe.	lah greep
...food poisoning.	...empoisonement	ahn-pwah-zuh-mahnt
	alimentaire.	ah-lee-mahn-tair
...the giggles.	...le fou rire.	luh foo reer
...hay fever.	...le rhume des foins.	luh rewm day fwan
...a headache.	...mal à la tête.	mahl ah lah teht
...a heart condition.	...problème cardiaque.	proh-blehm kar-dee-ak
...hemorrhoids.	...hémorroïdes.	ay-mor-wahd
...high blood pressure.	...de l'hypertension.	duh lee-pehr-tahn-see-ohn

...indigestion.	...une indigestion.	ewn an-dee-zhuh-stee-ohn
...an infection.	...une infection.	ewn an-fehk-see-ohn
...inflammation.	...une inflation.	ewn an-flah-see-ohn
...a migraine.	...une migraine.	ewn mee-grayn
...nausea.	...la nausée.	lah noh-zay
...pneumonia.	...la pneumonie.	lah puh-noo-moh-nee
...a rash.	...des boutons.	day boo-tohn
...sinus problems.	...problèmes de sinus.	proh-blehm duh see-noo
...a sore throat.	...mal à la gorge.	mahl ah lah gorzh
...a stomach ache.	...mal à l'estomac.	mahl ah luh-stoh-mah
...sunburn.	...un coup de soleil.	uhn koo duh soh-lay
...a swelling.	...une enflure.	ewn ahn-flewr
...a toothache.	...mal aux dents.	mahl oh dahn
...a urinary infection.	...une infection urinarire.	ewn an-fehk-see-ohn ew-ree-nah-reer
...a venereal disease.	...une maladie vénérienne.	ewn mah-lah-dee vay-nay-ree-ehn
...vicious sunburn.	...un méchant coup de soleil.	uhn may-shahn koo duh soh-lay
...vomiting.	...le vomissement.	luh voh-mee-suh-mahn
...worms.	...des vers.	day vehr

Women's Health

menstruation	menstruation	mahn-stroo-ah-see-ohn
menstrual cramps	crampes de menstruation	krahmp duh mahn-stroo-ah-see-ohn
period	les règles	lay reh-gluh
pregnancy (test)	(test de) grossesse	(tehst duh) groh-sehs
miscarriage	fausse couche	fohs koosh
abortion	avortement	ah-vor-tuh-mahn
birth control pill	la pilule	lah pee-lewl
diaphragm	diaphragme	dee-ah-frahm
I'd like to see a female...	Je voudrais voir une femme-...	zhuh voo-dray vwar ewn fahm-
...doctor.	...docteur.	dohk-tur
...gynecologist.	...gynécologue.	zhee-nay-koh-lohg
I've missed a period.	J'ai du retard dans mes règles.	zhay dew ruh-tar dahn may reh-gluh

My last period started on ___.	Mes dernières règles étaient le ___.	may dehrn-yehr reh-gluh ay-tan luh
I am / She is...	Je suis / Elle	zhuh swee / ehl
pregnant.	est enceinte...	ay ahn-sant
...___ months	...de ___ mois.	duh ___ mwah

Parts of the Body

ankle	cheville	shuh-veel
arm	bras	brah
back	dos	doh
bladder	vessie	veh-see
breast	seins	san
buttocks	fesses	feh-say
chest	poitrine	pwah-treen
ear	oreille	oh-ray
elbow	coude	kood
eye / eyes	oeil / yeux	oy / yuh
face	visage	vee-sahzh
finger	doigt	dwat
foot	pied	pee-ay
hair	cheveux	shuh-vuh
hand	main	man
head	tête	teht
heart	coeur	koor
hip	hanche	ahnsh
intestines	intestins	an-tehs-tan
knee	genou	zhuh-noo
leg	jambe	zhahmb
lung	poumon	poo-mohn
mouth	bouche	boosh
neck	cou	koo
nose	nez	nay
penis	pénis	pay-nee
rectum	rectum	rehk-toom
shoulder	épaule	ay-pohl
stomach	estomac	ay-stoh-mah

teeth	dents	dah<u>n</u>
testicles	testicules	tehs-tee-kool
throat	gorge	gorzh
toe	doigt de pied	dwat duh pee-ay
urethra	urèthre	ew-reh-truh
uterus	utérus	ew-tay-rew
vagina	vagin	vah-zheen
waist	taille	tah-ee
wrist	poignet	pwah<u>n</u>-yay

Healthy Words

24-hour pharmacy	pharmacie de garde	far-mah-see duh gard
bleeding	saignement	sehn-yah-mah<u>n</u>
blood	sang	sa<u>n</u>
contraceptive	contraceptif	koh<u>n</u>-trah-sehp-teef
dentist	dentiste	dah<u>n</u>-teest
doctor	docteur	dohk-tur
health insurance	assurance maladie	ah-sew-rah<u>n</u>s mah-lah-dee
hospital	hôpital	oh-pee-tahl
medical clinic	clinique médicale	klee-neek may-dee-kal
medicine	médicament	may-dee-kah-mah<u>n</u>
nurse	infirmière	ah<u>n</u>-fehrm-yay
pain	douleur	doo-lur
pharmacy	pharmacie	far-mah-see
pill	pilule, comprimé	pee-lewl, koh<u>n</u>-pree-may
prescription	ordonnance	or-duh-nah<u>n</u>s
refill (v)	remplir de nouveau	rah<u>n</u>-pleer duh noo-voh
unconscious	inconscient	a<u>n</u>-koh<u>n</u>-see-ah<u>n</u>
X-ray	radio	rah-dee-oh

After 7:00 P.M., most pharmacies are closed, but you'll find the name, address, and phone number on their front door of the after-hours *pharmacie de garde.* In an emergency, go to the police station, which will call ahead to the pharmacist. At the pharmacy, ring the doorbell and the pharmacist will open the door. *Voilà.*

HEALTH

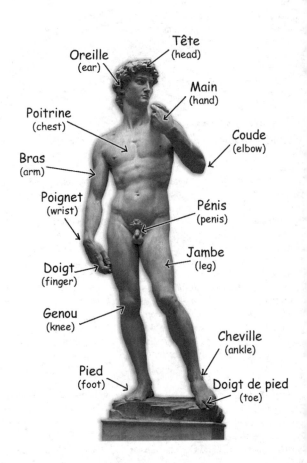

Tête
(head)

Oreille
(ear)

Main
(hand)

Poitrine
(chest)

Coude
(elbow)

Bras
(arm)

Poignet
(wrist)

Pénis
(penis)

Doigt
(finger)

Jambe
(leg)

Genou
(knee)

Cheville
(ankle)

Pied
(foot)

Doigt de pied
(toe)

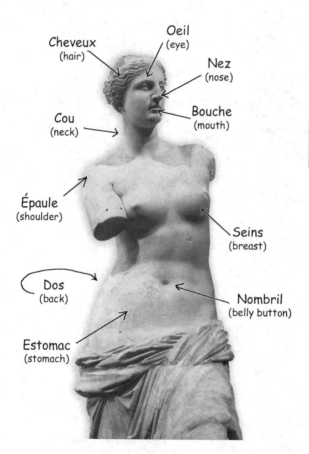

Cheveux
(hair)

Oeil
(eye)

Nez
(nose)

Cou
(neck)

Bouche
(mouth)

Épaule
(shoulder)

Seins
(breast)

Dos
(back)

Nombril
(belly button)

Estomac
(stomach)

First-Aid Kit

HEALTH

antacid	*anti-acide*	ahn-tee-ah-seed
antibiotic	*antibiotique*	ahn-tee-bee-oh-teek
aspirin	*aspirine*	ah-spee-reen
non-aspirin substitute	*Tylenol*	tee-luh-nohl
bandage	*bandage*	bahn-dahzh
Band-Aids	*pansements*	pahn-suh-mahn
cold medicine	*remède contre le rhume*	ruh-mehd kohn-truh luh rewm
cough drops	*pastilles pour la toux*	pah-steel poor lah too
decongestant	*décongestant*	day-kohn-zhehs-tahn
disinfectant	*désinfectant*	day-zan-fehk-tahn

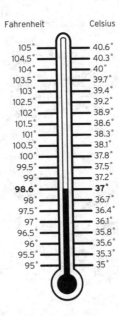

Fahrenheit	Celsius
105°	40.6°
104.5°	40.3°
104°	40°
103.5°	39.7°
103°	39.4°
102.5°	39.2°
102°	38.9°
101.5°	38.6°
101°	38.3°
100.5°	38.1°
100°	37.8°
99.5°	37.5°
99°	37.2°
98.6°	**37°**
98°	36.7°
97.5°	36.4°
97°	36.1°
96.5°	35.8°
96°	35.6°
95.5°	35.3°
95°	35°

first-aid cream	crème antiseptique	krehm ahn-tee-sehp-teek
gauze / tape	gaze / sparadra	gahz / spah-rah-drah
laxative	laxatif	lahk-sah-teef
medicine for diarrhea	médicament pour la diarrhée	may-dee-kah-mahn poor lah dee-ah-ray
moleskin	grain de beauté	gran duh boh-tay
pain killer	calmant	kahl-mahn
Preparation H	Préparation H (no kidding)	pray-pah-rah-see-ohn ahsh
support bandage	pansement élastique	pahn-suh-mahn ay-lah-steek
thermometer	thermomètre	tehr-moh-meh-truh
Vaseline	Vaseline	vah-zuh-leen
vitamins	vitamines	vee-tah-meen

Contacts and Glasses

glasses	lunettes	lew-neht
sunglasses	lunettes de soleil	lew-neht duh soh-lay
prescription	ordonnance	or-duh-nahns
contact lenses...	lentilles de contact...	lahn-tee duh kohn-tahkt
...soft	...souples	soop-luh
...hard	...dures	dewr
cleaning solution	solution nettoyante	soh-lew-see-ohn neh-toy-yahnt
soaking solution	solution à trempage	soh-lew-see-ohn ah trahn-pahzh
all-purpose solution (for cleaning and soaking)	solution pour tout (pour nettoyer et tremper)	soh-lew-see-ohn poor too (poor neh-toy-ay ay trahn-pay)
20/20 vision	vision vingt sur vingt	veez-yohn van sewr van
I've... a contact lens.	J'ai... une de mes lentilles de contact.	zhay... ewn duh may lahn-tee duh kohn-tahkt
...lost	...perdu	pehr-dew
...swallowed	...avalé	ah-vah-lay

HEALTH

Toiletries

comb	*peigne*	pehn-yuh
conditioner for hair	*après-shampoing*	ah-preh-shah<u>n</u>-pwa<u>n</u>
condoms	*préservatifs*	pray-zehr-vah-teef
dental floss	*fil dentaire*	feel dah<u>n</u>-tair
deodorant	*déodorant*	day-oh-doh-rah<u>n</u>
facial tissue	*kleenex*	klay-nehks
hairbrush	*brosse*	brohs
hand lotion	*crème pour les mains*	krehm poor lay ma<u>n</u>
lip salve	*beaume pour les lèvres*	bohm poor lay leh-vruh
mirror	*mirroir*	meer-war
nail clipper	*clip-ongles*	kleep-oh<u>n</u>-gluh
razor	*rasoir*	rah-zwahr
sanitary napkins	*serviettes hygiéniques*	sehrv-yeht ee-zhay-neek
scissors	*ciseaux*	see-zoh
shampoo	*shampoing*	shah<u>n</u>-pwa<u>n</u>
shaving cream	*mousse à raser*	moos ah rah-zehr
soap	*savon*	sah-voh<u>n</u>
sunscreen / suntan lotion	*crème solaire*	krehm soh-layr
tampons	*tampons*	tah<u>n</u>-poh<u>n</u>
tissues	*mouchoirs en papier*	moosh-wahr ah<u>n</u> pahp-yay
toilet paper	*papier hygiénique*	pahp-yay ee-zhay-neek
toothbrush	*brosse à dents*	brohs ah dah<u>n</u>
toothpaste	*dentifrice*	dah<u>n</u>-tee-frees
tweezers	*pince à épiler*	pa<u>n</u>s ah ay-pee-lay

Makeup

blush	*blush, rouge à joues*	bloosh, roozh ah zhoo
eye shadow	*ombre à paupières*	ohm-bruh ah pohp-yehr
eyeliner	*eyeliner, crayon pour les yeux*	"eyeliner," kray-oh<u>n</u> poor layz yuh
face cleanser	*lait nettoyant*	lay neh-toy-ah<u>n</u>

face powder	*fond de teint compact*	foh<u>n</u> duh ta<u>n</u> koh<u>n</u>-pahkt
foundation	*fond de teint*	foh<u>n</u>d duh ta<u>n</u>t
lipstick	*rouge à lèvres*	roozh ah leh-vruh
makeup	*maquillage*	mah-kee-ahzh
makeup remover	*lait démaquillant*	lay day-mah-kee-ah<u>n</u>
mascara	*mascara*	mas-kah-rah
moisturizer...	*crème hydratante...*	krehm ee-drah-tah<u>n</u>t
...with sun block	*...avec protection solaire*	ah-vehk proh-tehk-see-oh<u>n</u> soh-lair
nail polish	*vernis à ongles*	vehr-nee ah oh<u>n</u>-gluh
nail polish remover	*dissolvant*	dee-sohl-vah<u>n</u>
perfume	*parfum*	par-foom

For Babies

baby	*bébé*	bay-bay
baby food	*nourriture pour bébé*	noo-ree-tewr poor bay-bay
bib	*bavoir*	bah-vwar
bottle	*biberon*	bee-behr-oh<u>n</u>
diapers	*couches*	koosh
diaper wipes	*lingettes de couche*	la<u>n</u>-yeht duh koosh
diaper ointment	*pommade de couche*	poh-mahd duh koosh
formula...	*lait pour bébé...*	lay poor bay-bay
...powdered	*...en poudre*	ah<u>n</u> poo-druh
...liquid	*...liquide*	lee-keed
...soy	*...soja*	soh-zhah
medication for...	*médicament pour...*	may-dee-kah-mah<u>n</u> poor
...diaper rash	*...l'érythème fessier*	lay-ree-tehm fuh-see-ay
...teething	*...la poussée des dents*	lah poo-say day dah<u>n</u>
nipple	*tétine*	tay-teen
pacifier	*sucette*	soo-seht
Will you refrigerate this?	*Vous pouvez mettre ça au frigo?*	voo poo-vay meh-truh sah oh free-goh
Will you warm... for a baby?	*Vous pouvez réchauffer...pour un bébé?*	voo poo-vay ray-shoh-fay... poor uh<u>n</u> bay-bay

...this	*...ça*	sah
...some milk	*...un peu de lait*	uhn puh duh lay
...some water	*...un peu d'eau*	uhn puh doh
Not too hot, please.	*Pas trop chaud,*	pah troh shoh
	s'il vous plaît.	see voo play

More Baby Things

backpack to carry baby	*porte-bébé*	port-bay-bay
booster seat	*réhausseur*	ray-oh-sur
car seat	*siège voiture*	see-ehzh vwah-tewr
high chair	*chaise haute*	shehz oht
playpen	*parc*	park
stroller	*poussette*	poo-seht

HEALTH

CHATTING

My name is ___.	Je m'appelle ___.	zhuh mah-pehl
What's your name?	Quel est votre nom?	kehl ay voh-truh nohn
Pleased to meet you.	Enchanté.	ahn-shahn-tay
This is ___.	C'est ___.	say
How are you?	Comment allez-vous?	koh-mahnt ah-lay-voo
Very well, thanks.	Très bien, merci.	treh bee-an mehr-see
Where are you from?	D'où venez-vous?	doo vuh-nay-voo
What city?	Quelle ville?	kehl veel
What country?	Quel pays?	kehl pay-ee
What planet?	Quelle planète?	kehl plah-neht
I am...	Je suis...	zhuh swee
...a male American.	...américain.	zah-may-ree-kan
...a female American.	...américaine.	zah-may-ree-kehn
...a male Canadian.	...canadien.	kah-nah-dee-an
...a female Canadian.	...canadienne.	kah-nah-dee-ehn
...a pest.	...une peste.	ewn pehst
Where are you going?	Où allez-vous?	oo ah-lay-voo
I'm going to ___.	Je vais à ___.	zhuh vay ah
We're going to ___.	Nous allons à ___.	nooz ah-lohnz ah
Will you take my / our photo?	Vous pouvez prendre ma / notre photo?	voo-poo-vay prahn-druh mah / noh-truh foh-toh
Can I take a photo of you?	Je peux prendre votre photo?	zhuh puh prahn-druh noh-truh foh-toh
Smile!	Souriez!	soo-ree-ay

Key Phrases: Chatting

My name is ___.	*Je m'appelle ___.*	zhuh mah-pehl
What's your name?	*Quel est votre nom?*	kehl ay voh-truh nohn
Pleased to meet you.	*Enchanté.*	ahn-shahn-tay
Where are you from?	*D'où venez-vous?*	doo vuh-nay-voo
I'm from ___.	*Je viens de ___.*	zhuh vee-ahn duh
Where are you going?	*Où allez-vous?*	oo ah-lay-voo
I'm going to ___.	*Je vais à ___.*	zhuh vay ah
I like...	*J'aime...*	zhehm
Do you like...?	*Vous aimez...?*	vooz eh-may
Thank you very much.	*Merci beaucoup.*	mehr-see boh-koo
Have a good trip!	*Bon voyage!*	bohn voy-yahzh

CHATTING

Nothing More than Feelings...

I am / You are...	*Je suis / Vous êtes...*	zhuh swee / vooz eht
He / She is...	*Il / Elle est...*	eel / ehl ay
...happy. (m / f)	*...content / contente.*	kohn-tahn / kohn-tahnt
...sad.	*...triste.*	treest
...tired.	*...fatigué.*	fah-tee-gay
I am / You are...	*J'ai / Vous avez...*	zhay / vooz ah-vay
He / She is...	*Il / Elle a...*	eel / ehl ah
...hungry.	*...faim.*	fan
...thirsty.	*...soif.*	swahf
...lucky.	*...de la chance.*	duh lah shahns
...homesick.	*...le mal du pays.*	luh mahl dew pay-ee
...cold.	*...froid.*	frwah
...hot.	*...trop chaud.*	troh shoh

Who's Who

This is my friend.	*C'est mon ami.*	say mohn ah-mee
This is my... (m / f)	*C'est mon / ma...*	say mohn / mah

...boyfriend / girlfriend.	...petit ami / petite amie.	puh-teet ah-mee / puh-teet ah-mee
...husband / wife.	...mari / femme.	mah-ree / fahm
...son / daughter.	...fils / fille.	fees / fee
...brother / sister.	...frère / soeur.	frehr / sur
...father / mother.	...père / mère.	pehr / mehr
...uncle / aunt.	...oncle / tante.	oh<u>n</u>-kluh / tah<u>n</u>t
...nephew / niece.	...neveu / nièce.	nuh-vuh / nee-ehs
...male / female cousin.	...cousin / cousine.	koo-za<u>n</u> / koo-zeen
...grandfather / grandmother.	...grand-père / grand-mère.	grah<u>n</u>-pehr / grah<u>n</u>-mehr
...grandson / granddaughter.	...petit-fils / petite-fille.	puh-tee-fees / puh-teet-fee

Family

Are you married?	Vous êtes marié?	vooz eht mah-ree-ay
Do you have children?	Vous avez des enfants?	vooz ah-vay dayz ah<u>n</u>-fah<u>n</u>
How many boys / girls?	Combien de garçons / filles?	koh<u>n</u>-bee-a<u>n</u> duh gar-soh<u>n</u> / feel
Do you have photos?	Vous avez des photos?	vooz ah-vay day foh-toh
How old is your child?	Quel âge à votre enfant?	kehl ahzh ah voh-truh ah<u>n</u>-fah<u>n</u>
Beautiful child!	Quel bel enfant!	kehl behl ah<u>n</u>-fah<u>n</u>
Beautiful children!	Quels beaux enfants!	kehl bohz ah<u>n</u>-fah<u>n</u>

Work

What is your occupation?	Quel est votre métier?	kehl eh voh-truh may-tee-yay
Do you like your work?	Aimez-vous votre métier?	eh-may-voo voh-truh may-tee-yay
I'm a...	Je suis...	zhuh swee
...male student.	...étudiant.	zay-tew-dee-ah<u>n</u>
...female student.	...étudiante.	zay-tew-dee-ah<u>n</u>t

I work in...	Je travaille dans...	zhuh trah-vay-ee dahn
I'm studying to work in...	J'étudie pour travailler dans...	zhay-too-dee poor trah-vah-yay dahn
I used to work in...	Je travaillais dans...	zhuh trah-vah-yay dahn
I want to work in...	Je veux travailler dans...	zhuh vuh trah-vah-yay dahn
...accounting.	...la comptabilité.	lah kohmp-tah-bee-lee-tay
...the medical field.	...le secteur médical.	luh sehk-tur may-dee-kahl
...social services.	...le secteur social.	luh sehk-tur soh-see-ahl
...the legal profession.	...le secteur légal.	luh sehk-tur lay-gahl
...banking.	...le secteur bancaire.	luh sehk-tur bahn-kair
...business.	...le commerce.	luh koh-mehrs
...government.	...le gouvernement.	luh goo-vehr-nuh-mahn
...engineering.	...l'ingéniérie.	lan-zhay-nee-yay-ree
...public relations.	...les relations publiques.	lay reh-lah-see-ohn poob-leek
...science.	...les sciences.	lay see-ahns
...teaching.	...l'enseignement.	lahn-sehn-yuh-mahn
...the computer field.	...l'informatique.	lan-for-mah-teek
...the travel industry.	...le tourisme.	luh too-reez-muh
...the arts.	...les arts.	layz ar
...journalism.	...le journalisme.	luh zhoor-nahl-eez-muh
...a restaurant.	...un restaurant.	uhn rehs-toh-rahn
...a store.	...un magasin.	uhn mah-gah-zan
...a factory.	...une usine.	ewn oo-zeen
I am / We are...	Je suis / Nous sommes...	zhuh swee / noo suhm
...unemployed.	...au chômage.	oh shoh-mahzh
...retired.	...à la retraite.	ah lah ruh-trayt
I'm a professional traveler.	Je suis voyageur professionnel.	zhuh swee voy-yah-zhur proh-feh-see-oh-nehl
Do you have a...?	Vous avez...?	vooz ah-vay
Here is my / our...	C'est ma / notre...	say mah / noh-truh
...business card	...carte de visite	kart duh vee-zeet
...email address	...adresse email	ah-drehs ee-mayl

Chatting with Children

What's your first name?	Quel est ton prénom?	kehl ay tohn pray-nohn
My name is ___.	Je m'appelle ___.	zhuh mah-pehl
How old are you?	Quel âge as-tu?	kehl ahzh ah-tew
Do you have brothers and sisters?	Tu as des frères et soeurs?	tew ahz day frehr ay sur
Do you like school?	Tu aimes l'école?	tew ehm lay-kohl
What are you studying?	Tu étudies quoi?	tew ay-tew-dee kwah
I'm studying ___.	J'étudie ___.	zhay-too-dee
What's your favorite subject?	Quel est ton sujet préferé?	kehl ay tohn soo-zhay pray-fuh-ray
Do you have pets?	As-tu un animal chez toi?	ah-tew uhn ah-nee-mahl shay twah
I have a...	J'ai un...	zhay uhn
We have a...	Nous avons un...	nooz ah-vohn uhn
...cat / dog / fish / bird	...chat / chien / poisson / oiseau	shah / shee-an / pwah-sohn / wah-zoh
What is this?	Qu'est-ce que c'est?	kes kuh say
Will you teach me...?	Tu m'apprends...?	tew mah-prahn
Will you teach us...?	Tu nous apprend...?	tew nooz ah-prahn
...some French words	...quelques mots en français	kehl-kuh moh ahn frahn-say
...a simple French song	...une chanson française facile	ewn shahn-sohn frahn-sehz fah-seel
Guess which country I live in.	Devine mon pays.	duh-veen mohn pay-ee
Guess which country we live in.	Devine notre pays.	duh-veen noh-truh pay-ee
How old am I?	J'ai quel âge?	zhay kehl ahzh
I'm ___ years old.	J'ai ___ ans.	zhay ___ ahn
Want to hear me burp?	Veux-tu m'ententre roter?	vuh-tew mahn-tahn-truh roh-tay
Teach me a fun game.	Apprends-moi un jeu rigolo.	ah-prahn-mwah uhn zhuh ree-goh-loh

Got any candy?	*Tu as des bonbons?*	tew ah day bohn-bohn
Want to arm wrestle?	*Tu veux faire un bras de fer?*	tew vuh fair uhn brah duh fehr
Gimme five.	*Tape là.*	tahp lah

If you want to do a "high five" with a kid, hold up your hand and say, "Tape là" (Hit me here). For a French sing-along, you'll find the words for "Happy Birthday" on page 24 and a couple more songs on page 253.

Travel Talk

I am / Are you...?	*Je suis / Vous êtes...?*	zhuh sweez / vooz eht
...on vacation	*...en vacances*	ahn vah-kahns
...on business	*...en voyage d'affaires*	ahn voy-yahzh dah-fair
How long have you been traveling?	*Il y a longtemps que vous voyagez?*	eel yah lohn-tahn kuh voo voy-yah-zhay
day / week	*jour / semaine*	zhoor / suh-mehn
month / year	*mois / année*	mwah / ah-nay
When are you going home?	*Quand allez-vous rentrer?*	kahn ah-lay-voo rahn-tray
This is my first time in ___.	*C'est ma première fois en ___.*	say mah pruhm-yehr fwah ahn
This is our first time in ___.	*C'est notre première fois en ___.*	say noh-truh pruhm-yehr fwah ahn
It's / It's not a tourist trap.	*C'est / Ce n'est pas un piège à touristes.*	say / suh nay pah uhn pee-ehzh ah too-reest
This is paradise.	*Ceci est le paradis.*	say-see ay luh pah-rah-deez
France is wonderful.	*La France est magnifique.*	lah frahns ay mahn-yee-feek
The French are friendly / boring / rude.	*Les Français sont gentils / ennuyeux / impolis.*	lay frahn-say sohn zhahn-tee / ahn-noo-yuh / an-poh-lee
So far...	*Jusqu'à maintenant...*	zhews-kah man-tuh-nahn
Today...	*Aujourd'hui...*	oh-zhoor-dwee
...I have / We have seen ___ and ___.	*...j'ai / nous avons vu ___ et ___.*	zhay / nooz ah-vohn vew ___ ay ___

Next...	Après...	ah-preh
Tomorrow...	Demain...	duh-man
...I will / We will see ___.	...je vais / nous allons voir ___.	zhuh vay / nooz ahl-lohn vwar
Yesterday...	Hier...	yehr
...I saw / We saw ___.	...j'ai vu / nous avons vu ___.	zhay vew / nooz ah-vohn vew
My / Our vacation is ___ days long, starting in ___ and ending in ___.	J'ai / Nous avons ___ jours de vacances, qui commence à ___ et qui finissent à ___.	zhay / nooz ah-vohn ___ zhoor duh vah-kahns kee kohn-mahn-sahn ah ___ ay kee fee-nee-sahn ah ___
To travel is to live.	Voyager c'est vivre.	voy-yah-zhay say vee-vruh
Travel is enlightening.	Voyager ouvre l'esprit.	voy-yah-zhay oo-vruh luh-spree
I wish all (American) politicians traveled.	Je souhaite que tous les politiciens (américains) voyagent.	zhuh soo-ayt kuh too lay poh-lee-tee-see-an (ah-may-ree-kan) voy-yah-zhahn
Have a good trip!	Bon voyage!	bohn voy-yahzh

Map Musings

Use the following maps to delve into family history and explore travel dreams.

I live here.	J'habite ici.	zhah-beet ee-see
We live here.	Nous habitons ici.	nooz ah-bee-tohn ee-see
I was born here.	Je suis né là.	zhuh swee nay lah
My ancestors came from ___.	Mes ancêtres viennent de ___.	mayz ahn-seh-truh vee-ehn duh
I've traveled to ___.	J'ai visité à ___.	zhay vee-zee-tay ah
We've traveled to ___.	Nous avons visité à ___.	nooz ah-vohn vee-zee-tay ah
Next I'll go to ___.	Et puis je vais à...	ay pwee zhuh vay ah
Next we'll go to ___.	Et puis nous allons à...	ay pwee nooz ahl-lohn ah

France

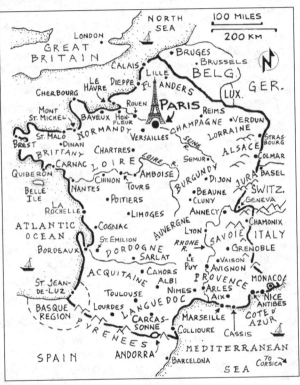

Europe

The United States

The World

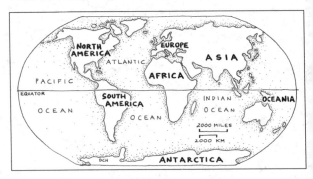

I'd like / We'd like to go to ___.	Je voudrais / Nous voudrions aller à ___.	zhuh voo-dray / noo voo-dree-ohn ah-lay ah
Where do you live?	Où est-ce que vous vivez?	oo ehs kuh voo vee-vay
Where were you born?	Où êtes-vous né?	oo eht-voo nay
Where did your ancestors come from?	D'où viennent vos ancêtres?	doo vee-ehn vohz ahn-seh-truh
Where have you traveled?	Où avez-vous voyagé?	oo ah-vay-voo voy-yah-zhay
Where are you going?	Où allez-vous?	oo ah-lay-voo
Where would you like to go?	Où voudriez-vous voyager?	oo voo-dree-yay-voo voy-yah-zhay

CHATTING

Favorite Things

What kind...	Quelle sorte...	kehl sort...
do you like?	vous aimez?	vooz eh-may
...of art	...d'art	dar
...of books	...de livres	duh lee-vruh
...of hobby	...de hobby, passe temps	duh oh-bee, pahs tahn
...of ice cream	...de glace	duh glahs
...of food	...de nourriture	duh noo-ree-tewr
...of movies	...de films	duh feelm
...of music	...de musique	duh mew-zeek
...of sports	...de sports	duh spor
...of vices	...de vices	duh vees
Who is your favorite...?	Qui est votre... préféré?	kee ay voh-truh... pray-fay-ray
...artist	...artiste	ar-teest
...author	...auteur	ow-tur
...male singer	...chanteur	shahn-tur
...female singer	...chanteuse	shahn-tuhz
...male movie star	...acteur	ahk-tur

...female movie star	*...actrice*	ahk-trees
Can you recommend	*Vous pouvez me*	voo poo-vay muh
a good...?	*conseiller un bon...?*	koh<u>n</u>-seh-yay uh<u>n</u> boh<u>n</u>
...French CD	*...français CD*	frah<u>n</u>-say say day
...French book	*...livre français*	lee-vruh frah<u>n</u>-say
translated	*traduit*	trah-dwee
in English	*en anglais*	ah<u>n</u> ah<u>n</u>-glay

Thanks a Million

Thank you	*Merci beaucoup.*	mehr-see boh-koo
very much.		
You are...	*Vous êtes...*	vooz eht
...helpful.	*...serviable.*	sehr-vee-ah-bluh
...wonderful.	*...magnifique.*	mah<u>n</u>-yee-feek
...generous. (m / f)	*...généreux /*	zhay-nay-ruh /
	généreuse.	zhay-nay-ruhz
You spoil me / us.	*Vous me / nous gâtez.*	voo muh / noo gah-tay
You've been a	*Vous m'avez*	voo mah-vay
great help!	*beaucoup aider!*	boh-koo ay-day
You are an angel	*Vous êtes un ange*	vooz eht uh<u>n</u> ah<u>n</u>zh
from heaven.	*venu du ciel.*	vuh-new duh see-ehl
I will remember	*Je me souviendrai*	zhuh muh soov-ya<u>n</u>-dreh
you...	*de vous...*	duh voo
We will remember	*Nous nous*	noo noo
you...	*souviendrons*	soov-ya<u>n</u>-dreh
	de vous...	duh voo
...always.	*...toujours.*	too-zhoor
...till Tuesday.	*...jusqu'à mardi.*	zhews-kah mar-dee

Weather

What's the weather	*Quel temps fera-t-il*	kehl tah<u>n</u> fuh-rah-teel
tomorrow?	*demain?*	duh-ma<u>n</u>
sunny / cloudy	*ensoleillé /*	ah<u>n</u>-soh-lay-yay /
	nuageux	nwah-zhuh
hot / cold	*chaud / froid*	shoh / frwah
muggy / windy	*humide / venteux*	oo-meed / vah<u>n</u>-tuh

CHATTING

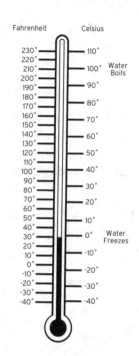

rain / snow	*pluie / neige*	ploo-ee / nehzh
It's raining like	*Il pleut comme*	eel pluh kohm
cow's piss.	*vâche qui pisse.*	vahsh kee pees
(French saying)		

Smoking

Do you smoke?	*Vous fumez?*	voo few-may
Do you smoke pot?	*Vous fumez*	voo few-may
	de l'herbe?	duh lehrb
I (don't) smoke.	*Je (ne) fume (pas).*	zhuh (nuh) fewm (pah)

We (don't) smoke.	*Nous (ne) fumons (pas).*	noo (nuh) few-moh<u>n</u> (pah)
lighter	*briquet*	bree-kay
cigarettes	*cigarette*	see-gah-reht
marijuana	*de l'herbe, marijuana*	duh lehrb, mah-ree-wah-nah
hash	*hachisch*	hah-sheesh
joint	*joint*	"joint"
stoned	*stoned*	"stoned"
Wow!	*Wow!*	"Wow"

Responses for All Occasions

I like that.	*Ça me plaît.*	sah muh play
We like that.	*Ça nous plaît*	sah noo play
I like you.	*Je vous aime bien.*	zhuh vooz ehm bee-a<u>n</u>
We like you.	*Nous vous aimons bien.*	noo vooz ehm-oh<u>n</u> bee-a<u>n</u>
That's cool.	*C'est chouette.*	say shweht
Great!	*Formidable!*	for-mee-dah-bluh
What a nice place.	*Quel endroit sympa.*	kehl ah<u>n</u>-dwah sah<u>n</u>-pah
Perfect.	*Parfait.*	par-fay
Funny.	*Amusant.*	ah-mew-zah<u>n</u>
Interesting.	*Intéressant.*	a<u>n</u>-tay-reh-sah<u>n</u>
Really?	*Vraiment?*	vray-mah<u>n</u>
Wow!	*Wow!*	"Wow"
Congratulations!	*Félicitations!*	fay-lee-see-tah-see-oh<u>n</u>
Well done!	*Bien joué!*	bee-a<u>n</u> zhoo-ay
You're welcome.	*Je vous en prie.*	zhuh vooz ah<u>n</u> pree
It's nothing.	*De rien.*	duh ree-a<u>n</u>
Bless you! (sneeze)	*À vos souhaits!*	ah voh sway
What a pity.	*Quel dommage.*	kehl doh-mahzh
That's life.	*C'est la vie.*	say lah vee
No problem.	*Pas de problème.*	pah duh proh-blehm
O.K.	*D'accord.*	dah-kor
This is the good life!	*Que la vie est belle!*	kuh lah vee ay behl
Have a good day!	*Bonne journée!*	buh<u>n</u> zhoor-nay

CHATTING

| Good luck! | *Bonne chance!* | buhn shahns |
| Let's go! | *Allons-y!* | ah-lohn-zee |

Conversing with Animals

rooster / cock-a-doodle-doo	*coq / cocorico*	kohk / koh-koh-ree-koh
bird / tweet tweet	*oiseau / cui cui*	wah-zoh / kwee kwee
cat / meow	*chat / miaou*	shah / mee-ah-oo
dog / woof woof	*chien / ouah ouah*	shee-an / wah wah
duck / quack quack	*canard / coin coin*	kah-nar / kwan kwan
cow / moo	*vache / meu*	vahsh / muh
pig / oink oink	*cochon / groin groin*	koh-shohn / grwan grwan

Profanity

People make animal noises, too. These words will help you understand what the more colorful locals are saying...

Damn! (Good God!)	*Bon Dieu!*	bohn dee-uh
bastard	*salaud*	sah-loh
bitch	*salope*	sah-lohp
breasts (colloq.)	*tétons*	tay-tohn
big breasts	*grands tétons*	grahn tay-tohn
penis (colloq.)	*bite*	beet
butthole	*sale con*	sahl kohn
drunk	*bourré*	boo-ray
idiot	*idiot*	ee-dee-oh
imbecile	*imbécile*	an-bay-seel
jerk	*connard*	kuh-nar
stupid	*stupide*	stew-peed
Did someone fart?	*Est-ce que quelqu'un à péter?*	ehs kuh kehl-kuhn ah pay-tay
I burped.	*J'ai roté.*	zhay roh-tay
This sucks.	*C'est dégueulasse.*	say day-gewl-ahs
Shit.	*Merde.*	mehrd
Bullshit.	*C'est de la merde.*	say duh lah mehrd
You are...	*Vous êtes...*	vooz eht

Don't be...	*Ne soyez pas...*	nuh soh-yay pah
...a son of a bitch.	*...un batard.*	uh<u>n</u> bah-tar
...an asshole.	*...un vieux con.*	uh<u>n</u> vee-uh koh<u>n</u>
...an idiot.	*...un idiot.*	uh<u>n</u> ee-dee-oh
...a creep.	*...un vicieux.*	uh<u>n</u> vee-see-uh
...a cretin.	*...un crétin.*	uh<u>n</u> kray-teen
...a pig.	*...un cochon.*	uh<u>n</u> koh-shoh<u>n</u>

Sweet Curses

My goodness.	*Mon Dieu.*	moh<u>n</u> dee-uh
Goodness gracious.	*Mon bon Dieu.*	moh<u>n</u> boh<u>n</u> dee-uh
Oh, my gosh.	*Oh la la.*	oo lah lah
Shoot.	*Zut.*	zewt
Darn it!	*Mince!*	ma<u>n</u>s

CREATE YOUR OWN CONVERSATION

The French enjoy good conversations. Join in! You can mix and match these words into a conversation. Make it as deep or silly as you want.

Who

I / you	*je / vous*	zhuh / voo
he / she	*il / elle*	eel / ehl
we / they	*nous / ils*	noo / eel
my / your...	*mes / vos...*	may / voh
...parents / children	*...parents / enfants*	pah-rah<u>n</u> / zah<u>n</u>-fah<u>n</u>
men / women	*hommes / femmes*	ohm / fahm
rich / poor people	*riches / pauvres*	reesh / poh-vruh
young people	*jeunes*	zhuh<u>n</u>
middle-aged / old	*d'âge mur / vieux*	dahzh mewr / vee-uh
the French	*les Français*	lay frah<u>n</u>-say
the Austrians	*les Autrichiens*	layz oh-treesh-ee-a<u>n</u>
the Belgians	*les Belges*	lay behlzh
the Czechs	*les Tchèques*	lay chehk

the Germans	*les Allemands*	layz ahl-mah<u>n</u>
the Italians	*les Italiens*	layz ee-tah-lee-a<u>n</u>
the Spanish	*les Espagnols*	layz eh-spahn-yohl
the Swiss	*les Suisses*	lay swees
the Europeans	*les Européens*	layz ur-oh-pee-ehn
EU	*UE*	ew uh
(European Union)	*(l'Union Européenne)*	(lewn-yun ur-oh-pee-ehn)
the Americans	*les Américains*	layz ah-may-ree-kan
liberals	*libéraux*	lee-bay-roh
conservatives	*conservateurs*	koh<u>n</u>-sehr-vah-tur
radicals	*radicaux*	rah-dee-koh
terrorists	*terroristes*	teh-roh-reest
politicians	*politiciens*	poh-lee-tee-see-a<u>n</u>
big business	*grosses affaires*	grohs ah-fair
multinational	*corporations*	kor-por-ah-see-oh<u>n</u>
corporations	*multinationales*	mewl-tee-nah-see-oh-nahl
military	*militaire*	mee-lee-tair
mafia	*mafia*	"mafia"
refugees	*réfugiés*	ray-few-zhee-ay
travelers	*voyageurs*	voy-yah-zhur
God	*Dieu*	dee-uh
Christian	*chrétien*	kray-tee-a<u>n</u>
Catholic	*catholique*	kah-toh-leek
Protestant	*protestant*	proh-tehs-tah<u>n</u>
Jew	*juif*	zhweef
Muslim	*musulmans*	mew-zewl-mah<u>n</u>
everyone	*tout le monde*	too luh moh<u>n</u>d

What

buy / sell	*acheter / vendre*	ah-shuh-tay / vah<u>n</u>-druh
have / lack	*avoir / manquer de*	ahv-wahr / mah<u>n</u>-kay duh
help / abuse	*aider / abuser*	ay-day / ah-boo-zay
learn / fear	*apprendre / craindre*	ah-prah<u>n</u>-druh / cra<u>n</u>-druh
love / hate	*aimer / détester*	eh-may / day-tehs-tay
prosper / suffer	*prospérer / souffrir*	proh-spay-ray / soo-freer
take / give	*prendre / donner*	prah<u>n</u>-druh / duh-nay

CHATTING

want / need	*vouloir / avoir*	vool-wahr / ahv-wahr
	besoin de	buh-swa<u>n</u> duh
work / play	*travailler / jouer*	trah-vah-yay / zhoo-way

Why

(anti-)	*(anti-)*	(ah<u>n</u>-tee-)
globalization	*globalisation*	gloh-bah-lee-zah-see-oh<u>n</u>
class warfare	*lutte sociale*	luht soh-see-ahl
corruption	*corruption*	koh-rewp-see-oh<u>n</u>
democracy	*démocratie*	day-moh-krah-tee
education	*éducation*	ay-dew-kah-see-oh<u>n</u>
family	*famille*	fah-mee-ee
food	*nourriture*	noo-ree-tewr
guns	*armes*	arm
happiness	*bonheur*	boh<u>n</u>-ur
health	*santé*	sah<u>n</u>-tay
hope	*espoir*	ehs-pwahr
imperialism	*impérialisme*	a<u>n</u>-pay-ree-ahl-eez-muh
lies	*mensonges*	mah<u>n</u>-soh<u>n</u>zh
love / sex	*amour / sexe*	ah-moor / "sex"
marijuana	*marijuana*	mah-ree-wah-nah
money / power	*argent / pouvoir*	ar-zhah<u>n</u> / poov-wahr
pollution	*pollution*	poh-lew-see-oh<u>n</u>
racism	*racisme*	rah-seez-muh
regime change	*changement*	shah<u>n</u>-zhuh-mah<u>n</u>
	de régime	duh ray-zheem
relaxation	*relaxation*	ruh-lahk-sah-see-oh<u>n</u>
religion	*religion*	ruh-lee-zhee-oh<u>n</u>
respect	*respect*	ruh-speh
taxes	*taxes*	tahks
television	*télévision*	tay-lay-vee-zee-oh<u>n</u>
violence	*violence*	vee-oh-lah<u>n</u>s
war / peace	*guerre / paix*	gehr / peh
work	*travail*	trah-vah-ee
global perspective	*perspective*	pehr-spehk-teev
	globale	gloh-bahl

CHATTING

You Be the Judge

(no) problem	(pas de) problème	(pah duh) proh-blehm
(not) good	(pas) bon	(pah) bohn
(not) dangerous	(pas) dangereux	(pah) dahn-zhay-ruh
(not) fair	(pas) juste	(pah) zhewst
(not) guilty	(pas) coupable	(pah) koo-pah-bluh
(not) powerful	(pas) puissant	(pah) pwee-sahn
(not) stupid	(pas) stupide	(pah) stew-peed
(not) happy	(pas) content	(pah) kohn-tahn
because / for	parce que / pour	pars kuh / poor
and / or / from	et / ou / de	ay / oo / duh
too much	trop	troh
(never) enough	(jamais) assez	(zhah-may) ah-say
same	même	mehm
better / worse	mieux / pire	mee-uh / peer
here / everywhere	ici / partout	ee-see / par-too

Beginnings and Endings

I like...	J'aime...	zhehm
We like...	Nous aimons...	nooz eh-mohn
I don't like...	Je n'aime pas...	zhuh nehm pah
We don't like...	Nous n'aimons pas...	noo neh-mohn pah
Do you like...?	Vous aimez...?	vooz eh-may
In the past...	Dans le passé...	dahn luh pah-say
When I was younger,	Quand j'étais jeune,	kahn zhay-tay zhuhn
I thought...	je pensais...	zhuh pahn-say
Now, I think...	Maintenant,	man-tuh-nahn
	je pense...	zhuh pahns
I am / Are you...?	Je suis / Vous êtes...?	zhuh swee / vooz eht
...optimistic /	...optimiste /	ohp-tee-meest /
pessimistic	pessimiste	peh-see-meest
I believe...	Je crois...	zhuh krwah
I don't believe...	Je ne crois pas...	zhuh nuh krwah pah
Do you believe...?	Croyez-vous...?	krwah-yay-voo
...in God	...en Dieu	ahn dee-uh
...in life after death	...en la vie après	ahn lah vee ah-preh
	la mort	lah mor

...in extraterrestrial life	...dans la vie extraterrestre	dahn lah vee ehk-strah-tuh-rehs-truh
...in Santa Claus	...au Père Noël	oh pehr noh-ehl
Yes. / No.	Oui. / Non.	wee / nohn
Maybe. / I don't know.	Peut-être. / Je ne sais pas.	puh-teh-truh / zhuh nuh say pah
What's most important in life?	Quel est le plus important dans la vie?	kehl ay luh plewz an-por-tahn dahn lah vee
The problem is...	Le problème, c'est que...	luh proh-blehm say kuh
The answer is...	La solution, c'est...	luh soh-lew-see-ohn say
We have solved the world's problems.	Nous avons résolu les problèmes du monde.	nooz ah-vohn ray-zoh-lew lay proh-blehm dew mohnd

CHATTING

The French Political Scene

These are the top six political parties in France, listed the same way you read, from left to right.

Parti Communiste: Beloved by labor unions, the communist party has become almost irrelevant.

Parti Écologiste: Also known as *Les Vert* (the greens), this is France's environmental party.

Parti Socialiste: The socialist party is France's mainstream left-leaning party.

Républicains pour la Rassemblement (RPR): Founded by Charles de Gaulle, this traditionally conservative party vies with the Parti Socialiste for control.

Front Nationale: Headed by Jean-Marie le Pen, this racist extreme right party advocates deportation of North African residents. Drawing about 10 to 15 percent of the vote, this party is fueled mainly by France's southern regions.

A FRENCH ROMANCE

Words of Love

I / me / you / we	je / moi / tu / nous	zhuh / mwah / tew /noo
flirt	flirter	fleer-tay
kiss	baiser	bay-zay
hug	se serrer dans les bras	suh suh-ray dahn lay brah
love	amour	ah-moor
make love	faire l'amour	fair lah-moor
condom	préservatif	pray-zehr-vah-teef
contraceptive	contraceptif	kohn-trah-sehp-teef
safe sex	safe sex	"safe sex"
sexy	sexy	"sexy"
cozy	douillet	doo-yay
romantic	romantique	roh-mahn-teek
my angel	mon ange	mohn ahnzh
my doe	ma biche	mah beesh
my love	mon amour	mohn ah-moor
my little cabbage	mon petit chou	mohn puh-tee shoo
my flea (endearing)	ma puce	mah poos
my treasure	mon trésor	mohn tray-sor

CHATTING

Ah, l'Amour

What's the matter?	Qu'est-ce qu'il y a?	kehs keel yah
Nothing.	Rien.	ree-an
I am / Are you...?	Je suis / Vous êtes...?	zhuh swee / vooz eht
...gay	...homosexual, gay	oh-moh-sehk-soo-ehl, "gay"
...straight	...hétéro	ay-tay-roh
...bisexual	...bisexuel	bee-sehk-swehl
...undecided	...indécis	an-day-see
...prudish (m / f)	...pudibond / pudibonde	pew-dee-bohn / pew-dee-bohnd
...horny	...excité	ehk-see-tay
We are on our honeymoon.	C'est notre lune de miel.	say noh-truh lewn duh mee-ehl

I have a boyfriend.	J'ai un petit ami.	zhay uhn puh-teet ah-mee
I have a girlfriend.	J'ai une petite amie.	zhay ewn puh-teet ah-mee
I'm married.	Je suis marié.	zhuh swee mah-ree-ay
I'm married (but...).	Je suis marié (mais...).	zhuh swee mah-ree-ay (may)
I'm not married.	Je ne suis pas marié.	zhuh nuh swee pah mah-ree-ay
Do you have a boyfriend / a girlfriend?	Vous avez un petit ami / une petite amie?	vooz ah-vay uhn puh-teet ah-mee / ewn puh-teet ah-mee
I am adventurous. (m / f)	Je suis aventureux(se).	zhuh swee ah-vahn-too-ruh(z)
I'm lonely (tonight).	Je me sens seul (ce soir).	zhuh muh sahn suhl (suh swar)
I am rich and single.	Je suis riche et célibataire.	zhuh swee reesh ay say-lee-bah-tair
Do you mind if I sit here?	Ça vous embête si je m'assieds ici?	sah vooz ahn-beht see zhuh mah-seed ee-see
Would you like a drink?	Vous voulez un verre?	voo voo-lay uhn vehr
Will you go out with me?	Vous voulez sortir avec moi?	voo voo-lay sor-teer ah-vehk mwah
Would you like to go out tonight for...?	Vous voulez m'accompagner ce soir pour...?	voo voo-lay mah-kohn-pahn-yay suh swar poor
...a walk	...une promenade	ewn proh-muh-nahd
...dinner	...dîner	dee-nay
...a drink	...boire un pot	bwar uhn poh
Where's the best place to dance nearby?	Où est le meilleur endroit pour danser?	oo ay luh meh-yur ahn-dwah poor dahn-say
Do you want to dance?	Vous voulez danser?	voo voo-lay dahn-say
Again?	De nouveau?	duh noo-voh
Let's celebrate!	Faisons la fête!	fay-zohn lah feht
Let's have fun like idiots!	Amusons-nous comme des fous!	ah-mew-zohn-noo kohm day foo

Let's have a wild and crazy night!	On va s'éclater ce soir!	ohn vah say-klah-tay suh swar
I have no diseases.	Je n'ai pas de maladies.	zhuh nay pah duh mah-lah-dee
I have many diseases.	J'ai plusieurs maladies.	zhay plewz-yur mah-lah-dee
I have only safe sex.	Je pratique que le safe sex.	zhuh prah-teek kuh luh "safe sex"
Can I take you home?	Tu veux venir chez moi?	tew vuh vuh-neer shay mwah
Why not?	Pourquoi pas?	poor-kwah pah
How can I change your mind?	Qu'est-ce que je peux faire pour te faire changer d'avis?	kehs kuh zhuh puh fair poor tuh fair shan-zhay dah-vee
Kiss me.	Embrasse-moi.	ahn-brah-say-mwah
May I kiss you?	Je peux t'embrasser?	zhuh puh tahn-brah-say
Can I see you again?	On peut se revoir?	ohn puh suh ruh-vwahr
Your place or mine?	Chez toi ou chez moi?	shay twah oo shay mwah
How does this feel?	Comment tu te sens?	koh-mahn tew tuh sahn
Is this an aphrodisiac?	C'est un aphrodisiaque?	sayt uhn ah-froh-dee-zee-yahk
This is my first time.	C'est la première fois.	seht lah pruhm-yehr fwah
This is not my first time.	Ce n'est pas la première fois.	seh nay pah lah pruhm-yehr fwah
You are my most beautiful souvenir.	Tu es mon plus beau souvenir.	tew ay mohn plew boh soo-vuh-neer
Do you do this often?	Tu fais ça souvent?	tew fay sah soo-vahn
How's my breath?	Comment tu trouves mon haleine?	koh-mahn tew troo-vay mohn ah-lehn
Let's just be friends.	Soyons amis.	swah-yohnz ah-mee

I'll pay for my share.	*Je paie mon partage.*	zhuh pay moh<u>n</u> par-tahzh
Would you like a massage...?	*Tu veux un massage...?*	tew vuh uh<u>n</u> mah-sahzh
...for your back	*...pour le dos*	poor luh doh
...for your feet	*...des pieds*	day pee-yay
Why not?	*Pourquoi pas?*	poor-kwah pah
Try it.	*Essaies.*	eh-say
That tickles.	*Ça chatouille.*	sah shah-too-ee
Oh my God.	*Mon Dieu.*	moh<u>n</u> dee-uh
I love you.	*Je t'aime.*	zhuh tehm
Darling, will you marry me?	*Chéri, tu veux m'épouser?*	shay-ree tew vuh may-poo-zay

DICTIONARY

FRENCH/ENGLISH

A

à	to; at
à la retraite	retired
à l'heure	on time
à remplir de nouveau	refill (v)
à travers	through
abstrait	abstract
abuser	abuse (v)
accès internet	Internet access
accessible à un fauteuil roulant	wheelchair-accessible
accident	accident
acheter	buy
adaptateur électrique	electrical adapter
addition	bill (payment)
adolescent	teenager
adresse	address
adresse email	email address
adulte	adult
aéroport	airport
affaires	business
affiche	poster
Afrique	Africa
âge	age
agence de voyage	travel agency
âgés, gens	seniors
aggressif	aggressive
agneau	lamb
agnostique	agnostic
agraffeuse	stapler
aider	help (v)
aigre	sour
aiguille	needle
aile	wing
aimable	kind
aimer	love (v)
aimer bien	like (v)
air	air
alcool	alcohol
Allemagne	Germany
aller	go
aller simple	one way (ticket)
allergies	allergies

French	English
allergique	allergic
aller-retour	round trip
allumettes	matches
amant	lover
ambassade	embassy
ami	friend
amitié	friendship
amour	love (n)
ampoule	bulb, light bulb
ampoules	blisters
amusement	fun
ancêtre	ancestor
ancien	ancient
âne	donkey
anglais	English
année	year
anniversaire	birthday
annuler	cancel; delete
anti-acide	antacid
antibiotique	antibiotic
antiquités	antiques
août	August
appareil-photo	camera
appartement	apartment
apprécier	enjoy
apprendre	learn
après	after, afterwards
après demain	day after tomorrow
après rasage	aftershave
après-midi	afternoon
après-shampoing	conditioner (hair)
araignée	spider
arbre	tree
arc-en-ciel	rainbow
argent	money; silver

French	English
arobase, signe	"at" sign (@)
arrêt	stop (n)
arrêt de bus	bus stop
arrêt de Métro	subway stop
arrêter	stop (v)
arrivées	arrivals
arriver	arrive
art	art
arthrite	arthritis
artiste	artist
arts	crafts
ascenseur	elevator
aspirine	aspirin
assez	enough
assiette	plate
assurance	insurance
assurance maladie	health insurance
assuré	insured
asthme	asthma
athée	atheist
attendre	wait
attirant	attractive
attraper	catch (v)
au chômage	unemployed
au dessus	above
au lieu de	instead
au revoir	goodbye
aube	sunrise
auberge de jeunesse	youth hostel
aujourd'hui	today
autel	altar
authentique	genuine
automne	autumn
autostop, faire de l'	hitchhike
autre	other

DICTIONARY

French / English

Autriche	Austria
aux urgences	emergency room
avaler	swallow (v)
avant	before
avec	with
avenir	future
avion	plane
avion, par	air mail
avocat	lawyer
avoir	have
avoir besoin de	need (v)
avoir sommeil	sleepy
avortement	abortion
avril	April

B

bac	ferry
bagage	baggage
bagage en cabine	carry-on luggage
bague	ring (n)
baignoire	bathtub
bain	bath
baiser	kiss (n, v)
balcon	balcony
balle	ball
banane	banana
bandage adhésif	Band-Aid
banque	bank
barbe	beard
bas	low
bas, en	down
basket	basketball
baskettes	tennis shoes
bateau	boat
bâtiment	building
batterie	battery

bavoir	bib
beau	handsome
beaucoup	much; many
beaume pour les lèvres	lip salve
beau-père	father-in-law
bébé	baby
Belgique	Belgium
belle	beautiful
belle-mère	mother-in-law
besoin de, avoir	need (v)
bibliothèque	library
bien	good
bientôt	soon
bienvenue	welcome
bière	beer
bijouterie	jewelry shop
bijoux	jewelry
billet	ticket
bizarre	strange
blague	joke (n)
blanc	white
blessé	injured
bleu	blue
blonde	blond
blush	blush (makeup)
boeuf	beef
boire	drink (v)
bois	wood
boisson	drink (n)
boîte	box
boîte de conserve	can (n)
bol	bowl
bombe	bomb
bombe contre les insectes	insect repellant
bon	fine (good); valid

bon marché	cheap
bonbon	candy
bonheur	happiness
bonjour	hello, good day
bonne santé	healthy
bottes	boots
bouche	mouth
bouchon	cork
bouchon pour le lavabo	sink stopper
boucle d'oreille	earrings
bougies	sparkplugs
bouilli	boiled
bouilloire	kettle
boulangerie	bakery
boules quiès	earplugs
boulot	job
bouteille	bottle
boutique	clothing boutique
boutique de souvenirs	souvenir shop
bouton	button
boutons	rash
bracelet	bracelet
bras	arm
briquet	lighter (n)
broche	brooch
bronzage	suntan (n)
brosse	hairbrush
brosse à dents	toothbrush
brouillard	fog
bruillant	noisy
brûlure	burn (n)
brun	brown
bruyant	loud
bureau	office
bus	city bus

C

cabine téléphonique	phone booth
cachot	dungeon
cadeau	gift
cafards	cockroach
café	coffee; coffee shop
caisse	cashier
calendrier	calendar
calepin	notebook
calmant	pain killer
camp, lit de	cot
camping-car	R.V.
canoë	canoe
canot	rowboat
capitaine	captain
car	long-distance bus
carafe	carafe
caroussel des bagages	baggage claim
carrefour	intersection
carte	card; menu; map
carte de crédit	credit card
carte de visite	business card
carte postale	postcard
carte téléphonique	telephone card
cascade	waterfall
casquette	cap
cassette	tape (cassette)
cathédrale	cathedral
catholique	Catholic (adj)
caution	deposit
cave	cellar
ce soir	tonight
ceinture	belt

célibataire	single	chaussures de tennis	tennis shoes
cendrier	ashtray		
centre	center	chef	boss
centre commercial	shopping mall	chemin de fer	railway
		chemise	shirt
centre-ville	downtown	chemise de nuit	nightgown
céramique	ceramic	chèque	check
chaire	pulpit	chèque de voyage	travelers check
chaise	chair		
chaise haute	high chair	cher	expensive
chambre	room	cheval	horse
chambre libre	vacancy (hotel)	chevalier	knight
champ	field	cheveux	hair
championnat	championship	cheveux, coupe de	haircut
chance	luck	cheville	ankle
chandelle	candle	chien	dog
change	change (n); exchange (n)	chinois	Chinese
		chocolat	chocolate
changer	change (v)	choeur	choir
chanson	song	chômage, au	unemployed
chanter	sing	chose	thing
chanteur	singer	chose, quelque	something
chapeau	hat	chrétien	Christian (adj)
chapelle	chapel	ciel	sky; heaven
chaque	each, every	cigarette	cigarette
charcuterie-traiteur	delicatessen	cinéma	cinema
		cintre	coat hanger
charmant	charming	circulation	traffic
chat	cat	ciseaux	scissors
château	castle	clair	clear
chaud	hot	classe	class
chauffage	heat (n)	classe, deuxième	second class
chauffer	heat (v)	classe, première	first class
chauffeur	driver	classique	classical
chaussettes	socks	clef	key
chaussons	slippers	clignotant	turn signal
chaussures	shoes	climatisé	air-conditioned

French	English
clinique médicale	medical clinic
cloches	bells
cloître	cloister
cochon	pig
code	PIN code
code postal	zip code
coeur	heart
coiffeur	barber, barber shop
coiffeur pour dames	beauty salon
coin	corner
coincé	stuck
colis	package
collants	nylons (pantyhose)
collier	necklace
colline	hill
combattre	fight (v)
combien	how many, how much
commencer	begin
comment	how
compagne	company
compartiment privé	sleeper (train)
complet	no vacancy
compliqué	complicated
composter	validate
comprendre	understand
comptable	accountant
compteur	taxi meter
concert	concert
conducteur	conductor
conduire	drive (v)
confirmer	confirm
confiserie	sweets shop
confortable	comfortable, cozy

French	English
congestion	congestion (sinus)
conserve, boîte de	can (n)
consigne	lockers
constipation	constipation
contagieux	contagious
contraceptif	contraceptive
coquille	shell
corde	rope
corde à linge	clothesline
corps	body
correspondance	connection, transfer (n) (train)
correspondance, prendre une	transfer (v)
corruption	corruption
costume de bain	swimsuit
côte	coast
coton	cotton
cou	neck
couche	diaper
coucher de soleil	sunset
couchette	berth (train)
coude	elbow
couleurs	colors
couloir	aisle
coup de soleil	sunburn
coupable	guilty
coupe de cheveux	haircut
courir	run (v)
courrier	mail (n)
courroie du ventilateur	fan belt
court	short
couteau	knife
coûter	cost (v)
couverture	blanket
craindre	fear (v)

crampes	cramps
crampes de menstruation	menstrual cramps
crayon	pencil
crayon pour les yeux	eyeliner
crème	cream
crème à raser	shaving cream
crème antiseptique	first-aid cream
crème chantilly	whipped cream
crème hydratante	moisturizer
crème pour les mains	hand lotion
croix	cross
cru	raw
crypte	crypt
cuillère	spoon
cuir	leather
cuisine	kitchen
cuisinier	cook (v)
cuisse	thigh
cuivre	copper
cuivre jaune	brass
cure-dent	toothpick

D

d'accord	agree; O.K.
dames	women
dangereux	dangerous
dans	in
danser	dance (v)
de	of; from
de l'herbe	marijuana
décembre	December

déclarer	declare (customs)
décongestant	decongestant
dedans	inside
déjà	already
délicieux	delicious
demain	tomorrow
demain, après	day after tomorrow
demander	ask
démangeaison	itch (n)
démocratie	democracy
dent	tooth
dentelle	lace
dentifrice	toothpaste
dentiste	dentist
dents	teeth
dents, mal aux	toothache
dépanneur	tow truck
départs	departures
dépêcher (se)	hurry (v)
dépenser	spend
déranger	disturb
dernier	last (adj.)
derrière	behind
désinfectant	disinfectant
désodorisant	deodorant
désolé	sorry
dessus, au	above
détester	hate (v)
deuxième	second
deuxième classe	second class
déviation	detour (n)
diabète	diabetes
diabétique	diabetic
diamant	diamond
diaphragme	diaphragm (birth control)

diarrhée	diarrhea
dictionnaire	dictionary
Dieu	God
difficile	difficult
dimanche	Sunday
dîner	dinner; dine
direct	direct
directeur	manager
disque compact	compact disc
dissolvant	nail polish remover
distributeur automatique	cash machine
divorcé	divorced
docteur	doctor
doigt	finger
dôme	dome
dommage, quel	it's a pity
donner	give
dormir	sleep (v)
dortoire	dormitory
dos	back
douane	customs
douche	shower
douleur	pain
doux	sweet; mild
douzaine	dozen
drapeau	flag
draps	sheets
droit	straight
droite	right (direction)
drôle	funny
dur	hard; tough

E

eau	water
eau du robinet	tap water
eau minérale	mineral water
eau potable	drinkable water
échelle	ladder
école	school
écouter	listen
écrire	write
éducation	education
église	church
elle	she; her
email, adresse	email address
emballer	wrap (v)
emplacement	campsite
emploi	occupation
empoisonement alimentaire	food poisoning
emporter	take out (food)
emprunter	borrow
en	in; by (train, car, etc.)
en bas	down
en haut	up; upstairs
en panne	broken
en plein air	outdoors
en sécurité	safe
enceinte	pregnant
encore	again; more
enfants	children
enflure	swelling (n)
ensemble	together
ensoleillé	sunny
entendre	hear
enterrement	funeral
entrée	entrance
enveloppe	envelope
envoyer	send
épais	thick
épaule	shoulder

DICTIONARY

French / English

épicerie	grocery store
épilepsie	epilepsy
épingle	pin (n)
épingle à nourrice	safety pin
épuisé	exhausted
équipe	team
équitation	horse riding
erreur	mistake (n)
érythème fessier	diaper rash
escalier	stairs
Espagne	Spain
espoir	hope
essence	fuel
essuie-glace	windshield wiper
est	is; east
estomac	stomach
estomac, mal à l'	stomachache
et	and
étage	story (floor)
état	state (n)
États-Unis	United States
été	summer
éternuer	sneeze (v)
étoile	star (in sky)
étranger	foreign
étroit	narrow
étudiant	student
exactement	exactly
excuse	apology
exemple	example
expliquer	explain

F

fâché	angry
facile	easy
faim	hungry

faire	make (v)
faire bronzer (se)	sunbathe
faire du ski	ski (v)
fait à la maison	homemade
falaise	cliff
fameux	famous
famille	family
fantastique	fantastic
fatigué	tired
fausse couche	miscarriage
fauteuil roulant, accessible à un	wheelchair-accessible
faux	false
félicitations	congratulations
femelle	female
femme	woman, wife
femme de sciences	female scientist
fenêtre	window
ferme	farm (n)
fermé	closed
fermer à clef	lock (v)
fermeture éclair	zipper
fermier	farmer
fesses	buttocks
feu	fire; stoplight
feux arrières	tail lights
feux d'artifices	fireworks
février	February
ficelle	string (n)
fièvre	fever
fil	thread (n)
fil dentaire	dental floss
fille	girl; daughter
film	movie
fils	son
fini	over (finished)

finir	finish (v)
flash	flash (camera)
fleur	flower
fois, une	once
fond	bottom
fond de teint	foundation (makeup)
fond de teint compact	face powder
fontaine	fountain
football	soccer
football américain	American football
fort	strong
fossé	moat
foule	crowd (n)
four	oven
fourchette	fork
fraîche	fresh
frais	cool
français	French
freins	brakes
frère	brother
frissons	chills
froid	cold (adj)
fromage	cheese
fromagerie	cheese shop
frontière	border (n)
fruit	fruit
fruits de mer	seafood
fumée	smoke (n)
fumeur	smoking
fumeur, non	non-smoking
fusibles	fuses
fusil	gun

G

gallerie	gallery
gallerie d'art	art gallery
gants	gloves
garçon	boy; waiter
garder	keep
gare routière	bus station
garer	park (v)
gauche	left
gaze	gauze
gênant	embarrassing
généreux	generous
genou	knee
gens	people
gens âgés	seniors
gilet	vest
glace	ice cream
glaçons	ice
glissant	slippery
gomme	eraser
gorge	throat
gorge, mal à la	sore throat
gothique	Gothic
goût	taste (n)
goûter	taste (v)
grain de beauté	moleskin
graisseux	greasy
grammaire	grammar
grand	big; tall
grand magasin	department store
grande route	highway
Grande-Bretagne	Great Britain
grand-mère	grandmother
grand-père	grandfather
grasse, matière	fat (n)
gratuit	free (no cost); toll-free

Grèce	Greece
grippe	flu
gris	gray
gros	fat (adj)
grossesse	pregnancy
grotte	cave
guarantie	guarantee (n)
guerre	war
guide	guide; guidebook
guide audio	audioguide
guitare	guitar
gymnastique	gymnastics
gynécologue	gynecologist

H

hachisch	hash
haleine	breath
handicapé	handicapped
haut	high
haut, en	up; upstairs
hémorroïdes	hemorrhoids
herbe	marijuana
heure	hour
heure, à l'	on time
heures d'ouverture	opening hours
heureux	happy
hier	yesterday
histoire	history
hiver	winter
homme	man
homme de sciences	male scientist
hommes	men
homosexuel	gay
honnête	honest
hôpital	hospital

horaire	timetable
horloge	clock
horrible	horrible
hors taxe	duty free
hors d'oeuvre	appetizer
hôtel	hotel
huile	oil
huile solaire	sunscreen
humide	muggy
hydroptère	hydrofoil
hypertension	high blood pressure

I

ici	here
il	he
île	island
immédiatement	immediately
imperméable	raincoat
importé	imported
impressionniste	Impressionist
imprimer	print
inclus	included
inconscient	unconscious
incroyable	incredible
indépendant	independent
indiquer	point (v)
industrie	industry
infection urinarire	urinary infection
infirmière	nurse
inflation	inflammation
ingénieur	engineer
insecte	insect
insolation	sunstroke
inspection des bagages	baggage check

French / English

DICTIONARY

interdit	prohibited
intéressant	interesting
intestins	intestines
invité	guest
Irlande	Ireland
Italie	Italy
ivre	drunk

J

jamais	never
jambe	leg
janvier	January
jardin	garden
jardinage	gardening
jaune	yellow
je	I
jeter	throw (v)
jeton	token
jeu	game
jeu de cartes	cards (deck)
jeudi	Thursday
jeune	young
jeunes	youths
jeunesse, auberge de	youth hostel
jeux, parc avec des	playground
joint	joint (marijuana)
jolie	pretty
jouer	play (v); athlete
jouet	toy
jour	day
jour férié	holiday
journal	newspaper
juif	Jewish
juillet	July
juin	June

jumeaux	twins
jupe	skirt
jupon	slip (n)
jus	juice
juste	fair (just)

L

la pilule	birth control pill
lac	lake
lacets	shoelaces
laid	ugly
laine	wool
lait nettoyant	face cleanser
lait pour bébé	baby formula
laiton	pewter
lampe de poche	flashlight
langue	language
lapin	rabbit
lavabo	sink
laver	wash (v)
laverie	launderette
laxatif	laxative
le meilleur	best
le pire	worst
lent	slow
lentilles de contact	contact lenses
lessive	laundry detergent
lettre	letter
lèvre	lip
l'heure, à	on time
librairie	book shop
libre	vacant
libre service	self-service
lieu de, au	instead
ligne aérienne	airline
lin	linen

DICTIONARY

French / English

liquide	cash
liquide de transmission	transmission fluid
liste	list
lit	bed
lit de camp	cot
litre	liter
lits superposés	bunk beds
livre	book (n)
loin	far
lotion solaire	suntan lotion
louer	rent (v)
lourd	heavy
lumière	light (n)
lundi	Monday
lune	moon
lune de miel	honeymoon
lunettes	glasses (eye)
lunettes de soleil	sunglasses
lutte	fight (n)

M

ma	my
machine à laver	washer
machine à sécher	dryer
machoire	jaw
Madame	Mrs.
Mademoiselle	Miss
magasin	shop (n), store
magasin d'antiquités	antiques shop
magasin de jouets	toy store
magasin de photo	camera shop
magasin de photocopie	photocopy shop
magasin de portables	cell phone shop
magasin de vêtements	clothing boutique
magnétoscope	video recorder
mai	May
maigre	skinny
maillot de bain	swim trunks
main	hand
maintenant	now
mais	but
maison	house
maison de la presse	newsstand
maison, fait à la	homemade
mal à la gorge	sore throat
mal à l'estomac	stomachache
mal aux dents	toothache
mal aux oreilles	earache
mal de tête	headache
malade	sick
maladie	disease
maladie vénérienne	venereal disease
mâle	male
malentendu	misunderstanding
malheureuse-ment	unfortunately
manches	sleeves
manger	eat
maquillage	makeup
marbre	marble (material)
marchand de vin	wine shop
marché	market
marché aux fleurs	flower market
marché aux puces	flea market

French / English

DICTIONARY

marché en plein air	open-air market
marché, bon	cheap
marcher	walk (v)
mardi	Tuesday
mari	husband
mariage	wedding
marié	married
mars	March
matière grasse	fat (n)
matin	morning
mauvais	bad
maux de poitrine	chest pains
maximum	maximum
mécanicien	mechanic
médicament pour la diarrhée	diarrhea medicine
médicaments	medicine
médiéval	medieval
meilleur	better
meilleur, le	best
mélange	mix (n)
même	same
mensonges	lies
mer	sea
merci	thanks
mercredi	Wednesday
mère	mother
mesdames	ladies
messe	church service
métal	metal
météo	weather forecast
Métro	subway
meubles	furniture
midi	noon
migraine	migraine
militaire	military

mince	thin
minuit	midnight
miroir	mirror
mode	fashion; style
moderne	modern
mois	month
mon	my
monastère	monastery
monde	world
monsieur	gentleman; sir
Monsieur	Mr.
montagne	mountain
montre	watch (n)
montrer	show (v)
moquette	carpet
morceau	piece
mort	dead
mosquée	mosque
mot	word
motocyclette	motorcycle
mouchoirs en papier	facial tissue
mouillé	wet
mourir	die
moustache	moustache
moustique	mosquito
moyen	medium
mûr	ripe
musée	museum
musique	music
musulman	Muslim (n, adj)
mycose	athlete's foot

N

nager	swim
nationalité	nationality
nature	nature

naturel	natural
nausée	nausea
navire	ship (n)
nécessaire	necessary
néoclassique	Neoclassical
nerveux	nervous
neveu	nephew
nez	nose
nièce	niece
Noël	Christmas
noir	black
nom	name
non	no
non fumeur	non-smoking
nord	north
normale	normal
nourriture	food
nourriture pour bébé	baby food
nous	we; us
nouveau	new
novembre	November
nu	naked
nuageux	cloudy
nuit	night
nylon	nylon (material)

O

occupé	occupied
océan	ocean
octobre	October
odeur	smell (n)
oeil	eye
oiseau	bird
Olympiques	Olympics
ombre à paupières	eye shadow

oncle	uncle
ongle	fingernail
opéra	opera
opticien	optician
or	gold
ordinateur	computer
ordonnance	prescription
oreille	ear
oreiller	pillow
oreilles, mal aux	earache
orgue	organ
orteil	toe
ou	or
où	where
oublier	forget
ouest	west
oui	yes
ouvert	open (adj)
ouvre-boîte	can opener
ouvrir	open (v)

P

pain	bread
paix	peace
palais	palace
panne, en	broken
panneau	sign
pannier	basket
pansement élastique	support bandage
pantalon	pants
papa	dad
papeterie	office supplies store
papier	paper
papier hygiénique	toilet paper
Pâques	Easter
par avion	air mail

paradis	heaven
parapluie	umbrella
parc	park (garden); playpen
parc avec des jeux	playground
parce que	because
pardon	excuse me
paresseux	lazy
parfait	perfect
parfum	flavor (n); perfume
parking	parking lot
parler	talk
partir	leave
pas	not
passager	passenger
passé	past
passeport	passport
passer	go through
pastille	cough drop
paté de maisons	block (street)
patinage	skating
patins à roulettes	roller skates
pâtisserie	pastry shop
pauvre	poor
payer	pay
pays	country
Pays-Bas	Netherlands
péage	toll
peau	skin
pêcher	fish (v)
pédalo	paddleboat
peigne	comb (n)
peignoir de bain	bathrobe
pénis	penis
penser	think
perdu	lost
père	father

Père Noël	Santa Claus
période	period (time)
personne	person
pétillant	fizzy
petit	small
petit déjeuner	breakfast
petite-fille	granddaughter
petit-fils	grandson
peu	few
peur	afraid
peut-être	maybe
phares	headlights
pharmacie	pharmacy
photocopie	photocopy (n)
pièces	coins
pied	foot
piéton	pedestrian
pilule	pill
pilule, la	birth control pill
pince à épiler	tweezers
pince à linge	clothes pins
pince à ongles	nail clipper
pinces	pliers
piquant	spicy
pique-nique	picnic (n)
piquets de tente	tent pegs
pire	worse
pire, le	worst
piscine	swimming pool
place	square (town); seat
plage	beach
plaindre (se)	complain
plaisant	nice
plaît, s'il vous	please
plan du Métro	subway map
planche à voile	windsurfing
planche de surf	surfboard

plante	plant	poussée	teething (baby)
plastique	plastic	des dents	
plein air, en	outdoors	pousser	push
pleurer	cry (v)	poussette	stroller
pluie	rain (n)	pouvoir	can (v); power
plus tard	later	pratique	practical
pneu	tire	premier	first
pneumonie	pneumonia	première classe	first class
poche	pocket	premiers secours	first aid
poids	weight	prendre	take
poignée	handle (n)	prendre une	transfer (v)
poignet	wrist	correspondance	(train)
point	dot (computer)	près	near
poisson	fish (n)	préservatif	condom
poitrine	chest	presque	approximately
poitrine, maux de	chest pains	prêt	ready
politiciens	politicians	prêter	lend
pomme	apple	prêtre	priest
pompe	pump (n)	principal	main
pont	bridge	printemps	spring
porc	pork	privé	private
porcelaine	porcelain	prix	price
port	harbor	problème	problem
portable	cell phone	problème	heart condition
porte	door	cardiaque	
portefeuille	wallet	prochain	next
porter	carry	produits	handicrafts
posséder	own (v)	artisanaux	
potable, eau	drinkable water	professeur	teacher
poul	pulse	propre	clean (adj)
poulet	chicken	propriétaire	owner
poumons	lungs	prospérer	prosper
poupée	doll	prudent	careful
pour	for	publique	public
pourcentage	percent	puce	flea
pourquoi	why	puissant	powerful
pourri	rotten	pullover	sweater

Q

quai	platform (train)
qualité	quality
quand	when
quart	quarter (¼)
que	what
quel dommage	it's a pity
quelque chose	something
quelques	some
queue	tail
qui	who
quiès, boules	earplugs
quincaillerie	hardware store

R

racisme	racism
radeau	raft
radiateur	radiator
radio	radio; X-ray
rasage, après	aftershave
rasoir	razor
réceptioniste	receptionist
recette	recipe
recevoir	receive
reçu	receipt
réduction	discount (n)
réfugiés	refugees
regarder	look, watch (v)
régional	local
règles	period (woman's)
réhausseur	booster seat
reine	queen
relaxation	relaxation
relique	relic
remboursement	refund (n)
remède contre le rhume	cold medicine
remparts	foritifed wall
remplir	refill (v)
renaissance	Renaissance
rendez-vous	appointment
réparer	repair (v)
répéter	repeat (v)
réponse	answer (n)
reposer (se)	relax (v)
reproduction	copy (n)
Republique Tchéque	Czech Republic
réservation	reservation
reserver	reserve
retardement	delay (n)
retraite, à la	retired
rêve	dream (n)
réveille-matin	alarm clock
réveiller (se)	wake up
rêver	dream (v)
revoir, au	goodbye
rhume	cold (n)
rhume des foins	hay fever
riche	rich
rien	nothing
rire	laugh (v)
rivière	river
robe	dress (n)
robinet	faucet
robinet, eau du	tap water
robuste	sturdy
rocade	ring road
rocher	rock (n)
roi	king
romanesque	Romanesque
romantique	romantic; Romantic
rondpoint	roundabout

ronfler	snore (v)
rose	pink
roue	wheel
rouge	red
rouge à joues	blush (makeup)
rouge à lèvres	lipstick
routière, gare	bus station
rue	street
ruines	ruins
ruisseau	stream (n)
Russie	Russia

S

sac	bag, purse
sac à dos	backpack
sac de couchage	sleeping bag
sac en plastique	plastic bag
sac en plastique à fermeture	Ziplock bag
saignement	bleeding
sale	dirty
salle	hall (big room)
salle d'attente	waiting room
salle de bains	bathroom
salut	hi
samedi	Saturday
sandales	sandals
sang	blood
sans	without
santé	health
Santé!	Cheers!
santé, en bonne	healthy
sauf	except
sauter	jump (v)
sauvage	wild
sauver	save (computer)

savoir	know
savon	soap
scandaleux	scandalous
Scandinavie	Scandinavia
scotch	scotch tape
sculpteur	sculptor
sculpture	sculpture
se dépêcher	hurry (v)
se faire bronzer	sunbathe
se plaindre	complain
se reposer	relax (v)
se réveiller	wake up
se souvenir	remember
seau	bucket
sec	dry (adj)
sécher	dry (v)
secours	help (n)
sécurité, en	safe
seins	breast
semaine	week
semblable	similar
sens unique	one way (street)
séparé	separate (adj)
septembre	September
sérieux	serious
serré	tight
serrure	lock (n)
serveuse	waitress
serviable	helpful
serviette	napkin
serviette de bain	towel
serviettes hygiéniques	sanitary napkins
seule	alone
seulement	only
sexe	sex
sexy	sexy

shampooing	shampoo
short	shorts
si	if
SIDA	AIDS
siècle	century
siège voiture	car seat (baby)
signe arobase	"at" sign (@)
s'il vous plaît	please
simple, aller	one way (ticket)
site web	website
ski	skiing
ski nautique	waterskiing
slip	underwear
sobriquet	nickname
soeur	sister
soie	silk
soif	thirsty
soir	evening
soir, ce	tonight
soirée	party (n)
solaire, huile	sunscreen
solaire, lotion	suntan lotion
solde	sale
soleil	sun; sunshine
soleil, coucher de	sunset
soleil, coup de	sunburn
soleil, lunettes de	sunglasses
sombre	dark
sommeil, avoir	sleepy
sortie	exit (n)
sortie de secours	emergency exit
soudain	suddenly
souffrir	suffer
souhaiter	wish (v)
souligne	underscore (_)
sourire	smile (v)

sous	under; below
sous vêtements	underwear
sous-sol	basement
soutien-gorge	bra
souvenir (se)	remember
spécialement	especially
spécialité	specialty
spectacle	show (n)
standardiste	operator
station de Métro	subway station
station de service	gas station
stoned	stoned
stupide	stupid
stylo	pen
sud	south
suggérer	recommend
Suisse	Switzerland
super	great
supermarché	supermarket
supplément	supplement
sur	on
surfeur	surfer
synthétique	synthetic

T

tableau	painting
taille	size; waist
talc	talcum powder
tante	aunt
tapis	rug
tard	late
tard, plus	later
tasse	cup
taxe	tax
taxe, hors	duty free

teinture d'iode	iodine
télécharge	download (n)
téléphone	telephone
télévision	television
température	temperature
tempête	storm
temps	weather
tendre	tender (adj.)
tennis	tennis
tente	tent
terre	earth
terroristes	terrorists
test de grossesse	pregnancy test
testicules	testicles
tête	head
tête, mal de	headache
tétine	pacifier
théâtre	theater; play (n)
thermomètre	thermometer
tiède	lukewarm
timbre	stamp
timide	shy
tire-bouchon	corkscrew
tirer	pull
tiret	hyphen (-)
tissu	cloth
toilette	toilet
toit	roof
tomber	fall (v)
tongues	flip-flops
tôt	early
total	total
toucher	touch (v)
toujours	always
tour	tour; tower
touriste	tourist

tournevis	screwdriver
tousser	cough (v)
tout	everything
toux	cough (n)
traditionnel	traditional
traduire	translate
train	train
tranche	slice (n)
transpirer	sweat (v)
travail	work (n)
travailler	work (v)
travaux	construction (sign)
travers, à	through
trépied	tripod
très	very
trésorerie	treasury
triste	sad
trombone	paper clip
trop	too (much)
trou	hole
tu	you (informal)
tuba	snorkel
tuer	kill (v)
Turquie	Turkey

U

une fois	once
univiersité	university
urèthre	urethra
urgence	emergency
urgences, aux	emergency room
urgent	urgent
usine	factory
utérus	uterus
utiliser	use (v)

V

vacances	vacation
vache	cow
vagin	vagina
valise	suitcase
vallée	valley
végétarien	vegetarian (n)
vélo	bicycle
vélomoteur	motor scooter
velours	velvet
vendre	sell
vendredi	Friday
venir	come
vent	wind (n)
venteux	windy
vernis à ongles	nail polish
verre	glass
vert	green
vertige	dizziness
vessie	bladder
veste	jacket
vêtements	clothes
veuf	widower
veuve	widow
viande	meat
vide	empty
vidéo	video
vie	life
vieux	old
vignoble	vineyard
village	town
ville	city
vin	wine
viol	rape (n)
violet	purple
visage	face

visite	visit (n)
visite guidée	guided tour
visiter	visit (v)
vitamines	vitamins
vitesse	speed
voie	track (train)
voile	sailing
voilier	sailboat
voir	see
voiture	car; train car
voiture restaurant	dining car (train)
voix	voice
vol	flight
volé	robbed
voler	fly (v)
voleur	thief
vomir	vomit (v)
vouloir	want (v)
vous	you (formal)
voyage	trip
voyage, agence de	travel agency
voyage, chèque de	travelers check
voyager	travel
voyageurs	travelers
vue	view (n)

W

wagon-lit	sleeper car (train)

Z

zéro	zero
zoo	zoo

ENGLISH/FRENCH

A

abortion	avortement
above	au dessus
abstract	abstrait
abuse (v)	abuser
accident	accident
accountant	comptable
adapter, electrical	adaptateur électrique
address	adresse
address, email	adresse email
adult	adulte
afraid	peur
Africa	Afrique
after	après
afternoon	après-midi
aftershave	après rasage
afterwards	après
again	encore
age	âge
aggressive	aggressif
agnostic	agnostique
agree	d'accord
AIDS	SIDA
air	air
air mail	par avion
air-conditioned	climatisé
airline	ligne aérienne
airport	aéroport
aisle	couloir
alarm clock	réveille-matin
alcohol	alcool
allergic	allergique
allergies	allergies
alone	seule
already	déjà
altar	autel
always	toujours
ambulance	ambulance
ancestor	ancêtre
ancient	ancien
and	et
angry	fâché
animal	animal
ankle	cheville
another	encore
answer	réponse
antacid	anti-acide
antibiotic	antibiotique
antiques	antiquités
antiques shop	magasin d'antiquités
apartment	appartement
apology	excuses
appetizer	hors d'oeuvre
apple	pomme
appointment	rendez-vous
approximately	presque
April	avril
arm	bras
arrivals	arrivées
arrive	arriver
art	art
art gallery	gallerie d'art
Art Nouveau	art nouveau
arthritis	arthrite
artificial	artificial
artist	artiste
ashtray	cendrier

English / French

DICTIONARY

ask	demander
aspirin	aspirine
asthma	asthme
at	à
"at" sign (@)	signe arobase
atheist	athée
athlete	jouer
athlete's foot	mycose
attractive	attirant
audioguide	guide audio
August	août
aunt	tante
Austria	Autriche
autumn	automne

B

baby	bébé
baby booster seat	réhausseur
baby car seat	siège voiture
baby food	nourriture pour bébé
baby formula	lait pour bébé
babysitter	babysitter
babysitting service	service de babysitting
back	dos
backpack	sac à dos
bad	mauvais
bag	sac
bag, plastic	sac en plastique
bag, Ziplock	sac en plastique à fermeture
baggage	bagages
baggage check	inspection des bagages
baggage claim	carousel des bagages
bakery	boulangerie

balcony	balcon
ball	balle
banana	banane
bandage	bandage
bandage, support	pansement élastique
Band-Aid	bandage adhésif
bank	banque
barber	coiffeur
barber shop	coiffeur
baseball	baseball
basement	sous-sol
basket	pannier
basketball	basket
bath	bain
bathrobe	peignoir de bain
bathroom	salle de bain
bathtub	baignoire
battery	batterie
beach	plage
beard	barbe
beautiful	belle
beauty salon	coiffeur pour dames
because	parce que
bed	lit
bedbugs	insectes
bedroom	chambre
bedsheet	draps
beef	boeuf
beer	bière
before	avant
begin	commencer
behind	derrière
Belgium	Belgique
bells	cloches
below	sous

belt	ceinture	**boutique,**	boutique; magasin
berth (train)	couchette	**clothing**	de vêtements
best	le meilleur	**bowl**	bol
better	meilleur	**box**	boîte
bib	bavoir	**boy**	garçon
bicycle	vélo	**bra**	soutien-gorge
big	grand	**bracelet**	bracelet
bill (payment)	addition	**brakes**	freins
bird	oiseau	**brass**	cuivre jaune
birth control pill	la pilule	**bread**	pain
birthday	anniversaire	**breakfast**	petit déjeuner
black	noir	**breast**	seins
bladder	vessie	**breath**	haleine
blanket	couverture	**bridge**	pont
bleeding	saignement	**briefs**	slip
blisters	ampoules	**broken**	en panne
block (street)	paté de maisons	**bronze**	bronze
blond	blonde	**brooch**	broche
blood	sang	**brother**	frère
blood	hypertension	**brown**	brun
pressure, high		**bucket**	seau
blue	bleu	**building**	bâtiment
blush	blush, rouge à joues	**bulb, light**	ampoule
(makeup)		**bunk beds**	lits superposés
boat	bateau	**burn (n)**	brûlure
body	corps	**bus**	bus
boiled	bouilli	**bus station**	gare routière
bomb	bombe	**bus stop**	arrêt de bus
book (n)	livre	**bus, city**	bus
book shop	librairie	**bus, long-distance**	car
booster seat	réhausseur	**business**	affaires
boots	bottes	**business card**	carte de visite
border	frontière	**but**	mais
borrow	emprunter	**buttocks**	fesses
boss	chef	**button**	bouton
bottle	bouteille	**buy**	acheter
bottom	fond	**by (train, car, etc.)**	en

C

calendar	calendrier
calorie	calorie
camera	appareil-photo
camera shop	magasin de photo
camping	camping
campsite	emplacement
can (n)	boîte de conserve
can (v)	pouvoir
can opener	ouvre-boîte
Canada	Canada
canal	canal
cancel	annuler
candle	chandelle
candy	bonbon
canoe	canoë
cap	casquette
captain	capitaine
car	voiture
car (train)	voiture
car, dining (train)	voiture restaurant
car seat (baby)	siège voiture
car, sleeper (train)	wagon-lit
carafe	carafe
card	carte
card, telephone	carte téléphonique
cards (deck)	jeu de cartes
careful	prudent
carpet	moquette
carry	porter
carry-on luggage	bagage en cabine
cash	liquide
cash	distributeur

machine	automatique
cashier	caisse
cassette	cassette
castle	château
cat	chat
catch (v)	attraper
cathedral	cathédrale
Catholic (adj)	catholique
cave	grotte
cell phone	portable
cell phone shop	magasin de portables
cellar	cave
center	centre
century	siècle
ceramic	céramique
chair	chaise
championship	championnat
change (n)	change
change (v)	changer
chapel	chapelle
charming	charmant
cheap	bon marché
check	chèque
Cheers!	Santé!
cheese	fromage
cheese shop	fromagerie
chest	poitrine
chest pains	maux de poitrine
chicken	poulet
children	enfants
chills	frissons
Chinese	chinois
chocolate	chocolat
choir	choeur
Christian (adj)	chrétien
Christmas	Noël

church	église	compact disc	disque compact
church service	messe	complain	se plaindre
cigarette	cigarette	complicated	compliqué
cinema	cinéma	computer	ordinateur
city	ville	concert	concert
class	classe	conditioner (hair)	après-shampoing
classical	classique		
clean (adj)	propre	condom	préservatif
clear	clair	conductor	conducteur
cliff	falaise	confirm	confirmer
clinic, medical	clinique médicale	congestion (sinus)	congestion
		congratulations	félicitations
clock	horloge	connection (train)	correspondance
clock, alarm	réveille-matin		
cloister	cloître	constipation	constipation
closed	fermé	construction (sign)	travaux
cloth	tissu	contact lenses	lentilles de contact
clothes	vêtements		
clothes pins	pince à linge	contagious	contagieux
clothesline	corde à linge	contraceptive	contraceptif
clothing boutique	boutique, magasin de vêtements	cook (v)	cuisinier
		cool	frais
cloudy	nuageux	copper	cuivre
coast	côte	copy (n)	reproduction
coat hanger	cintre	copy shop	magasin de photocopie
cockroach	cafards		
coffee	café	cork	bouchon
coffee shop	café	corkscrew	tire-bouchon
coins	pièces	corner	coin
cold (adj)	froid	corridor	couloir
cold (n)	rhume	corruption	corruption
cold medicine	remède contre le rhume	cost (v)	coûter
		cot	lit de camp
colors	couleurs	cotton	coton
comb (n)	peigne	cough (n)	toux
come	venir	cough (v)	tousser
comfortable	confortable	cough drop	pastille

country	pays
countryside	compagne
cousin	cousin
cow	vache
cozy	confortable
crafts	arts
cramps	crampes
cramps, menstrual	crampes de menstruation
cream	crème
cream, first-aid	crème antiseptique
credit card	carte de crédit
cross	croix
crowd (n)	foule
cry (v)	pleurer
crypt	crypte
cup	tasse
customs	douane
Czech Republic	République Tchéque

D

dad	papa
dance (v)	danser
danger	danger
dangerous	dangereux
dark	sombre
dash (-)	tiret
daughter	fille
day	jour
day after tomorrow	après demain
dead	mort
December	décembre
declare (customs)	déclarer

decongestant	décongestant
delay (n)	retardement
delete	annuler
delicatessen	charcuterie-traiteur
delicious	délicieux
democracy	démocratie
dental floss	fil dentaire
dentist	dentiste
deodorant	désodorisant
depart	partir
department store	grand magasin
departures	départs
deposit	caution
dessert	dessert
detergent	lessive
detour (n)	déviation
diabetes	diabète
diabetic	diabétique
diamond	diamant
diaper	couche
diaper rash	érythème fessier
diaphragm (birth control)	diaphragme
diarrhea	diarrhée
diarrhea medicine	médicament pour la diarrhée
dictionary	dictionnaire
die	mourir
difficult	difficile
dine (v)	dîner
dining car (train)	voiture restaurant
dinner (n)	dîner
direct (adj)	direct
direction	direction

dirty	sale
discount (n)	réduction
disease	maladie
disease, venereal	maladie vénérienne
disinfectant	désinfectant
disturb	déranger
divorced	divorcé
dizziness	vertige
doctor	docteur
dog	chien
doll	poupée
dome	dôme
donkey	âne
door	porte
dormitory	dortoire
dot (computer)	point
double	double
down	en bas
download (n)	télécharge
downtown	centre-ville
dozen	douzaine
dream (n)	rêve
dream (v)	rêver
dress (n)	robe
drink (n)	boisson
drink (v)	boire
drive (v)	conduire
driver	chauffeur
drunk	ivre
dry (adj)	sec
dry (v)	sécher
dryer	machine à sécher
dungeon	cachot
duty free	hors taxe

E

each	chaque
ear	oreille
earache	mal aux oreilles
early	tôt
earplugs	boules quiès
earrings	boucle d'oreille
earth	terre
east	est
Easter	Pâques
easy	facile
eat	manger
education	éducation
elbow	coude
electrical adapter	adaptateur électrique
elevator	ascenseur
email	email
email address	adresse email
embarrassing	gênant
embassy	ambassade
emergency	urgence
emergency exit	sortie de secours
emergency room	aux urgences
empty	vide
engineer	ingénieur
English	anglais
enjoy	apprécier
enough	assez
entrance	entrée
entry	entrée
envelope	enveloppe
epilepsy	épilepsie
eraser	gomme
especially	spécialement

Europe	Europe
evening	soir
every	chaque
everything	tout
exactly	exactement
example	exemple
excellent	excellent
except	sauf
exchange (n)	change
excuse me	pardon
exhausted	épuisé
exit (n)	sortie
exit,	sortie de secours
emergency	
expensive	cher
explain	expliquer
eye	oeil
eye shadow	ombre à paupières
eyeliner	eyeliner, crayon
	pour les yeux

F

face	visage
face cleanser	lait nettoyant
face	fond de teint compact
powder	
facial	kleenex, mouchoirs
tissue	en papier
factory	usine
fair (just)	juste
fall (v)	tomber
false	faux
family	famille
famous	fameux
fan belt	courroie du ventilateur
fantastic	fantastique

far	loin
farm (n)	ferme
farmer	fermier
fashion	mode
fat (adj)	gros
fat (n)	matière grasse
father	père
father-in-law	beau-père
faucet	robinet
fax (n)	fax
fear (v)	craindre
February	février
female	femelle
ferry	bac
fever	fièvre
few	peu
field	champ
fight (n)	lutte
fight (v)	combattre
fine (good)	bon
finger	doigt
fingernail	ongle
finish (v)	finir
fire	feu
fireworks	feux d'artifices
first	premier
first aid	premiers secours
first class	première classe
first-aid	crème antiseptique
cream	
fish (n)	poisson
fish (v)	pêcher
fix (v)	réparer
fizzy	pétillant
flag	drapeau
flash (camera)	flash
flashlight	lampe de poche

flavor (n)	parfum
flea	puce
flea market	marché aux puces
flight	vol
flip-flops	tongues
floss, dental	fil dentaire
flower	fleur
flower market	marché aux fleurs
flu	grippe
fly (v)	voler
fog	brouillard
food	nourriture
food poisoning	empoisonement alimentaire
foot	pied
football, American	football américain
for	pour
forbidden	interdit
foreign	étranger
forget	oublier
fork	fourchette
formula (for baby)	lait pour bébé
foundation (makeup)	fond de teint
fountain	fontaine
fragile	fragile
free (no cost)	gratuit
French	français
fresh	fraîche
Friday	vendredi
friend	ami
friendship	amitié
Frisbee	frisbee
from	de

fruit	fruit
fuel	essence
fun	amusement
funeral	enterrement
funny	drôle
furniture	meubles
fuses	fusibles
future	avenir

G

gallery	gallerie
game	jeu
garage	garage
garden	jardin
gardening	jardinage
gas station	station de service
gauze	gaze
gay	homosexuel
generous	généreux
gentleman	monsieur
genuine	authentique
Germany	Allemagne
gift	cadeau
girl	fille
give	donner
glass (drinking)	verre
glasses (eye)	lunettes
gloves	gants
go	aller
go through	passer
God	Dieu
gold	or
golf	golf
good	bien
good day	bonjour
goodbye	au revoir

Gothic	gothique
grammar	grammaire
granddaughter	petite-fille
grandfather	grand-père
grandmother	grand-mère
grandson	petit-fils
gray	gris
greasy	graisseux
great	super
Great Britain	Grande-Bretagne
Greece	Grèce
green	vert
grocery store (n)	épicerie
guarantee	guarantie
guest	invité
guide (n)	guide
guidebook	guide
guided tour	visite guidée
guilty	coupable
guitar	guitare
gum	chewing-gum
gun	fusil
gymnastics	gymnastique
gynecologist	gynécologue

H

hair	cheveux
hairbrush	brosse
haircut	coupe de cheveux
hall (big room)	salle
hand	main
hand lotion	crème pour les mains
handicapped	handicapé
handicrafts	produits artisanaux
handle (n)	poignée
handsome	beau

happiness	bonheur
happy	heureux
harbor	port
hard	dur
hardware store	quincaillerie
hash	hachisch
hat	chapeau
hate (v)	détester
have	avoir
hay fever	rhume des foins
he	il
head	tête
headache	mal de tête
headlights	phares
health	santé
health insurance	assurance maladie
healthy	en bonne santé
hear	entendre
heart	coeur
heart condition	problème cardiaque
heat (n)	chauffage
heat (v)	chauffer
heaven	ciel
heavy	lourd
hello	bonjour
help (n)	secours
help (v)	aider
helpful	serviable
hemorrhoids	hémorroïdes
her	elle
here	ici
hi	salut
high	haut
high blood pressure	hypertension

high chair	chaise haute	ill	malade
highway	grande route	immediately	immédiatement
hill	colline	important	important
history	histoire	imported	importé
hitchhike	autostop	impossible	impossible
hobby	hobby	Impressionist	impressionniste
hockey	hockey	in	en; dans
hole	trou	included	inclus
holiday	jour férié	incredible	incroyable
homemade	fait à la maison	independent	indépendant
homesickness	mal de pays	indigestion	indigestion
honest	honnête	industry	industrie
honeymoon	lune de miel	infection	infection
hope (n)	espoir	infection, urinary	infection urinarire
horrible	horrible	inflammation	inflation
horse	cheval	information	information
horse riding	équitation	injured	blessé
hospital	hôpital	innocent	innocent
hot	chaud	insect	insecte
hotel	hôtel	insect repellant	bombe contre les insectes
hour	heure	inside	dedans
house	maison	instant	instant
how	comment	instead	au lieu de
how many	combien	insurance	assurance
how much ($)	combien	insurance, health	assurance maladie
hungry	faim	insured	assuré
hurry (v)	se dépêcher	intelligent	intelligent
husband	mari	interesting	intéressant
hydrofoil	hydroptère	Internet	internet
hyphen (-)	tiret	Internet access	accès internet
		Internet café	café internet
I		intersection	carrefour
I	je	intestines	intestins
ice	glaçons	invitation	invitation
ice cream	glace		
if	si		

iodine	teinture d'iode
Ireland	Irlande
is	est
island	île
Italy	Italie
itch (n)	démangeaison
it's a pity	quel dommage

J

jacket	veste
January	janvier
jaw	machoire
jeans	jeans
jewelry	bijoux
jewelry shop	bijouterie
Jewish	juif
job	boulot
jogging	jogging
joint (marijuana)	joint
joke (n)	blague
journey	voyage
juice	jus
July	juillet
jump (v)	sauter
June	juin

K

keep	garder
kettle	bouilloire
key	clef
kill (v)	tuer
kind	aimable
king	roi
kiss (n, v)	baiser
kitchen	cuisine
kitchenette	kitchenette

knee	genou
knife	couteau
knight	chevalier
know	savoir

L

lace	dentelle
ladder	échelle
ladies	mesdames
lake	lac
lamb	agneau
language	langue
large	grand
last	dernier
late	tard
later	plus tard
laugh (v)	rire
launderette	laverie
laundry soap	lessive
lawyer	avocat
laxative	laxatif
lazy	paresseux
learn	apprendre
leather	cuir
leave	partir
left	gauche
leg	jambe
lend	prêter
lenses, contact	lentilles de contact
letter	lettre
library	bibliothèque
lies	mensonges
life	vie
light (n)	lumière
light bulb	ampoule

DICTIONARY

English / French

lighter (n)	briquet	mail (n)	courrier
like	aimer bien	main	principal
linen	lin	make (v)	faire
lip	lèvre	makeup	maquillage
lip salve	beaume pour les lèvres	male	mâle
		mall (shopping)	centre commercial
lipstick	rouge à lèvres		
list (n)	liste	man	homme
listen	écouter	manager	directeur
liter	litre	many	beaucoup
little (adj)	petit	map	carte
local	régional	marble (material)	marbre
lock (n)	serrure	March	mars
lock (v)	fermer à clef	marijuana	herbe, marijuana
locker	consigne		
look (v)	regarder	market (n)	marché
lost	perdu	market, flea	marché aux puces
lotion, hand	crème pour les mains	market, flower	marché aux fleurs
loud	bruyant	market, open-air	marché en plein air
love (n)	amour		
love (v)	aimer	married	marié
lover	amant	mascara	mascara
low	bas	matches	allumettes
lozenges	pastilles	maximum	maximum
luck	chance	May	mai
luggage	bagage	maybe	peut-être
luggage, carry-on	baggage en cabine	meat	viande
		mechanic	mécanicien
lukewarm	tiède	medicine	médicaments
lungs	poumons	medicine for a cold	remède contre le rhume
		medicine, non-aspirin substitute	Tylenol
M		medieval	médiéval
macho	macho	medium	moyen
mad	fâché	men	hommes
magazine	magazine		

menstrual cramps	crampes de menstruation
menstruation	menstruation
menu	carte
message	message
metal	métal
meter, taxi	compteur
midnight	minuit
migraine	migraine
mild	doux
military	militaire
mineral water	eau minérale
minimum	minimum
minutes	minutes
mirror	miroir
miscarriage	fausse couche
Miss	Mademoiselle
mistake	erreur
misunderstanding	malentendu
mix (n)	mélange
moat	fossé
modern	moderne
moisturizer	crème hydratante
moleskin	grain de beauté
moment	moment
monastery	monastère
Monday	lundi
money	argent
month	mois
monument	monument
moon	lune
more	encore
morning	matin
mosque	mosquée
mosquito	moustique
mother	mère
mother-in-law	belle-mère

motor scooter	vélomoteur
motorcycle	motocyclette
mountain	montagne
moustache	moustache
mouth	bouche
movie	film
Mr.	Monsieur
Mrs.	Madame
much	beaucoup
muggy	humide
muscle	muscle
museum	musée
music	musique
Muslim (n, adj)	musulman
my	mon; ma

N

nail (finger)	ongle
nail clipper	pince à ongles
nail polish	vernis à ongles
nail polish remover	dissolvant
naked	nu
name	nom
napkin	serviette
narrow	étroit
nationality	nationalité
natural	naturel
nature	nature
nausea	nausée
near	près
necessary	nécessaire
neck	cou
necklace	collier
need (v)	avoir besoin de
needle	aiguille

DICTIONARY

English / French

Neoclassical	néoclassique
nephew	neveu
nervous	nerveux
Netherlands	Pays-Bas
never	jamais
new	nouveau
newspaper	journal
newsstand	maison de la presse
next	prochain
nice	plaisant
nickname	sobriquet
niece	nièce
night	nuit
nightgown	chemise de nuit
no	non
no vacancy	complet
noisy	bruillant
non-aspirin substitute	Tylenol
non-smoking	non fumeur
noon	midi
normal	normale
north	nord
nose	nez
not	pas
notebook	calepin
nothing	rien
November	novembre
now	maintenant
nurse	infirmière
nylon (material)	nylon
nylons (pantyhose)	collants

O

occupation	emploi
occupied	occupé
ocean	océan
October	octobre
of	de
offer (n)	offre
offer (v)	offrir
office	bureau
office supplies store	papeterie
oil	huile
O.K.	d'accord
old	vieux
Olympics	Olympiques
on	sur
on time	à l'heure
once	une fois
one way (street)	sens unique
one way (ticket)	aller simple
only	seulement
open (adj)	ouvert
open (v)	ouvrir
open-air market	marché en plein air
opening hours	heures d'ouverture
opera	opéra
operator	standardiste
optician	opticien
or	ou
orange	orange
organ	orgue
original	original
other	autre
outdoors	en plein air
oven	four
over (finished)	fini
own (v)	posséder
owner	propriétaire

P

pacifier	tétine
package	colis
paddleboat	pédalo
page	page
pail	seau
pain	douleur
pain killer	calmant
pains, chest	maux de poitrine
painting	tableau
pajamas	pyjama
palace	palais
panties	slip
pants	pantalon
paper	papier
paper clip	trombone
parents	parents
park (garden)	parc
park (v)	garer
parking lot	parking
party	soirée
passenger	passager
passport	passeport
past	passé
pastry shop	pâtisserie
pay	payer
peace	paix
pedestrian	piéton
pen	stylo
pencil	crayon
penis	pénis
people	gens
percent	pourcentage
perfect	parfait
perfume	parfum
period (time)	période
period (woman's)	règles

person	personne
pewter	laiton
pharmacy	pharmacie
phone booth	cabine téléphonique
phone, cellular	portable
photo	photo
photocopy (n)	photocopie
photocopy shop	magasin de photocopie
pickpocket	pickpocket
picnic	pique-nique
piece	morceau
pig	cochon
pill (n)	pilule
pill, birth control	la pilule
pillow	oreiller
pin	épingle
PIN code	code
pink	rose
pity, it's a	quel dommage
pizza	pizza
plain	simple
plane	avion
plant (n)	plante
plastic	plastique
plastic bag	sac en plastique
plate	assiette
platform (train)	quai
play (n)	théâtre
play (v)	jouer
playground	parc avec des jeux
playpen	parc
please	s'il vous plaît
pliers	pinces
pneumonia	pneumonie
pocket	poche

point (v)	indiquer
police	police
politicians	politiciens
pollution	pollution
polyester	polyester
poor	pauvre
porcelain	porcelaine
pork	porc
Portugal	Portugal
possible	possible
postcard	carte postale
poster	affiche
power	pouvoir
powerful	puissant
practical	pratique
pregnancy	grossesse
pregnancy test	test de grossesse
pregnant	enceinte
prescription	ordonnance
present (gift)	cadeau
pretty	jolie
price	prix
priest	prêtre
print (v)	imprimer
private	privé
problem	problème
profession	profession
prohibited	interdit
pronunciation	prononciation
prosper	prospérer
Protestant (adj)	protestant
public	publique
pull	tirer
pulpit	chaire
pulse	poul
pump (n)	pompe

punctual	à l'heure
purple	violet
purse	sac
push	pousser

Q

quality	qualité
quarter (¼)	quart
queen	reine
question (n)	question
quiet	silence

R

R.V.	camping-car
rabbit	lapin
racism	racisme
radiator	radiateur
radio	radio
raft	radeau
railway	chemin de fer
rain (n)	pluie
rainbow	arc-en-ciel
raincoat	imperméable
rape (n)	viol
rash	boutons
rash, diaper	érythème fessier
raw	cru
razor	rasoir
ready	prêt
receipt	reçu
receive	recevoir
receptionist	réceptioniste
recipe	recette
recommend	suggérer
rectum	rectum
red	rouge

refill (V)	à remplir de nouveau
refugees	réfugiés
refund (n)	remboursement
relax (v)	se reposer
relaxation	relaxation
relic	relique
religion	religion
remember	se souvenir
Renaissance	renaissance
rent (v)	louer
repair (v)	réparer
repeat (v)	répéter
reservation	réservation
reserve	reserver
respect	respect
retired	à la retraite
rich	riche
right (direction)	droite
ring (n)	bague
ring road	rocade
ripe	mûr
river	rivière
robbed	volé
rock (n)	rocher
roller skates	patins à roulettes
Romanesque	romanesque
Romantic (art)	romantique
romantic	romantique
roof	toit
room	chambre
rope	corde
rotten	pourri
round trip	aller-retour
roundabout	rondpoint
rowboat	canot
rucksack	sac à dos

rug	tapis
ruins	ruines
run (v)	courir
Russia	Russie

S

sad	triste
safe	en sécurité
safety pin	épingle à nourrice
sailboat	voilier
sailing	voile
saint	saint
sale	solde
same	même
sandals	sandales
sandwich	sandwich
sanitary napkins	serviettes hygiéniques
Santa Claus	Père Noël
Saturday	samedi
save (computer)	sauver
scandalous	scandaleux
Scandinavia	Scandinavie
school	école
science	science
scientist (m/f)	homme / femme de sciences
scissors	ciseaux
scotch tape	scotch
screwdriver	tournevis
sculptor	sculpteur
sculpture	sculpture
sea	mer
seafood	fruits de mer
seat	place

second	deuxième
second class	deuxième classe
secret	secret
see	voir
self-service	libre service
sell	vendre
send	envoyer
seniors	gens âgés
separate (adj)	séparé
September	septembre
serious	sérieux
service	service
service, church	messe
sex	sexe
sexy	sexy
shampoo	shampooing
shaving cream	crème à raser
she	elle
sheet	drap
shell	coquille
ship (n)	navire
shirt	chemise
shoelaces	lacets
shoes	chaussures
shoes, tennis	baskettes, chaussures de tennis
shop (n)	magasin
shop, antique	magasin d'antiquités
shop, barber	coiffeur
shop, camera	magasin de photo
shop, cell phone	magasin de portables
shop, cheese	fromagerie
shop, jewelry	bijouterie
shop, pastry	patisserie
shop, photocopy	magasin de photocopie
shop, souvenir	boutique de souvenirs
shop, sweets	confiserie
shop, wine	marchand de vin
shopping	shopping
shopping mall	centre commercial
short	court
shorts	short
shoulder	épaule
show (n)	spectacle
show (v)	montrer
shower	douche
shy	timide
sick	malade
sign	panneau
signature	signature
silence	silence
silk	soie
silver	argent
similar	semblable
simple	simple
sing	chanter
singer (male)	chanteur
single	célibataire
sink	lavabo
sink stopper	bouchon pour le lavabo
sinus problems	problèmes de sinus
sir	monsieur
sister	soeur
size	taille
skating	patinage
ski (v)	faire du ski

English	French
skiing	ski
skin	peau
skinny	maigre
skirt	jupe
sky	ciel
sleep (v)	dormir
sleeper (train)	compartiment privé
sleeper car (train)	wagon-lit
sleeping bag	sac de couchage
sleepy	avoir sommeil
sleeves	manches
slice (n)	tranche
slide (photo)	diapositive
slip (n)	jupon
slippers	chaussons
slippery	glissant
slow	lent
small	petit
smell (n)	odeur
smile (v)	sourire
smoke (n)	fumée
smoking	fumeur
snack	snack
sneeze (v)	éternuer
snore	ronfler
snorkel	tuba
soap	savon
soap, laundry	lessive
soccer	football
socks	chaussettes
some	quelques
something	quelque chose
son	fils
song	chanson
soon	bientôt

English	French
sore throat	mal à la gorge
sorry	désolé
sour	aigre
south	sud
souvenir shop	boutique de souvenirs
Spain	Espagne
sparkplug	bougies
speak	parler
specialty	spécialité
speed (n)	vitesse
spend	dépenser
spicy	piquant
spider	araignée
spoon	cuillère
sport	sport
spring	printemps
square (town)	place
stairs	escalier
stamp	timbre
stapler	agraffeuse
star (in sky)	étoile
state (n)	état
station	station
stomach	estomac
stomachache	mal à l'estomac
stoned	stoned
stop (n)	stop; arrêt
stop (v)	arrêter
stoplight	feu
stopper, sink	bouchon pour le lavabo
store (n)	magasin
store, department	grand magasin
store, hardware	quincaillerie
store, office supplies	papeterie

store, toy	magasin de jouets
storm	tempête
story (floor)	étage
straight	droit
strange	bizarre
stream (n)	ruisseau
street	rue
string	ficelle
stroller	poussette
strong	fort
stuck	coincé
student	étudiant
stupid	stupide
sturdy	robuste
style	mode
subway	Métro
subway entrance	l'entrée du Métro
subway exit	sortie
subway map	plan du Métro
subway station	station de Métro
subway stop	arrêt de Métro
suddenly	soudain
suffer	souffrir
suitcase	valise
summer	été
sun	soleil
sunbathe	se faire bronzer
sunburn	coup de soleil
Sunday	dimanche
sunglasses	lunettes de soleil
sunny	ensoleillé
sunrise	aube
sunscreen	huile solaire
sunset	coucher de soleil
sunshine	soleil

sunstroke	insolation
suntan (n)	bronzage
suntan lotion	lotion solaire
supermarket	supermarché
supplement (n)	supplément
surfboard	planche de surf
surfer	surfeur
surprise (n)	surprise
swallow (v)	avaler
sweat (v)	transpirer
sweater	pullover
sweet	doux
sweets shop	confiserie
swelling (n)	enflure
swim	nager
swim trunks	maillot de bain
swimming pool	piscine
swimsuit	costume de bain
Switzerland	Suisse
synagogue	synagogue
synthetic	synthétique

T

table	table
tail	queue
tail lights	feux arrières
take	prendre
take out (food) (v)	emporter
talcum powder	talc
talk	parler
tall	grand
tampons	tampons
tape (adhesive)	scotch
tape (cassette)	cassette
taste (n)	goût
taste (v)	goûter

tax	taxe	through	à travers
taxi	taxi	throw (v)	jeter
taxi meter	compteur	Thursday	jeudi
taxi stand	station de taxi	ticket	billet
teacher	professeur	tight	serré
team	équipe	time, on	à l'heure
teenager	adolescent	timetable	horaire
teeth	dents	tire	pneu
teething (baby)	poussée des dents	tired	fatigué
		tires	pneus
telephone	téléphone	tissue, facial	kleenex, mouchoirs en papier
telephone card	carte téléphonique	to	à
television	télévision	today	aujourd'hui
temperature	température	toe	orteil
tender (adj)	tendre	together	ensemble
tennis	tennis	toilet	toilette
tennis shoes	baskettes, chaussures de tennis	toilet paper	papier hygiénique
		token	jeton
tent	tente	toll	péage
tent pegs	piquets de tente	toll-free	gratuit
terrible	terrible	tomorrow	demain
terrorists	terroristes	tomorrow, day after	après demain
testicles	testicules		
thanks	merci	tonight	ce soir
theater	théâtre	too (much)	trop
thermometer	thermomètre	tooth	dent
thick	épais	toothache	mal aux dents
thief	voleur	toothbrush	brosse à dents
thigh	cuisse	toothpaste	dentifrice
thin	mince	toothpick	cure-dent
thing	chose	total	total
think	penser	touch (v)	toucher
thirsty	soif	tough	dur
thongs	tongues	tour	tour
thread (n)	fil	tour, guided	visite guidée
throat	gorge	tourist	touriste

DICTIONARY

English / French

tow truck	dépanneur
towel	serviette de bain
tower	tour
town	village
toy	jouet
toy store	magasin de jouets
track (train)	voie
traditional	traditionnel
traffic	circulation
train	train
train car	voiture
transfer (n)	correspondance
transfer (v)	prendre une correspondance
translate	traduire
transmission fluid	liquide de transmission
travel (v)	voyager
travel agency	agence de voyage
travelers	voyageurs
travelers check	chèque de voyage
treasury	trésorerie
tree	arbre
trip (n)	voyage
tripod	trépied
trouble	trouble
T-shirt	T-shirt
Tuesday	mardi
tunnel	tunnel
Turkey	Turquie
turn signal	clignotant
tweezers	pince à épiler
twins	jumeaux

U

ugly	laid
umbrella	parapluie
uncle	oncle
unconscious	inconscient
under	sous
underpants	slip
underscore (_)	souligne
understand	comprendre
underwear	sous vêtements
unemployed	au chômage
unfortunately	malheureusement
United States	États-Unis
university	université
up	en haut
upstairs	en haut
urethra	urèthre
urgent	urgent
urinary infection	infection urinarire
us	nous
use (v)	utiliser
uterus	utérus

V

vacancy (hotel)	chambre libre
vacant	libre
vacation	vacances
vagina	vagin
valid	bon
validate	composter
valley	vallée
Vaseline	Vaseline
vegetarian (n)	végétarien
velvet	velours

venereal disease	maladie vénérienne
very	très
vest	gilet
video	vidéo
video recorder	magnétoscope
view (n)	vue
village	village
vineyard	vignoble
violence	violence
virus	virus
visit (n)	visite
visit (v)	visiter
vitamins	vitamines
voice	voix
vomit (v)	vomir

W

waist	taille
wait (v)	attendre
waiter	garçon
waiting room	salle d'attente
waitress	serveuse
wake up	se réveiller
walk (v)	marcher
wall, fortified	remparts
wallet	portefeuille
want (v)	vouloir
war	guerre
warm (adj)	chaud
wash (v)	laver
washer	machine à laver
watch (n)	montre
watch (v)	regarder
water	eau

water, drinkable	eau potable
water, tap	eau du robinet
waterfall	cascade
waterskiing	ski nautique
we	nous
weather	temps
weather forecast	météo
website	site web
wedding	mariage
Wednesday	mercredi
week	semaine
weight	poids
welcome	bienvenue
west	ouest
wet	mouillé
what	que
wheel	roue
wheelchair-accessible	accessible à un fauteuil roulant
when	quand
where	où
whipped cream	crème chantilly
white	blanc
who	qui
why	pourquoi
widow	veuve
widower	veuf
wife	femme
wild	sauvage
wind	vent
window	fenêtre
windshield wiper	essuie-glace
windsurfing	planche à voile
windy	venteux
wine	vin

wine shop	marchand de vin
wing	aile
winter	hiver
wish (v)	souhaiter
with	avec
without	sans
women	dames
wood	bois
wool	laine
word	mot
work (n)	travail
work (v)	travailler
world	monde
worse	pire
worst	le pire
wrap	emballer
wrist	poignet
write	écrire

X

| X-ray | radio |

Y

year	année
yellow	jaune
yes	oui
yesterday	hier
you (informal)	tu
you (formal)	vous
young	jeune
youth hostel	auberge de jeunesse
youths	jeunes

Z

zero	zéro
zip code	code postal
Ziplock bag	sac en plastique à fermeture
zipper	fermeture éclair
zoo	zoo

TIPS FOR HURDLING THE LANGUAGE BARRIER

Don't Be Afraid to Communicate

Even the best phrase book won't satisfy your needs in every situation. To really hurdle the language barrier, you need to leap beyond the printed page, and dive into contact with the locals. Never allow your lack of foreign language skills to isolate you from the people and cultures you traveled halfway around the world to experience. Remember that in every country you visit, you're surrounded by expert, native-speaking tutors. Spend bus and train rides letting them teach you.

Start conversations by asking politely in the local language, "Do you speak English?" When you speak English with someone from another country, talk slowly, clearly, and with carefully chosen words. Use what the Voice of America calls "simple English." You're talking to people who are wishing it was written down, hoping to see each letter as it tumbles out of your mouth. Pronounce each letter, avoiding all contractions and slang. For bad examples, listen to other tourists.

Keep things caveman-simple. Make single nouns work as entire sentences ("Photo?"). Use internationally-understood words ("auto kaput" works in Bordeaux). Butcher the language if you must. The important thing is to make the effort. To get air mail stamps, you can flap your wings and say "tweet, tweet." If you want milk, moo and pull two imaginary udders. Risk looking like a fool.

If you're short on words, make your picnic a potluck. Pull out a map and point out your journey. Draw what you mean. Bring photos from home and introduce your family. Play cards or toss a Frisbee. Fold an origami bird for kids or dazzle 'em with sleight-of-hand magic.

Go ahead and make educated guesses. Many situations are easy-to-fake multiple choice questions. Practice. Read timetables, concert posters, and newspaper headlines. Listen to each language on a multi-lingual tour. Be melodramatic. Exaggerate the local accent. Self-consciousness is the deadliest communication killer.

Choose multilingual people to communicate with, such as students, business people, urbanites, or anyone in the tourist trade. Use a small note pad to jot down handy phrases and to help you communicate more clearly with the locals by scribbling down numbers, maps, and so on. Some travelers carry important messages written on a small card: allergic to nuts, strict vegetarian, your finest ice cream.

International Words

As our world shrinks, more and more words hop across their linguistic boundaries and become international. Savvy travelers develop a knack for choosing words most likely to be universally understood ("auto" instead of "car," "kaput" instead of "broken," "photo," not "picture"). Internationalize your pronunciation. "University," if you play around with its sound (oo-nee-vehr-see-tay), will be understood anywhere. The average American is a real flunky in this area. Be creative.

Here are a few internationally understood words. Remember, cut out the Yankee accent and give each word a pan-European sound.

Amigo	Bank	Casanova	Coke, Coca-Cola
Attila	Beer	(romantic)	Communist
(mean, crude)	Bill Gates	Central	Computer
Auto	Bon voyage	Chocolate	Disco
Autobus	Bye-bye	Ciao	Disneyland
("booos")	Camping	Coffee	(wonderland)

Elephant (big clod)	Mama mia	Passport	Stop
English ("Engleesh")	Mañana	Photo	Super
Europa	McDonald's	Photocopy	Taxi
Fascist	Michelangelo (artistic)	Picnic	Tea
Hello	Moment	Police	Telephone
Hercules (strong)	No	Post	Toilet
Hotel	No problem	Rambo	Tourist
Information	Nuclear	Restaurant	US profanity
Internet	OK	Rock 'n' roll	University
Kaput	Oo la la	Self-service	Vino
	Pardon	Sex / Sexy	Yankee,
		Sport	Americano

French Verbs

These conjugated verbs will help you assemble a caveman sentence in a pinch.

TO BE	*ÊTRE*	eh-truh
I am	*je suis*	zhuh swee
you are	*vous êtes*	vooz eht
(formal, singular or plural)		
you are	*tu es*	tew ay
(singular, informal)		
he / she / one is	*il / elle / on est*	eel / ehl / oh<u>n</u> ay
("one"–or in French, on–is colloquial for "we")		
we are	*nous sommes*	noo suhm
they (m / f) are	*ils / elles sont*	eel / ehl soh<u>n</u>

TO HAVE	*AVOIR*	ah-vwar
I have	*j'ai*	zhay
you have	*vous avez*	vooz ah-vay
(formal, singular or plural)		
you have	*tu as*	tew ah
(singular, informal)		
he / she / one has	*il / elle / on a*	eel / ehl / oh<u>n</u> ah

we have	*nous avons*	nooz ah-vohn
they (m / f) have	*ils / elles ont*	eelz / ehlz oh<u>n</u>

TO SPEAK	*PARLER*	par-lay
I speak	*je parle*	zhuh parl
you speak	*vous parlez*	voo par-lay
(formal, singular or plural)		
you speak	*tu parles*	tew parl
(singular, informal)		
he / she / one speaks	*il / elle / on parle*	eel / ehl / oh<u>n</u> parl
we speak	*nous parlons*	noo par-loh<u>n</u>
they (m / f) speak	*ils / elles parlent*	eel / ehl parl

TO WALK	*MARCHER*	mar-shay
I walk	*je marche*	zhuh marsh
you walk	*vous marchez*	voo mar-shay
(formal, singular or plural)		
you walk	*tu marches*	tew marsh
(singular, informal)		
he / she / one walks	*il / elle / on marche*	eel / ehl / ohn marsh
we walk	*nous marchons*	noo mar-shoh<u>n</u>
they (m / f) walk	*ils / elles marchent*	eel / ehl marsh

TO LIKE	*AIMER*	ehm-ay
I like	*j'aime*	zhehm
you like	*vous aimez*	vooz eh-may
(formal, singular or plural)		
you like	*tu aimes*	tew ehm
(singular, informal)		
he / she / one likes	*il / elle / on aime*	eel / ehl / ohn ehm
we like	*nous aimons*	nooz eh-moh<u>n</u>
they (m / f) like	*ils / elles aiment*	eelz / ehlz ehm

TO GO	*ALLER*	ah-lay
I go	*je vais*	zhuh vay
you go	*vous allez*	vooz ah-lay
(formal, singular or plural)		

LANGUAGE TIPS

you go (singular, informal)	*tu vas*	tew vah
he / she / one goes	*il / elle / on va*	eel / ehl / oh<u>n</u> vah
we go	*nous allons*	nooz ah-loh<u>n</u>
they (m / f) go	*ils / elles vont*	eel / ehl voh<u>n</u>

TO DO / TO MAKE	*FAIRE*	fair
I do	*je fais*	zhuh fay
you do (formal, singular or plural)	*vous faîtes*	voo feht
you do (singular, informal)	*tu fais*	tew fay
he / she / one does	*il / elle / on fait*	eel / ehl / oh<u>n</u> fay
we do	*nous faisons*	noo fuh-soh<u>n</u>
they (m / f) do	*ils / elles font*	eel / ehl foh<u>n</u>

TO SEE	*VOIR*	vwar
I see	*je vois*	zhuh vwah
you see (formal, singular or plural)	*vous voyez*	voo vwah-yay
you see (singular, informal)	*tu vois*	tew vwah
he / she / one sees	*il / elle / on voit*	eel / ehl / oh<u>n</u> vwah
we see	*nous voyons*	noo vwah-yoh<u>n</u>
they (m / f) see	*ils / elles voient*	eel / ehl vwah

TO BE ABLE	*POUVOIR*	poo-vwar
I can	*je peux*	zhuh puh
you can (formal, singular or plural)	*vous pouvez*	voo poo-vay
you can (singular, informal)	*tu peux*	tew puh
he / she / one can	*il / elle / on peut*	eel / ehl / oh<u>n</u> puh
we can	*nous pouvons*	noo poo-voh<u>n</u>
they (m / f) can	*ils / elles peuvent*	eel / ehl puhv

TO WANT	*VOULOIR*	vool-war
I want	*je veux*	zhuh vuh
you want (formal, singular or plural)	*vous voulez*	voo voo-lay

you want (singular, informal)	*tu veux*	tew vuh
he / she / one wants	*il / elle / on veut*	eel / ehl / ohn vuh
we want	*nous voulons*	noo voo-lohn
they (m / f) want	*ils / elles veulent*	eel / ehl vuhl
TO NEED	*AVOIR BESOIN DE*	ah-vwar buh-swan duh
I need	*j'ai besoin de*	zhay buh-swan duh
you need (formal, singular or plural)	*vous avez besoin de*	vooz ah-vay buh-swan duh
you need (singular, informal)	*tu as besoin de*	tew ah buh-swan duh
he / she / one needs	*il / elle / on a besoin de*	eel / ehl / ohn ah buh-swan duh
we need	*nous avons besoin de*	nooz ah-vohn buh-swan duh
they (m / f) need	*ils / elles ont besoin de*	eelz / ehlz ohn buh-swan duh

French Tongue Twisters

Tongue twisters are a great way to practice a language and break the ice with local Europeans. Here are a few French tongue twisters that are sure to challenge you, and amuse your hosts.

Bonjour madame la saucissonière!	Hello, madame sausage-seller!
Combien sont ces six saucissons-ci?	How much are these six sausages?
Ces six saucissons-ci sont six sous.	These six sausages are six cents.
Si ces saucissons-ci sont six sous, ces six saucissons-ci sont trop chers.	If these are six cents, these six sausages are too expensive.
Je veux et j'exige qu'un chasseur sachant chasser sans ses èchasses sache chasser sans son chien de chasse.	I want and demand that a hunter who knows how to hunt without his stilts knows how to hunt without his hunting dog.

Ce sont seize cent jacynthes sèches dans seize cent sachets secs.	These are 600 dry hyacinths in 600 dry sachets.
Ce sont trois très gros rats dans trois très gros trous roulant trois gros rats gris morts.	These are three very fat rats in three very fat rat-holes rolling three fat gray dead rats.

English Tongue Twisters

After your French friends have laughed at you, let them try these tongue twisters in English:

If neither he sells seashells, nor she sells seashells, who shall sell seashells? Shall seashells be sold?	Si ni lui ni elle ne vendent de coquillages, qui les vendra? Les coquillages seront-ils vendus?
Peter Piper picked a peck of pickled peppers.	Pierre Pipant a choisi un picotin de cornichons.
Rugged rubber baby buggy bumpers.	Des pare-chocs solides en caoutchoue pour les voitures d'enfants.
The sixth sick sheik's sixth sheep's sick.	Le sixième mouton du sixième sheik est malade.
Red bug's blood and black bug's blood.	Sang d'insecte rouge, sang d'insecte noir.
Soldiers' shoulders.	Epaules de soldats.
Thieves seize skis.	Les voleurs s'emparent de skis.
I'm a pleasant mother pheasant plucker. I pluck mother pheasants. I'm the	Je suis une plaisant plumeur de faisanes. Je plume les faisanes. Je suis

most pleasant mother pheasant plucker that ever plucked a mother pheasant.	le plumeur de faisanes le plus plaisant qui ait jamais plumé de faisanes.

French Songs

You probably know the nursery songs *Frere Jacques* and *Sur le Pont d'Avignon*. Here are a couple more French songs and their meanings. Ask a friendly local to teach you the tunes.

LA MARSEILLAISE

Allons enfants de la patrie,	Let's go, children of the fatherland,
Le jour de gloire est arrivé.	The day of glory has arrived.
Contre nous de la tyrannie	The blood-covered flagpole of tyranny
L'étendard sanglant est levé,	Is raised against us,
L'étendard sanglant est levé.	Is raised against us.
Entendez-vous dans nos campagnes	Do you hear what's happening in our countryside?
Mugir nos féroces soldats?	The ferocious soldiers are howling.
Qui viennent jusque dans nos bras.	They're nearly in our grasp.
Egorger nos fils et nos compagnes.	They're slitting the throats of our sons and our women.
Aux armes citoyens,	Grab your weapons, citizens,
Formez vos bataillons,	Form your battalions,
Marchons, marchons,	March on, march on,
Qu'un sang impur	So that their impure blood
Abreuve dans sillons.	Will fill our trenches.

CHEVALIERS DE LA TABLE RONDE

This is a great drinking song often sung when friends and families get together.

Chevaliers de la table ronde,	Knights of the round table,
Goûtons voir si le vin est bon.	Let's taste if the wine is good.
Goûtons voir, oui, oui, oui	Let's taste, yes, yes, yes
Goûtons voir, non, non, non	Let's taste, no, no, no

Goûtons voir si le vin est bon.	Let's taste if the wine is good.
Goûtons voir, oui, oui, oui	Let's taste, yes, yes, yes
Goûtons voir, non, non, non	Let's taste, no, no, no
Goûtons voir si le vin est bon.	Let's taste if the wine is good.
J'en boirais cinq à six bouteilles,	I will drink five to six bottles,
Une femme sur les genoux.	A woman on each knee.
Une femme, oui, oui, oui	A woman, yes, yes, yes
Une femme, non, non, non	A woman, no, no, no
Une femme sur les genoux.	A woman on each knee.
Si je meurs je veux qu'on m'enterre	If I die I want to be buried
Dans une cave où y'a du bon vin.	In a cave where the wine is good.
Dans une cave, oui, oui, oui	In a cave, yes, yes, yes
Dans une cave, non, non, non	In a cave, no, no, no
Dans une cave où y'a du bon vin.	In a cave where the wine is good.
Les deux pieds contre la muraille	The two feet against the wall
Et la tête sous le robinet.	And the head under the spigot.
Et la tête, oui, oui, oui	And the head, yes, yes, yes
Et la tête, non, non, non	And the head, no, no, no
Et la tête sous le robinet.	And the head under the spigot.
Sur ma tombe je veux qu'on écrive	On my tomb I want it to be written
Ici gît le roi des buveurs.	Here lies the king of the drinkers.
Ici gît, oui, oui, oui	Here lies, yes, yes, yes
Ici gît, non, non, non	Here lies, no, no, no
Ici gît le roi des buveurs.	Here lies the king of the drinkers.

French Gestures

Here are a few common French gestures and their meanings:

The Fingertips Kiss: Gently bring the fingers and thumb of your right hand together, raise to your lips, kiss lightly, and toss your fingers and thumb into the air. Be careful: Tourists look silly when they over-emphasize this subtle action. It can mean sexy, delicious, divine, or wonderful.

The Eyelid Pull: Place your extended forefinger below the center of your eye, and pull the skin downward. This means: "I'm alert. I'm looking. You can't fool me."

The Roto-Wrist: Hold your forearm out from your waist with your open palm down, and pivot your wrist clockwise and counter-clockwise like you're opening a doorknob. When a Frenchman uses this gesture while explaining something to you, he isn't sure of the information or it's complete B.S. He'll usually say, "*Bof!*" or "*Comme ci, comme ça.*"

The Hand Shave: Move the back of your hand gently up and down the side of your face as if checking a clean shave. This denotes a boring person, show, talk, or whatever, and is often accompanied by the expression "*La barbe*" (the beard).

The Shoulder Shrug: Move your shoulders up towards your ears and slightly lift your arms with palms up. This basically means, "I don't know and I don't care."

The Nose-Grab-and-Twist: Wrap your hand around your nose and twist it down. If someone does this to you, put down your wine glass—it means you're drunk.

To beckon someone: In northern Europe, you bring your palm up, and in France and the south, you wave it down. To Americans, this looks like "go away"—not the invitation it actually is.

Numbers and Stumblers

- Europeans write a few of their numbers differently than we do.
  1=_1_ , 4=_4_ , 7=_7_ .
- Europeans write the date in this order: day/month/year.
- Commas are decimal points and decimals are commas. A dollar
  in a mi le.
- The European "first floor" isn't the ground floor, but the first
  floor up.
- When counting with your fingers, start with your thumb. If you
  hold up only your first finger, you'll probably get two of
  something.

APPENDIX

LET'S TALK TELEPHONES

Making Calls within a European Country: About half of all European countries use area codes (like we do); the other half uses a direct-dial system without area codes.

To make calls within a country that uses a direct-dial system (Belgium, Czech Republic, Denmark, France, Greece, Italy, Norway, Poland, Portugal, Spain, and Switzerland), you dial the same number whether you're calling across the country or across the street.

In countries that use area codes (such as Austria, Britain, Croatia, Finland, Germany, Ireland, the Netherlands, Slovakia, Slovenia, and Sweden), you dial the local number when calling within a city, and you add the area code if calling long-distance within the country.

Making International Calls: You always start with the international access code (011 if you're calling from America or Canada, or 00 from Europe), then dial the country code of the country you're calling (see codes on next page).

What you dial next depends on the phone system of the country you're calling. If the country uses area codes, drop the initial zero of the area code, then dial the rest of the number.

Countries that use direct-dial systems (no area codes) vary in how they're accessed internationally by phone. You always start by dialing the international access code, followed by the country code.

Then, if you're calling the Czech Republic, Denmark, Italy, Norway, Portugal, or Spain, simply dial the phone number in its entirety. But if you're calling Belgium, France, Poland, or Switzerland, drop the initial zero of the phone number.

Country Codes

After you've dialed the international access code, dial the code of the country you're calling.

Austria—43	France—33	Poland—48
Belgium—32	Germany—49	Portugal—351
Bosnia-	Gibraltar—350	Slovakia—421
Herzegovina—387	Greece—30	Slovenia—386
Britain—44	Hungary—36	Spain—34
Canada—1	Ireland—353	Sweden—46
Croatia—385	Italy—39	Switzerland—41
Czech Rep.—420	Montenegro—382	Turkey—90
Denmark—45	Morocco—212	United States—1
Estonia—372	Netherlands—31	
Finland—358	Norway—47	

Useful Phone Numbers

Emergency (police): tel. 17
Emergency Medical Assistance: tel. 15
Directory Assistance: tel. 12
  (some English spoken)

Embassies

US Embassy/Consulate:
• tel. 01 43 12 22 22
• 4 avenue Gabriel, Paris
• Métro stop: Concorde
• http://france.usembassy.gov

Canadian Embassy/Consulate:
• tel. 01 44 43 29 00
• 35 avenue Montaigne, Paris
• Métro stop: Franklin-Roosevelt
• www.amb-canada.fr

Tear-Out Cheat Sheet

Keep this sheet of French survival phrases in your pocket, handy to memorize or use if you're caught without your phrase book.

Good day.	*Bonjour.*	bohn-zhoor
Do you speak English?	*Parlez-vous anglais?*	par-lay-voo ahn-glay
Yes. / No.	*Oui. / Non.*	wee / nohn
I don't understand.	*Je ne comprends pas.*	zhuh nuh kohn-prahn pah
Please.	*S'il vous plaît.*	see voo play
Thank you.	*Merci.*	mehr-see
You're welcome.	*De rien.*	duh ree-an
I'm sorry.	*Désolé.*	day-zoh-lay
Excuse me (to get attention).	*Excusez-moi.*	ehk-skew-zay-mwah
Excuse me (to pass).	*Pardon.*	pahr-dohn
No problem.	*Pas de problème.*	pah duh proh-blehm
Very good.	*Très bon.*	tray bohn
Goodbye.	*Au revoir.*	oh reh-vwahr
How much is it?	*C'est combien?*	kohn-bee-an
Write it?	*Ecrivez?*	ay-kree-vay
euro (€)	*euro*	oo-roo
one / two	*un / deux*	uhn / duh
three / four	*trois / quatre*	twah / kah-truh
five / six	*cinq / six*	sank / sees
seven / eight	*sept / huit*	seht / weet
nine / ten	*neuf / dix*	nuhf / dees
20	*vingt*	van
30	*trente*	trahnt
40	*quarante*	kah-rahnt
50	*cinquante*	san-kahnt
60	*soixante*	swah-sahnt
70	*soixante-dix*	swah-sahnt-dees
80	*quatre-vingts*	kah-truh-van
90	*quatre-vingt-dix*	kah-truh-van-dees
100	*cent*	sahn

I'd like...	*Je voudrais...*	zhuh voo-dray
We'd like...	*Nous voudrions...*	noo voo-dree-oh<u>n</u>
...this.	*...ceci.*	suh-see
...more.	*...plus.*	ploo
...a ticket.	*...un billet.*	uh<u>n</u> bee-yay
...a room.	*...une chambre.*	ewn shah<u>n</u>-bruh
...the bill.	*...l'addition.*	lah-dee-see-oh<u>n</u>
Is it possible?	*C'est possible?*	say poh-see-bluh
Where are the toilets?	*Où sont les toilettes?*	oo soh<u>n</u> lay twah-leht
men / women	*hommes / dames*	ohm / dahm
entrance / exit	*entrée / sortie*	ah<u>n</u>-tray / sor-tee
no entry	*défense d'entrer*	day-fah<u>n</u>s dah<u>n</u>-tray
open / closed	*ouvert / fermé*	oo-vehr / fehr-may
At what time does this open / close?	*À quelle heure c'est ouvert / fermé?*	ah kehl ur say oo-vehr / fehr-may
Just a moment.	*Un moment.*	uh<u>n</u> moh-mah<u>n</u>
Now.	*Maintenant.*	ma<u>n</u>-tuh-nah<u>n</u>
Soon.	*Bientôt.*	bee-a<u>n</u>-toh
Later.	*Plus tard.*	plew tar
Today.	*Aujourd'hui.*	oh-zhoor-dwee
Tomorrow.	*Demain.*	duh-ma<u>n</u>
Monday	*lundi*	luh<u>n</u>-dee
Tuesday	*mardi*	mar-dee
Wednesday	*mercredi*	mehr-kruh-dee
Thursday	*jeudi*	zhuh-dee
Friday	*vendredi*	vah<u>n</u>-druh-dee
Saturday	*samedi*	sahm-dee
Sunday	*dimanche*	dee-mah<u>n</u>sh

Making Your Hotel Reservation

Most hotel managers know basic "hotel English." Emailing or faxing are the preferred methods for reserving a room. They're clearer and more foolproof than telephoning. Photocopy and enlarge this form, or find it online at www.ricksteves.com/reservation.

One-Page Fax

To: _____   _____
           hotel   *email or fax*

From: _____   _____
           name   *email or fax*

Today's date: ____/____/____
                 day *month* *year*

Dear Hotel _____

Please make this reservation for me:

Name: _____

Total # of people: _____   # of rooms: _____   # of nights: _____

Arriving: ____/____/____   Arrival time: (24-hr clock): _____
             day *month* *year*   (I will telephone if I will be late)

Departing: ____/____/____
               day *month* *year*

Room(s): Single___ Double___ Twin___ Triple___ Quad___ Quint___

With: Toilet ___ Shower___ Bathtub___ Sink only___

Special needs: View ___ Quiet___ Cheapest___ Ground floor___

Please email or fax me confirmation of my reservation, along with the type of room reserved and the price. Please also inform me of your cancellation policy. After I hear from you, I will quickly send my credit-card information as a deposit to hold the room. Thank you.

Name _____

Address _____

City _____ State____ Zip Code_____ Country_____

Email address _____

NOTES

NOTES

NOTES

NOTES

NOTES

Start your trip at

Free information and great gear to

▶ Plan Your Trip

Browse thousands of articles and a wealth of money-saving tips for planning your dream trip. You'll find up-to-date information on Europe's best destinations, packing smart, getting around, finding rooms, staying healthy, avoiding scams and more.

▶ Eurail Passes

Find out, step-by-step, if a railpass makes sense for your trip—and how to avoid buying more than you need. Get a bunch of free extras!

▶ Graffiti Wall & Travelers' Helpline

Learn, ask, share— our online community of savvy travelers is a great resource for first-time travelers to Europe, as well as seasoned pros.

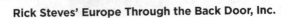

Rick Steves' Europe Through the Back Door, Inc.

The perfect complement
to your phrase book

Travel with Rick Steves' candid, up-to-date advice on the best places to eat and sleep, the must-see sights, getting off the beaten path—and getting the most out of every day and every dollar while you're in Europe.